DEA

DEA
The War against Drugs

Jessica de Grazia

BBC BOOKS

TO

District Attorney Robert M. Morgenthau

ISBN 0 563 36080 1

Published by BBC Books
a division of BBC Enterprises Ltd
Woodlands, 80 Wood Lane, London W12 OTT

Set in Monophoto Laser Times 327 by Butler & Tanner Ltd, Frome, Somerset
Printed and bound in Great Britain by Butler & Tanner Ltd, Frome, Somerset
Jacket printed by Lawrence Allen Ltd, Weston-super-Mare

Contents

Maps

Maps

Abbreviations used in this book

CI	Confidential Informant
CIA	Central Intelligence Agency
DAS	Departamento Administrativo de Seguridad (Colombian anti-narcotics force)
DEA	Drug Enforcement Administration
FBI	Federal Bureau of Investigation
INM	International Narcotics Matters (US Bureau of)
INS	Immigration and Naturalization Service (US)
IRS	Inland Revenue Service
NADDIS	Narcotics and Dangerous Drugs Information System
NAU	Narcotics Assistance Unit (US State Department)
SCA	Servizio Centrale Antidroga (Italian anti-narcotics force)
TDY	Temporary Duty
UC	Undercover Cop
UMOPAR	Unidad Movil de Patrullaje Rural (Mobile Rural Patrol Units: Bolivian anti-narcotics force)

Acknowledgements

This book grew out of a television series conceived by Paul Hamann and Roger Courtiour but ultimately produced by Christopher Jeans. Each, along with Sally Benge, has played an important role in nurturing the project, researching and critically evaluating the manuscript. Many of the photographs that appear in these pages were taken by Christopher Jeans. The rest were provided by the DEA.

I am indebted to Sheila Ableman of BBC Enterprises for making this book possible; to Martha Caute who, by gentle prodding, succeeded in editing this book on a very tight schedule; to Ann Wilson who helped translate the colourful but sometimes incomprehensible idiom of the DEA agents. As a result of Ann's skill as an editor, I hope I am a better writer.

Many law enforcement agents assisted this project. Bill Alden, Kenny Robinson, Gary Hale, Jerry McArdle and Don Ferrarone of the DEA read the manuscript and double checked facts. John Capers, Richard Girgenti, Bob Silbering and Connie Cucchiara of the Manhattan District Attorney's Office have kept me informed of the latest developments in New York City. Many other former colleagues have shaped my views. Among them are John Fried and Michael Cherkasky, but especially Bob Morgenthau, 'the dean of American prosecutors', to whom this book is dedicated.

Finally, I would like to thank the past and present fellows of the Institute for the Study of Drug Dependence and the Latin American Bureau, especially Nicholas Dorn, James Dunkerley and James Painter who, with his wife Sophia, were very helpful to me in Bolivia. They all opened my eyes to the difference between the British and American perspective, thereby helping me to shed some of my biases.

Jessica de Grazia

'It was like a plague, and the plague usually afflicted the eldest child of every family, like the one of the first born with Pharaoh's people in the bible. Sometimes it was even worse than the biblical plague. In Danny Rogers' family, it had everybody. There were four boys, and it had all of them. It was a disheartening thing for a mother and father to see all their sons strung out on drugs at the same time. It was as though drugs were a ghost, a big ghost, haunting the community.

People were more afraid than they'd ever been before. Everybody was afraid of this drug thing, even the older people who would never use it. They were afraid to go out of their houses with just one lock on the door. They had two, three and four locks. People had guns in their houses because of the junkies. The junkies were committing almost all the crimes in Harlem. ...

Then money became more of a temptation. The young people out in the streets were desperate for it. If a cat took out a twenty dollar bill on Eighth Avenue in broad daylight, he could be killed. ...

Cats were taking butcher knives and going at their fathers because they had to have money to get drugs. Anybody who was standing in the way of a drug addict when his habit was down on him – from mother or father on down – was risking his life.'

Claude Brown, *Manchild in the Promised Land*, 1965

1 The Tidal Wave

This book is about the Drug Enforcement Administration, the US government's anti-narcotics police force. There are in the DEA, as in every other law enforcement agency, people with good, bad and indifferent qualities; mistakes are made, there are errors of judgement, instances of negligence and incompetence. Very occasionally, DEA agents have been corrupted. (In the years 1973–91, fifteen agents were convicted of crimes.) But this book is not about the defects of the Drug Enforcement Administration. It is about the efforts of 'good cops' – idealistic, enterprising, aggressive, experienced DEA agents and analysts – to devise effective strategies to fight the war against narcotics; it describes the obstacles they face, their efforts to circumvent them, the difficulty of their work, how they cope with the frustration. It is about a police agency's best hopes for solving the narcotics problem but also it is about the limits of law enforcement.

Since this book describes the US anti-narcotics police force, it focuses on the American drug scene and perspective. Qualitatively and quantitatively, Britain's drug problem is different – historical and modern distinctions will be discussed in this chapter and the conclusion – but throughout the 1980s drug use has increased in Britain. In 1989–90 there was a jump of twenty per cent in the number of English and Welsh addicts notified to the government and according to a 1990 report by the Institute for the Study of Drug Dependence, Britain has approximately 100,000, mainly young heroin addicts.[1] In its effort to contain heroin use and forestall the cocaine epidemic that some DEA agents have warned will eventually cross the Atlantic, the British government has adopted some American strategies. These include attempts to reduce the supply of heroin and cocaine from the producing countries through diplomatic pressure coupled with economic assistance, tougher sentences for drug traffickers, confiscation of traffickers' assets, more resources for HM Customs and Excise to prevent and deter drug smuggling, and the creation of specialized drug squads and dedicated 'drug wings' to target trafficking organizations within the country. Yet the DEA operations covered in this book – Operations Snowcap, Tandem, Calico and Offsides – which are imaginative and, within the limits of available resources, well-executed programmes, provide little comfort to individuals on either side of the Atlantic who think that once a drug problem is deeply entrenched, it can be substantially affected by increased law enforcement.

At the outset, I should say that my perceptions of police work and the drug problem have been shaped by three experiences. I was once a law enforcement agent; my own family was affected by heroin addiction; and as a resident of New York, I observed the devastation wreaked on that city by thirty-five years of a drug epidemic.

As the daughter of a university professor, I grew up in a succession of college towns – St Paul, Minnesota; West Barrington, Rhode Island; Stanford, California – until finally, in the late 1950s, my family settled in Princeton, New Jersey. My parents were from New York and Chicago, cities which have suffered greatly from sucessive waves of heroin, cocaine and now crack abuse and consumption, but when they were growing up and when I was a child, in the span of years from 1925 to 1965 (the year I graduated from high school), the drug problem in the United States was almost negligible. My family did not know anyone who was addicted to drugs. We had no close friend, no family member, no acquaintance who suffered from this affliction. We were never warned against experimenting with drugs. In fact, the whole subject of drug addiction was not discussed. It was rarely reported in the newspapers, it was not mentioned on television, it was not a part of my state high school's health curriculum. Where drugs were concerned, my family was like a *tabula rasa* and in this respect we mirrored society at large, which had no historical memory of America's experience with narcotics in the nineteenth century.

Before Congress passed the Harrison Act of 1914 which outlawed the use and sale of opium (the dried juice of the opium poppy), morphine (the chief active ingredient of opium), heroin (a derivative of morphine discovered in the last quarter of the nineteenth century) and cocaine (the active alkaloid of coca leaf, isolated in the mid-nineteenth century), these drugs were widely consumed both for medical reasons and for pleasure. Doctors freely prescribed opiates as tranquillizers and pain-killers, and as antidotes to the symptoms of food poisoning and gastrointestinal diseases such as cholera. They recommended cocaine as a tonic, to relieve sinusitis and hay fever – it was the official remedy of the Hay Fever Association – and as a cure for addiction to opium, morphine and alcohol. Many of these drugs were components of patent medicines. Heroin was first marketed as a cough suppressant. (Its name derives from the German '*heroisch*', meaning 'powerful, with effect even in small doses'.) Cocaine, which was peddled door to door and, in 'dry' states, used as a substitute for hard liquor, was a favourite ingredient of wines and alcoholic beverages – some bars served a shot of whiskey laced with a pinch of cocaine – and of soft drinks, including until 1903 Coca Cola.[2]

As a result, there was widespread addiction in the United States, with an estimated 250,000 narcotic addicts in 1900. They tended to be middle-class, middle-aged women from rural areas or small towns who had become addicted to opiates by consuming patent medicine. Gradually, as the physically destructive qualities of these drugs became apparent, there was public agitation among doctors, pharmacologists, religious leaders and progressive politicians for strict controls on the use of opiates and cocaine. The fact that opium and cocaine were associated with two despised races, Chinese immigrant labourers and American blacks, exacerbated popular antipathy.

These domestic developments coincided with the United States' expansion into the Far East, where the desire to open up the Chinese market (hitherto cornered by the major European powers and Japan) prompted America to ally itself with China, which was probably the first nation to be concerned about the social consequences of opium use.

In 1898, following its four-month war with Spain, the United States acquired the Philippines and, with this new imperial power base, responsibility for managing the islanders' use of opium.

Under Spanish rule, Chinese inhabitants had been permitted to purchase opium. The tax on its sale was a source of government revenue. In the interregnum between the end of Spanish rule and the crushing of a nationalist-inspired insurrection against the US Colonial government in 1902, opium addiction spread among native Filipinos, who relied on the drug's constipating qualities to stave off a cholera epidemic. When the US Governor of the Philippines, William Howard Taft, proposed reinstituting a government monopoly restricted to the Chinese, there was moral outrage within the United States. Taft then appointed the Philippine Commission, comprising two doctors and the islands' first Episcopal Bishop, Charles Henry Brent, who visited Japan, Formosa, Shanghai, Hong Kong, Saigon, Singapore, Burma and Java to see how other colonial powers were handling their dependencies' opium problem. (Bishop Brent later reported to Taft how disgusted he was with the French in Saigon, who 'paid no attention whatever to the moral aspects of the question'. He was favourably impressed, however, by the 'courtesy and interest that characterizes all the English officials with whom we have been brought into contact'.)[3]

The Philippine Commission's conclusion that opium was one of the gravest evils in the Orient led Congress in 1905 to prohibit the opium trade in the islands. It also encouraged the British anti-opium movement. Throughout the nineteenth century Britain had paid for imports of tea and silk and financed the government of India through revenues generated by the sale of Bengal opium to China. (Exports of opium produced under a state-administered monopoly accounted for one-seventh of the revenue of British India.)[4] There was some opposition to what Gladstone called 'this most infamous and atrocious trade' but most public officials, including Palmerston, damped their qualms with an argument one hears today in Latin America – that it was up to the consuming country, in this instance, China, to end the traffic by suppressing its people's desire to consume the product.

The Chinese did indeed attempt to curb opium demand. After a drive in the early 1830s to eradicate its poppy crop, the Emperor in 1839 promulgated the thirty-nine Regulations. This law imposed Draconian penalties, usually death, for importing, wholesale dealing, retailing, smoking and inciting others to smoke opium, as well as for keeping an opium den. Government officials under whose jurisdiction these offences took place would be punished by decreases in salary or loss of rank.

Before the Commissioner of Canton, Lin Tse-hsu, moved to implement the new law, he sent the following communiqué to the British merchants in Canton who traded in opium:

> It is wrong to make profit out of what is harmful to others, to bring opium (which you do not smoke in your own land) to our country, swindle people out of their money and endanger their lives. You have been doing this for twenty or thirty years, accumulating an untold amount of wrongful gain, incurring the universal resentment of man and the certain retribution of Heaven. However the days when opium was saleable in China are now over. The death penalty for opium offences has been approved and will shortly come into force. The new regulations will apply just as much to you as to the Chinese themselves. I now call upon you to hand over for destruction all the opium you have on your ships and sign an undertaking that you will never bring opium here again, and that you are aware that if you are found to have done so your goods will be confiscated and you yourselves dealt with according to the law.[5]

In the weeks following this notice, Lin Tse-hsu had 20,000 chests of opium, whose contents were first polluted with salt and lime, dumped into the sea. It was a Chinese version of the Boston Tea Party but the war that was triggered did not end so happily. With command of the sea and major waterways, superior firepower and military technology, the British had an easy victory in the Chinese Opium War of 1840–41. Under the humiliating terms of the Treaty of Nanking, China was forced to pay reparations, cede the island of Hong Kong and admit British opium trading ships to several of its ports. After the second Opium War of 1856, opium was made legal and trading rights conceded for eleven more ports.

Between the beginning and the end of the nineteenth century, there was an extraordinary increase of opium imports to China, from 350 tons per year in the period 1811–21 to 6500 tons in 1880.[6] To save foreign exchange, China repealed its own ban on opium cultivation in the 1860s. By 1885 it was producing twice as much opium as it imported. Two missionaries travelling through West China in the early 1880s reported that three-quarters of the land they saw was devoted to poppy growing.[7] According to one estimate, the Chinese addict population exceeded 15 million.[8]

The British debate over the morality of opium trafficking, which was almost as old as the trade itself (in 1839 A. S. Thelwall published in London *The Iniquities of the Opium Trade with China*, an eloquent appeal for the suppression of opium production in India), was finally decided by the parliamentary elections of 1906. The Liberal Party, which had long proposed to eliminate Indian opium exports to China, won an overwhelming victory. By the end of that year China and Britain agreed to a gradual phasing out of the trade. Spurred by hatred of foreign domination and the perception that opium contributed to the nation's technological and military backwardness by sapping its strength and initiative, the Chinese government, with popular support, ruthlessly extirpated its own opium industry. In 1916 Britain ended its exports of Indian opium to China. (India remains today the major source of opium for the legal market.)

The 1912 Hague Convention, which was eventually signed by forty-four countries, called for controls of the non-medical use of opiates and cocaine. The United States, which had chaired the Convention, complied with its terms when it passed the Harrison Act in 1914 making the importation, sale or possession of opiates and cocaine illegal except for medical reasons. In 1920 the British Parliament passed the Dangerous Drug Act, a similar law.

These statutes, which provided the legislative framework for the criminalization of drugs in both countries, left open a substantial question: whether doctors should be permitted to maintain addicts on morphine or heroin in order to 'treat' them. The United States Supreme Court, in Webb et al vs. US, 249 US 96 (1919), ruled that this practice was illegal but in Britain the opposite conclusion was reached by the Rolleston Committee, a distinguished group of physicians led by Lord Humphrey Rolleston, President of the Royal College of Physicians.

In nineteenth-century England opium was almost as widely used, and for the same reasons, as aspirin – discovered in 1899 – is today. Working people relied on opiates to relieve depression, sleeplessness and as a cure-all for many complaints. Among the Fen country's labouring population, its use was endemic. A report to the Privy Council in 1864 noted: 'A man in South Lincolnshire complained that his wife had spent 100 pounds in opium since he married. A man may be seen occasionally asleep in a field leaning on his hoe. He starts when approached, and works vigorously for a while. A man who is setting about a hard job takes his pill as a preliminary, and many never take their beer without dropping a piece of opium into it.' Among all classes, mothers and nurses quietened fractious infants with a potion consisting of laudanum (opium in an alcoholic tincture) or crude opium mixed with aniseed, treacle and sugar.[9]

But by the time the Rolleston Committee was convened in 1924 to decide what role doctors should play in the implementation of the Dangerous Drugs Act, the general use of opiates had greatly declined. Addiction was a very minor problem, a middle-class phenomenon confined largely to the medical profession. Understandably, the Committee concluded that addiction 'must be regarded as a manifestation of disease', more appropriately controlled by the medical profession than by policemen, courts and prisons.[10] In 1926, following the Committee's recommendations, the British government permitted doctors to prescribe opiates for addicted patients. This system, under which an addict could obtain his supply from a pharmacy just as he would any other medicine, lasted until the 1960s.

After the passage of the Harrison Act in the United States, which was the culmination of twenty-five years of an anti-narcotics movement, the use of narcotics slowly declined. It reached a nadir during World War Two. Then, during the late 1950s, there was a surge in heroin use in poor inner city areas like Harlem to which southern blacks had immigrated in large numbers in the 1930s and 1940s. The first post-war heroin epidemic is documented in *Manchild in the Promised Land*, the autobiography of a black American lawyer, Claude Brown, who eloquently describes the racism, de facto segregation and breakdown of traditional southern rural black culture with subsequent loss of identity and self-destructiveness that made so many young people in his community vulnerable to heroin abuse.

In the mid-1960s this heroin epidemic spread into suburban and ex-urban middle-class neighbourhoods. White kids began experimenting with heroin. The decade from 1960 to 1970 was a period of extraordinary prosperity and social upheaval. In the space of ten years the US gross national product doubled. The post-war 'baby-boomers' reached adolescence; the number of youths in the turbulent age group fifteen to twenty-four increased by fifty per cent. The decade saw the beginning and end of the civil rights movement, with peaceful sit-ins and demonstrations to desegregate schools, hotels, buses, parks, swimming pools and public toilets, which were met by bombings, beatings and murder. There were race riots in New York, Detroit, Chicago and Newark. President John Kennedy, Senator Robert Kennedy and Martin Luther King Junior were assassinated. It was the decade when America became embroiled in the Vietnam conflict, losing fifty thousand soldiers in a war that many Americans believed was illegal and immoral. Students took over university buildings to demonstrate against the draft.

Out of ignorance, in defiance, in pursuit of pleasure, many young people experimented with marijuana, LSD (Lysergic acid diethylamide, a natural hallucinogen derived from ergot, a fungus) and heroin. Between 1960 and 1970 the number of heroin users rose from about fifty thousand to approximately half a million.[11] The situation was made worse by widespread use of the narcotic among GIs in Vietnam. Some fourteen per cent of ground troops became addicted to heroin in Vietnam.[12]

On a much smaller scale, heroin use in Britain suddenly increased. Between 1961 and 1969 the number of British addicts grew five-fold and while the total number of addicts was only about three thousand, a figure which could be matched in a five-block area of Harlem, Parliament was moved in 1967 to make major changes in the British system. It had functioned well when there were only a few hundred addicts whose addiction derived from medical treatment – usually opiates prescribed for chronic pain – but it broke down under pressure from the new class of addicts, pleasure seekers belonging to a distinctive subculture who helped spread addiction by selling their excess supplies of heroin. Under the revised British system, GPs no longer had powers to prescribe opiates. Responsibility for heroin addicts was shifted to Drug Dependency Units, clinics staffed by addiction specialists whose policy was eventually to substitute methadone (a synthetic opiate discovered by the Germans during the Second World War) for heroin. Thus the distinctive feature of the British system – the control and treatment of addiction by prescribing heroin – was removed.

The dozens of studies of the spread of heroin use show that it runs through peer groups like a contagious disease. Adolescents – angry, bored, insecure, miserable, rebellious, daring – are the most vulnerable. One person in a group of friends injects himself with heroin (the majority of heroin users are young males) and within a very short time, often four or five days, the entire group will have experimented with the drug. Thereafter, its use spreads like a brush fire in parched summer weather, leaping dirt boundaries to consume one field after another. This pattern holds true for Britain as well as the States.[13] There is very little evidence to support the view that commercially motivated drug-pushers lure adolescents into drug use.[14]

In 1967 the heroin epidemic in the United States hit my home town of Princeton, New Jersey. When I went to the University of Chicago in 1965, I left four brothers, aged sixteen to eleven, behind. At home for the summer in 1967, I realized that the three older boys, along with most of their friends, were smoking marijuana. From the traffic in and out of their bedrooms, the furtive discussions, it seemed likely they were also selling the drug. That September, Paul, the oldest of my younger brothers, joined me at the University of Chicago. After a few months he dropped out. At first I thought it was because the environment was too intellectual. My brother was bold, adventurous, a good athlete, but he had little interest in the academic world. The war in Vietnam – students were then exempt from the draft – and pressure from my father were the only reasons he found himself at university.

The knowledge that someone you love is a heroin addict dawns very slowly. My family was large; as an older sister, I helped care for my younger brothers and was close to them all, but especially to Paul, my playmate when we were small, whose dark good looks and daring character, so different from mine, I admired.

Since he had no place to live, I offered to let him stay in my flat. I would leave early in the morning to go to classes and return when the library closed at eleven. Often when I came in, I would find him lying on the sofa in a daze. He brought 'druggie' friends into the flat. He talked admiringly of an acquaintance, a pilot, who was smuggling marijuana from Mexico to California. He himself was selling marijuana. (I didn't know then that many heroin users turn to drug selling to support their habit.) He brought it into the flat to break it down into bags; the place was filled with its sweet, sickly smell. He did not even bother to sweep up the residue; my feet crunched on the seeds when I walked through the living room. I reached the point where I could stand it no longer. I came home tired one night, saw him nodding out on the sofa, and screamed at him, 'You have to get out.' He mumbled, 'ok, ok', and left. I saw him once a few months later, then not again for another ten years.

It is a terrible thing to cast someone you love on to the street. Fear gave me the courage to be cruel. (The Chicago police were not noted for their humanity; I thought that if they found drugs in the apartment, I would also be arrested.) Fear and the pain of seeing his degradation. A heroin addict doesn't think of anyone. He doesn't care about his mother, his father, his brothers or sisters, his friends, himself. He doesn't care where he sleeps, what he eats, whether he's clean. All a heroin addict cares about is how to get his next fix. A heroin addict has no moral sense. I felt as though the brother I loved was one of the walking dead.

In 1969, my youngest brother Christopher, a gentle, loving, obliging child, began using heroin. At the age of fourteen, he was an addict. I was now studying for my law degree at the Yale Law School. Christopher was hanging around Princeton, having dropped out of high school. Like the mothers of black teenagers in Harlem who send their delinquent children 'down south', thinking life in small rural towns will straighten them out, I thought a different environment might alter Christopher's course. For a few weeks during the summer of 1970, a brief period when he was drug-free, he lived with me in New Haven, Connecticut. We rarely discussed his drug problem – it was a taboo subject, as though he was suffering from cancer – but once I asked him, 'Why did you use heroin?'

'No one paid me much attention,' he said. 'Mom and Dad were fighting. I was always alone, I felt empty and heroin filled me up, it made me warm.' Later, he told me, 'Heroin is the slowest form of suicide.'

Christopher went back to using heroin. Both he and Paul left the United States, searching for places where there was less pressure on addicts, where they did not have to scour for drugs in dangerous inner city neighbourhoods. I moved to New York City and married an Englishman who was working there for the British Broadcasting Corporation. By then, Christopher had settled in a junkie community in Amsterdam. Paul was serving a prison sentence in Thailand.

In January 1975 I was sworn in as Assistant District Attorney in the Manhattan District Attorney's Office. For the next twelve years I worked as a prosecutor in one of the world's greatest cities, the commercial, cultural and financial capital of the United States and also the hub of its drug trafficking network. Many of the cases I was prosecuting, thefts, burglaries, armed robberies, assaults and murders, had some connection with the drug problem – addicts stealing to support their habit, stick-up boys robbing drug dealers, drug dealers killing other drug dealers, innocent bystanders injured or killed in this maelstrom of violence.

Between 1975 and 1980 the focus of law enforcement was the heroin problem. Heroin was the drug that was most abused. While no one knew the causal relationship – did criminals become addicts or did addicts turn to crime? – many studies had established that addicts committed a disproportionate number of crimes and that criminals, when they were using heroin, offended at two to six times their usual level.[15]

Heroin was also thought to be the 'hardest' drug, the most physically and morally destructive, the least susceptible to treatment, the most addictive. With some exceptions – addicts who survived into their thirties and forties when addiction tends to burn out naturally or the small number who benefited from therapeutic treatment – once a person was an addict, there were only three roads to travel. One led to death, the second to prison, the third to methadone maintenance programmes. (During President Nixon's administration the federal government saw methadone as a solution to the heroin problem. Dispensed by clinics, ingested orally – it was given to addicts diluted in orange juice – methadone produced a mild euphoria similar to heroin but legally obtainable and thus it was hoped that addicts would be able to lead more or less normal and relatively crime-free lives.)

When drugs were first made illegal in 1914, heroin and cocaine were deemed equally pernicious, but during the ensuing sixty years, the experiential and scientific basis for this conclusion was lost. By that time, the mid-1970s, there was widespread support for decriminalizing marijuana. The only significant, well-established risk of marijuana smoking is damage to the respiratory system. Cigarette smoking, however, constitutes a graver public health problem. Moreover, marijuana smoking seems to suppress aggression and is rarely implicated in the violent behaviour and reckless driving tragedies associated with alcohol consumption.[16]

Many public health experts put cocaine on a par with marijuana. In September 1975 a Task Force established by President Ford published a White Paper on drug abuse. After studying the federal government's anti-drug efforts since 1969, the White Paper concluded that since all drugs were not equally dangerous and destructive, priority should be given to suppress the supply and demand for heroin, amphetamines and mixed barbiturates. None of the White Paper's seventy-seven specific recommendations made any mention of cocaine. President Carter's drug abuse adviser, Dr Peter G. Bourne, who shaped the federal government's drug abuse policy from 1976 to 1978, described cocaine as 'probably the most benign of illicit drugs currently in widespread use. At least as strong a case could be made for legalizing it as for legalizing marijuana. Short acting – about fifteen minutes – not physically addicting, and acutely able, cocaine has found increasing favour at all socioeconomic levels.'[17]

The heroin epidemic of the 1960s had begun in the inner city ghettos, spreading outwards in concentric circles to middle-class suburbs. The cocaine epidemic's course was the mirror image. Beginning in the mid-1970s, it became a fashionable drug among jet-setters, rock stars, athletes, entertainers and middle-class professionals. (It caused the downfall of Dr Peter Bourne, who resigned as the White House drug adviser after the *Washington Post* alleged that he had snorted cocaine at a party.) It was a luxury drug, costing over $100 a gram in 1978.

Middle-class drug consumption habits were popularized through the mass media and by word of mouth, and by the end of the 1970s street distribution gangs in Harlem were selling and using cocaine rather than heroin. By the time its physiological impact was understood, the market of consumers and suppliers was thoroughly entrenched.

When cocaine is frequently used, it is as physically damaging and probably more socially destructive than intravenous heroin abuse. Heroin is a depressant. When injected intravenously, it produces a rush of euphoria, likened by addicts to an intense sexual orgasm, followed by languorous oblivion, a sense of detachment from one's problems. Cocaine is a stimulant. It results in feelings of euphoria and exhilaration; it produces hyperactivity and intensifies experience, making sex more exciting and loosening inhibitions. Long-term use often produces short-temperedness, paranoia, aggression and delusions.[18] Chronic cocaine use creates a strong psychological dependence akin to addiction. Studies of monkeys have found that it is very difficult to induce animals to drink alcohol but they will do enormous amounts of work to earn their cocaine shots, more even than monkeys addicted to heroin.[19]

Demand stimulates supply, supply excites demand. The suppliers of cocaine came from Colombia and were a group of entrepreneurs from the lower and criminal classes who thought of themselves as 'cocaine capitalists'. They paid peasants in Bolivia and Peru, where the coca bush is indigenous, to cultivate the crop. The leaves were processed into cocaine with commercial chemicals manufactured mainly by US and German companies. At first, most of the cocaine was processed in laboratories in Colombia.

In less than a decade cocaine overtook coffee, Colombia's top-ranking export, as the country's chief foreign exchange earner. But whereas coffee, which had been planted in Colombia in the 1870s, had provided the economic basis to forge a nation out of a fractured and backward nineteenth-century republic, the impact of the cocaine industry was profound political destabilization.

By 1980 there were two identifiable Colombian cocaine distribution rings which were responsible for exporting eighty per cent of the cocaine that reached America. They were named after the cities from which their leaders hailed – the Medellin and the Cali Cartels. These organizations were run on different operational principles. The Medellin Cartel was extraordinarily vicious. They used threats, torture, bombings and assassinations to protect and promote the cocaine industry. The Cali Cartel, on the other hand, eschewed terrorism. Like any other criminal group, it used murder to enforce organizational discipline, and in the late 1980s it became engaged in a bloody trade war with the Medellin Cartel, but it did not attack the government of Colombia. As much as possible, it operated its drug distribution organization like a legitimate business.

For historical and constitutional reasons, responsibility for narcotics law enforcement in the United States is divided among state, local and federal police forces and prosecutors – lawyers who have powers associated in the English system only with the police and judges. In conjunction with the police, prosecutors carry out investigations; they decide on the charges after the police make an arrest and they play a major role in plea bargaining, the pre-trial negotiation between prosecutor, defence attorney and judge in which the defendant agrees to plead guilty in exchange for a lesser sentence – and by which the vast majority of cases are resolved. Prosecutors also take cases to trial and recommend sentences.

In Manhattan, the New York Police Department and the District Attorney's Office are responsible for arresting and prosecuting street dealers – the individuals and gangs who retail drugs. The Drug Enforcement Administration and the US Attorney's Office for the Southern and Eastern Districts of New York make cases against and prosecute import organizations and bulk dealers.[20] Both agencies are subdivisions of the Justice Department, located in Washington and headed by the Attorney General, a presidential appointee.

Other federal agencies – the Coast Guard, the main policing agency on the high seas; the Customs Service, whose role is equivalent to HM Customs and Excise; and the Border Patrol which enforces immigration policy on the US – Mexican border – are responsible for stopping the movement of drugs across sea, air and land borders.

Since the District Attorney (unlike the Attorney General) is an elected official and the Police Chief is appointed by another elected official, the Mayor, they are sensitive, if not always responsive, to the concerns of the community. If, for example, a gang starts peddling drugs in front of a church on 131st Street in Harlem, the pastor calls the 28th Precinct. If the commander tells him, 'We are locking them up, but the courts are letting them go,' an irate community group demands a meeting with the DA.

There are other factors which make local law enforcement agents more sensitive than their federal counterparts to the needs of the community. Residency laws require policemen and prosecutors to live within the city or state, and every day, on the streets, in the DA's office and in the police station, city police and prosecutors witness the suffering of the victims of street crimes – the murders, assaults, robberies, burglaries, rapes, over which local law enforcement has jurisdiction.

Local police and prosecutors saw what cocaine was doing to New York City several years before federal law enforcement agencies did. We saw it first in an upsurge of drug-related murders. The street gangs that were dealing cocaine were much more violent. They murdered with impunity, sometimes torturing their victims. They indiscriminately killed innocent civilians. They were committing scores of crimes, besides selling drugs, and getting away with murder, because the Precinct Investigative Units were swamped with cases and had neither the manpower nor the incentive to investigate drug-related killings. (The New York Police Department measures the productivity of its commanders by the number of cases cleared by an arrest. This practice discourages commanders from allocating resources to hard-to-solve cases which have not made the front pages of the daily newspapers – and drug-related murders are notoriously difficult to solve because the only witnesses are usually other gang members.)

In 1980 I was assigned to work with Operation Trinity, a small team of homicide detectives attached to the District Attorney's Office with the task of identifying the most vicious street distribution gangs; we were to build cases against them, arrest, convict and incarcerate them. Our goal was to reduce the mayhem on the streets by taking out of circulation the most violent gangs.

We spent two years working on a single 'crew' whose members, *modus operandi* and impact on the Harlem community were characteristic of the new generation of cocaine gangs. Their leader was a thirty-year-old Harlemite, Walter Tyrone Smith, known as Smitty, a semi-literate high school drop-out for whom drugs and money were a means of accumulating power. He gathered round him a crew of like-minded people, the youngest of whom was a fourteen-year-old contract killer. When not selling or using cocaine, they passed their time discussing how to kill people.

We were able to attribute a dozen murders, although there were probably more, to Smitty's crew. Most of the victims were other street people. The reasons they died were often trivial. A young man was shot because he sat on a gang member's car. Another young man, who fancied one of Smitty's girls, was kidnapped, bound, gagged, taken to Smitty's house and forced to perform fellatio on the gang leader. Then they suffocated him by encasing his head in a plastic bag. His corpse was found in a rubbish-strewn alley in the Bronx.

Although certain streets in Harlem are notorious for drug dealing and violence, there are many other blocks (or were, because the number is rapidly diminishing) where working-class blacks live in relative peace. One of these was 151st Street and St Nicholas Place, a tree-lined street of nineteenth-century brownstone houses converted into flats in the 1940s. A sixteen-year-old schoolboy named Ronnie Blake lived in this neighbourhood. His father, a man of sixty-odd years, had worked as a waiter in the Union Club in mid-town Manhattan for twenty-five years. (When he came to my office, he was always dressed in a suit; he had retained the courteous manners of the rural southern community from which he had emigrated to New York in the 1940s.) On an early spring afternoon in 1981 Ronnie Blake walked home from his school around the corner, talked over his homework with his mother, then ate a snack and fell asleep on the sofa. His mother went out to do some shopping, leaving a scribbled note on the table beside the sofa, 'Don't leave the house, I've gone to the store.' The last thing she did before pulling the flat door closed was to remove the glasses from her sleeping son's face and place them on the table next to her note.

But it was the first fine weather of the season and when Ronnie woke up, he ignored his mother's note and, taking his radio, stepped into the street and headed towards the corner where the neighbourhood kids played. A few hundred feet from his house, he was caught in a hail of gunfire as Walter Tyrone Smith and his gang, high on cocaine, their faces masked by Balaclavas, drove past firing wildly at the cab company near the corner whose taxis were occasionally commissioned by a rival drug dealer. Half an hour later, when Mr Blake returned from work, he saw blue and white radio cars opposite his building. The police were collecting bullets, cordoning off the crime scene, asking people on the block what they had seen. The neighbourhood kids ran over to him shouting 'Mr Blake, Ronnie's been shot.' The ambulance had already come and gone. Mr Blake next saw his only child in a city hospital's morgue.

It took two years to bring Ronnie Blake's murderers to justice. Because the men who shot him were wearing masks, it seemed at first a hopeless task. We had to take the word on the street, build cases against people who might be informants, convince them to turn state's evidence and testify against the killers, then, because under New York law a person cannot be convicted only on an accomplice's word, develop independent evidence to corroborate their testimony. Eventually, every member of Smitty's gang except one was convicted and sent to prison.

When Smitty was sentenced to two consecutive life terms, which would make him eligible for parole when he was eighty years old, the detectives and I were tremendously elated. We rejoiced in having been the instruments of justice for a grief-stricken couple; we saw it as a great moral victory, the triumph of good over evil. But we had had no impact on New York City's narcotics problem. Within a few months of Smitty's arrest his crew had been replaced by half a dozen new gangs.

In 1986 I was appointed First Assistant District Attorney. I was no longer working in the courtroom, I was now absorbed by issues of criminal justice policy and administration. Much of my time was spent on the narcotics problem, which had grown steadily worse in the five years since Ronnie Blake's death.

With the appearance in 1985 of crack – a crystallized form of cocaine which, instead of being snorted like cocaine or injected intravenously like heroin, is smoked in pipes or cigarettes – a new epidemic of drug abuse, worse than anything previously seen, was sweeping through the city. The cost of heroin and cocaine had discouraged many potential consumers (in 1985, in New York City a gram of heroin retailed for $115–130 and a gram of cocaine sold for $75–100)[21] but crack was comparatively cheap. In 1985 a vial containing about a quarter gram, which could produce a twelve-minute high, sold for $5. (By 1991 the price had dropped to $2 a vial.) Crack was also much more likely than cocaine to result in dependency. (Smoking delivers the drug to the brain more quickly than sniffing. This intensifies both the 'high' and the 'rebound effect' of depression and anxiety, which users then attempt to alleviate by smoking more crack. In a random sample of 458 crack abusers in America, eighty-two per cent reported drug craving.)[22] Unlike heroin, there was no synthetic substitute, no equivalent of methadone, that would permit a partial cure. It was also more appealing than heroin since it did not involve intravenous injection and could be easily ingested.

The social consequences of this new epidemic of drug addiction were devastating, particularly for economically depressed communities like Harlem which already suffered from a plethora of social problems; educational opportunities, unemployment, housing, literacy rates, rivalled conditions in an underdeveloped country.

Whereas the vast majority of heroin addicts had been young men, some fifty per cent of crack users were women. Many were young and sexually active – sex is often sold in crack houses in exchange for drugs – and they gave birth to crack-addicted babies. In a two-year period, from 1986 to 1988, the number of babies born in New York City who tested positive for drugs (mainly cocaine) leaped from 1325 to 5088.[23] (Babies exposed to crack prior to birth may develop a range of health problems including kidney damage, low birth weight and mental retardation.) The incidence of child abuse also shot up. Between 1984 and 1988 the number of neglect petitions in the Family Court increased by nearly four hundred per cent.[24]

Crack was both easy to produce and very profitable. It could be made with the simplest of implements and ingredients: a cooker, a pot, a stirrer, cocaine, baking soda and water. An ounce of cocaine (price $600) could be converted into 350 crack vials retailing for $5 a vial, which produced a tidy profit of $1150. The number of street dealers multiplied as a new industry was created which produced thousands of jobs for the forty per cent of minority-group teenagers who could not find employment in the legitimate economy. They sold drugs openly, and not just in Harlem but in parks and streets all over Manhattan. And with the increase in distributors, there was an increase in violence. In 1981 a gang like Walter Tyrone Smith's was somewhat unusual but now there were scores of equally vicious gangs fighting for territorial markets.

Consumers could be as violent as dealers. A third of the admissions to New York's psychiatric hospitals were of individuals suffering from cocaine-induced psychosis. The indiscriminate violence that cost Ronnie Blake his life had become a ubiquitous feature of New York life.

Community leaders from Harlem, the Lower East Side, Washington Heights, the Upper West Side, came to the District Attorney's Office asking for help. They represented the Mr and Mrs Blakes of the city, hard-working, respectable people who were terrified of leaving their homes at night, frightened to walk to the shops in the day, afraid to let their children outside lest they be caught in the cross-fire of a drug gang's territorial battle or seduced into smoking crack or peddling drugs. They wanted more police on the streets, more arrests, tougher prosecutions, more convictions, more and longer prison sentences. Tougher law enforcement, they thought, was the solution; this was how to rid their streets of traffickers.

How do you explain to irate citizens that the public officials, whom they think of as omnipotent, feel equally helpless? A tidal wave had burst over New York City and with a mop and bucket, local law enforcement officials were trying to turn back the sea.

I knew from my experience as an investigator and trial lawyer the limits of the effectiveness of local law enforcement. It had taken two years and the full-time labour of three detectives and a prosecutor to bring to justice Ronnie Blake's killers, and that was just one crime. The year that Ronnie Blake was killed, there were 558 murders in Manhattan, 1003 rapes, 35,856 armed robberies and muggings, and 52,397 burglaries, plus thousands more major crimes that were not reported.

New York State had the toughest drug laws in the country, with mandatory life prison terms for the sale of small amounts of cocaine or heroin. Since 1981 we had tripled the number of people charged with serious drug dealing offences. In 1987 6,600 people were charged with felony offences related to drug-trafficking; sixty-nine per cent of the cases involved crack. The jails and prisons were overflowing. The Manhattan District Attorney had a large staff – four hundred prosecutors in 1987 – and there were thirty thousand police in the New York City Police Department, but local law enforcement still did not have the resources to stop street drug dealing. Nor was it likely it ever would. The problem had been allowed to grow too big.

Depending on which neighbourhood group complained the most, we would increase the pressure on a particular block. We would step up arrests, refuse to plea bargain, ask the judges to impose a stiffer sentence. (More often than not the judges ignored us, not out of malice or lack of concern for the city, but because their chief way of preventing the collapse of the inadequately staffed court system was to dismiss cases or induce defendants to plead guilty by offering them light sentences.) But all our efforts did was push the traffickers into a different neighbourhood, into the vestibules of buildings or into apartments. This made the streets slightly more civilized but was, in fact, counter-productive because it made it more difficult to make 'buy and bust cases'. (This is the main technique of street drug law enforcement: an informant introduces an undercover policeman (UC) to a dealer, the 'UC' makes a buy and a back-up team arrests the seller.)

Our inability to perform our duty and the depressing condition of our city were a constant source of frustration for local law enforcement officials. We were angry with the federal government. President Reagan's anti-Welfare State policies had stripped communities like Harlem of after-school programmes, job training, financial support for new public housing, food stamps and welfare benefits. He and his wife Nancy were promoting as a solution a derisively inadequate educational programme – 'Just Say No' – which might have some appeal to middle-class people but had no relevance to the drug problem of New York City. The State Department's subdivision, the Bureau of International Narcotics Matters (INM), was the main agency for coordinating American narcotics policy overseas, including suppressing drug production and controlling drug crops in the source countries, but under the Regan administration the State Department was obsessed with the expansion of communism in Central and Latin America; at the bottom of its agenda was suppression of the cocaine industry. (In 1990 an internal State Department report confirmed what local law enforcement officials had long said, that under the Reagan administration INM had done 'a poor job of managing an expensive program with little to show for it, with other foreign policy concerns systematically overriding the narcotics aspect'.)[25]

In 1986, halfway through Reagan's second term, police and prosecutors in New York, the city's Mayor and Governor, and the editorial boards of its daily newspapers were all calling for the federal government to do much more. We wanted Customs, the Coast Guard and the Border Patrol to make our borders less porous. We wanted the State Department to put pressure on the cocaine source countries – Colombia, Bolivia, Peru – to quash the industry there. We wanted the federal government to put more resources into the Drug Enforcement Administration. (Because of its small size – 2800 agents in 1988 – my boss, District Attorney Robert Morgenthau, often likened the federal government's anti-narcotics police force to a 'corporal's guard'.)

In 1987 I left the District Attorney's Office and moved to England with my husband and children. My husband began making a series of documentaries on the Drug Enforcement Administration for the BBC and I was engaged to write a companion book on the agency.

One's perspective is both enriched and circumscribed by experience. After twelve years as a local prosecutor I thought I knew some of the answers to the narcotics problem. It was not until I accompanied DEA agents on operations in Bolivia, New York and Italy that I realized that the solutions I had thought most hopeful were as unrealistic as the expectation that we could clean up the streets of New York with a mop and bucket.

As the research for this book began in the late summer of 1989, President Bush, in a much heralded televised speech to the nation, announced his plans for coping with the nation's drug problem. This was nine months into his administration, after a presidential campaign in which drugs had been a significant issue and one on which the Democrats had the advantage. The Democratic Congress rather than the White House had been responsible for the legislative innovations and budget increases for drug law enforcement, treatment and prevention that took place under the Reagan administration. During the campaign, there had also been embarrassing media reports of links between Vice-President Bush and the Panamanian dictator, Manuel Noriega (since indicted by a Florida federal Grand Jury for drug trafficking crimes), who claimed to have worked for the CIA when the Vice-President headed that agency.

In the summer months of 1989 major American cities, including Washington, DC, reported record high numbers of drug-related murders. The often sensational coverage of the drug problem by television, the daily papers and weekly news magazines such as *Time* and *Newsweek*, helped whip up anti-drug sentiment. In an unprecedented full-page editorial, the *New York Times* wrote of crack: 'It is reaching out to destroy the quality of life, and life itself, at all levels of American society. Crack may be to the 80s and 90s what the Great Depression was to the 30s or the Vietnam War was to the 60s and 70s.'[26] By the end of the summer, opinion polls showed that many Americans considered drugs the country's most pressing problem.

President Bush's National Drug Control Strategy called for more police, more prisons, stiffer sentences for traffickers, harsher penalties for drug consumers. He urged increased military and economic assistance to the Andean source countries to stem the flow of cocaine out of Latin America. Of the additional money to be allocated to the drug problem – a $2.2 billion increase to be phased in over several years – he proposed that seventy per cent be spent on law enforcement.

This is the policy context in which the DEA operations described in this book take place.

PART I

GOING TO THE SOURCE

DRUG TRAFFICKING

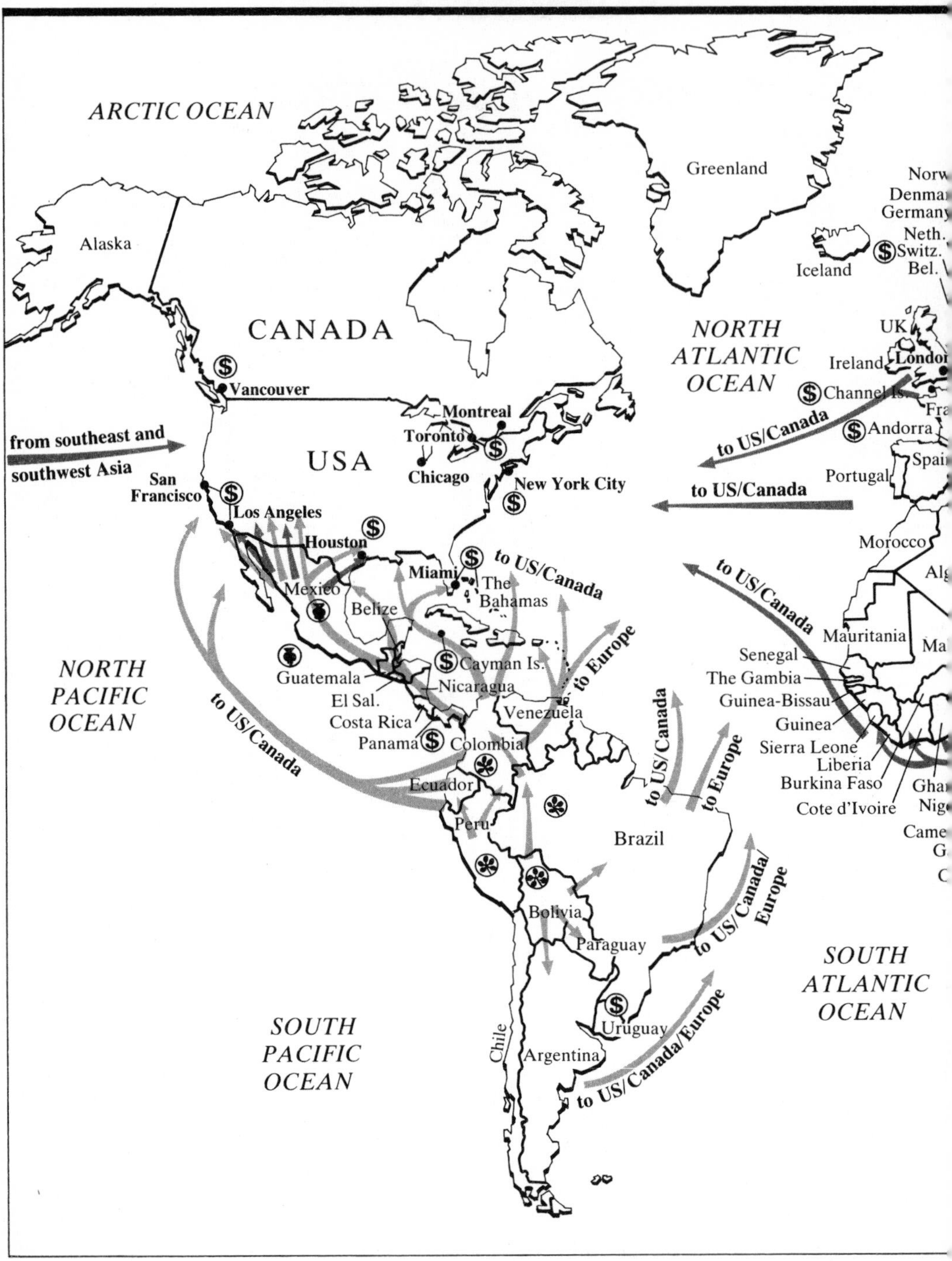

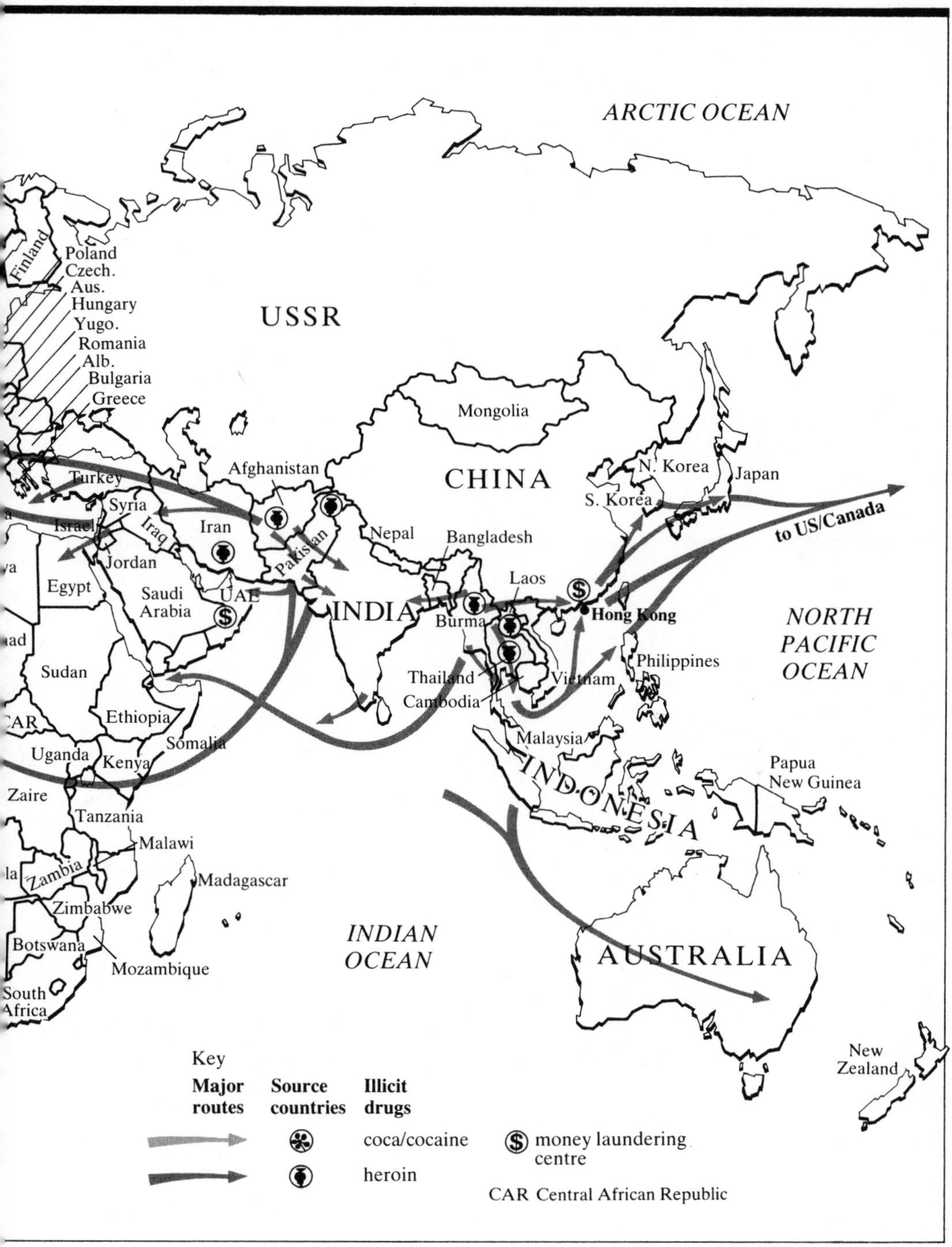

ARCTIC OCEAN
USSR
Finland
Poland
Czech.
Aus.
Hungary
Yugo.
Romania
Alb.
Bulgaria
Greece
Turkey
Syria
Israel
Iraq
Jordan
Egypt
Saudi Arabia
UAE
Iran
Afghanistan
Pakistan
Nepal
Bangladesh
INDIA
Mongolia
CHINA
N. Korea
S. Korea
Japan
to US/Canada
Laos
Burma
Hong Kong
Thailand
Cambodia
Vietnam
Philippines
NORTH PACIFIC OCEAN
Malaysia
INDONESIA
Papua New Guinea
Sudan
Ethiopia
Somalia
CAR
Uganda
Kenya
Zaire
Tanzania
Malawi
Zambia
Madagascar
Zimbabwe
Botswana
Mozambique
South Africa
INDIAN OCEAN
AUSTRALIA
New Zealand
Key
Major routes
Source countries
Illicit drugs
coca/cocaine
heroin
money laundering centre
CAR Central African Republic

BOLIVIA

Key
coca growing areas
entry of precursor chemicals
laboratories where cocaine produced
BRAZIL
PERU
PANDO
Guayaramerin
Rio Itenez
San Joaquin
San Ramon
R. Machupo
Santa Ana de Yacuma
BENI
Trinidad
LA PAZ
Yungas
BOLIVIA
La Paz
El Alto Airport
THE ANDES
COCHABAMBA
Chapare
Cochabamba
Santa Cruz
SANTA CRUZ
Oruro
ORURO
Sucre
Puerto Suarez
PACIFIC OCEAN
CHUQUISACA
PARAGUAY
TARIJA
POTOSI
CHILE
ARGENTINA
N
0 150 300 kilometres
0 100 200 miles

2 Lawrence of Latin America

It was the last Monday in October 1989 and Special Agent Don Ferrarone, chief of the DEA's operations in Bolivia, sat at his desk in the American Embassy in La Paz gloomily reading a newspaper that was spread open before him. He was an unusual looking man with a strong jaw and a big brow, made higher by thin black hair that was beginning to recede. He had an arrestingly open and intelligent face.

The newspaper was the Sunday edition of *Opinion*, a provincial paper published in Cochabamba, a little city, both pretty and shabby, in the foothills of the Andes. It was known as the City of Eternal Spring because of its year-round temperate weather but in recent years it had developed a less savoury reputation as a market town for the workers involved in the cultivation of coca leaf and its processing into cocaine.

Opinion had devoted a centre spread to Yayo Rodriguez, one of Bolivia's major drug traffickers. An eye-catching headline, inked in red and blue, declared, 'LA MISTERIOSA DESAPARACION DE 36 PILOTOS BRASILENOS ORIGINA UNA NUEVA PAGINA EN EL NEGOCIO DE LA COCAINA' (The mysterious disappearance of thirty-six Brazilian pilots opens a new page in the cocaine industry). There were photographs and vivid drawings to illustrate the lurid story of how this 'mysterious major trafficker' had killed at least thirty Brazilian pilots. He had hired their private aeroplanes, twin-engined Cessnas, duped them into flying into Bolivia and then shot them in the head, burying their bodies in the jungle; he was now using the planes to transport narcotics.

As Don read the story, he shook his head in dismay – the timing of the article could not have been worse. The DEA and the UMOPAR (the Bolivian anti-narcotics police) were about to launch Operation Tandem, an airborne assault involving almost the entire UMOPAR force, every US agent in the country, all their aircraft and three C-130 troop transports rented from the Bolivian Air Force. The intended target of this battalion-sized operation was Yayo Rodriguez, the hitherto obscure '*mega-traficante*' – major drug trafficker – who had suddenly been elevated to public enemy number one.

A handful of DEA employees – three agents, two pilots, an intelligence analyst – were now sitting in Don's small and sparsely furnished office. In a corner of the room was a pile of boxes. They contained books, photographs, personal mementoes, which Don would eventually unpack when he found an hour of leisure. From the street below the sound of traffic seeped through the loose sash of the room's dirty window, which was protected by thick metal mesh, supposedly bomb-proof, ugly but practical.

The men in the room were a tough and fit-looking group, all but one casually dressed in boots, blue jeans and sweatshirts. They were not youthful. Most had celebrated their fortieth birthday. Most had seen combat, either in Vietnam or in the war against narcotics. None were newcomers to Bolivia and their faces showed it. They were weathered by exposure to the sun and by the stress of life in this remote and abjectly underdeveloped country.[1] Separated from the sea, locked between the Andes mountains and the Amazonian jungle, at times Bolivia seemed to them as if it was located at the end of the world.

Gary Hale De Los Santos, Don's intelligence chief, stood out among them, perhaps because he was dressed in a suit and tie, perhaps because he looked more vulnerable. He had small, sharp, brown eyes which were set deep in an intense, pale-skinned face.

In another few weeks he would be sitting behind a desk in DEA headquarters in Washington; his three-year tour in Bolivia was almost finished. During his stint he had seen very few successes. Of everything he had worked on, Operation Tandem seemed to have the most potential. Now he anxiously awaited his boss's reaction to the *Opinion* article.

Gary was a Mexican-American, born on the wrong side of the tracks in Laredo, Texas, who owed his middle name to his great-great-grandfather, an Irishman who had emigrated to America to work on the railroads. From this distant relation Gary had inherited distinctly non-Mexican features; in fact, the only clue to his Hispanic origins was a slight slurring of consonants and the lilt of his accent.

In one way or another most of Gary's family were connected to the military. His father had been a civilian Air Force mechanic; one brother was a marine, the other a helicopter gunner. When Gary was seventeen and graduating from high school, he had decided to become an intelligence officer. This aspiration had been roughly dismissed by an Army recruitment officer, accustomed to routing Mexican-American youths into infantry service; he suggested Gary should try for the motor pool instead. But Gary was determined to take the examination for intelligence school and when the results came back, his marks were in the 90s.

Between his stint in the Army (during which he had been assigned to GCHQ Cheltenham) and his service in the DEA (which he joined after leaving the Army), Gary had seventeen years' experience in the intelligence field and he had retained a passionate enthusiasm for his chosen profession. His exceptional talents had been recognized by DEA headquarters, who had sent him to Bolivia to create an intelligence division. But his first boss, Don Ferrarone's predecessor, had not been supportive and many plans that Gary proposed were greeted with scepticism or derision.

Don, in every respect, was the opposite of his predecessor. He considered Gary unique among analysts because of his ability to bridge the gap between intelligence and operations, and when he had seen the file on Yayo Rodriguez, he had immediately told Gary and Jim Nims, one of the dozen agents stationed in Bolivia on long-term assignments, to update the intelligence in order to mount an operation.

Gary and Jim had set to work. They already had considerable information; for six months, sporadically, Gary had been collecting intelligence. They knew Yayo Rodriguez's rank among Bolivian traffickers (one of the top three) and they knew his headquarters were in San Ramon, a small town, hardly more than a break in the jungle. It was one of a complex of towns (San Joaquin and Santa Ana de Yacuma were two others) near the Brazilian border in a wild frontier region called the Beni, whose terrain was a mixture of dense jungle and savannah criss-crossed by numerous tributaries of the Amazon river and whose distance from La Paz and physicial isolation provided cocaine traffickers with safe havens.

The two Americans set up a network of informants which Jim organized from Santa Cruz where the DEA had a small office. Sited in the fertile agricultural plains of the eastern part of the country, Santa Cruz is Bolivia's second largest city and the home of many of the older *narcotraficante* (drug trafficking) families whose original wealth derived from cotton. When the cotton boom collapsed at the end of the 1970s, they switched to cocaine and, largely because of their new-found wealth, Santa Cruz is now Bolivia's most prosperous city.

One by one, Jim sent his CIs ('Confidential Informants') into San Ramon. These CIs were Bolivians, present or past residents of the town, involved in the narcotics industry, who were cultivated by the DEA and provided information for money or personal reasons. It would usually take a couple of days to make the trip because they had to travel by truck or bus along rutted dirt tracks, occasionally journeying by boat, sometimes by plane. They would stay a week, then return to Santa Cruz; Gary would make the forty-five-minute flight from La Paz for their debriefing.

It was from one of these informants that Gary first learned that Yayo Rodriguez was stealing Brazilian planes and killing their pilots. Several months before the press heard of the story, a CI photographed two twin-engined Brazilian aircraft in the San Ramon hangar. Their tail numbers had been painted over. When the Bolivian Air Force seized a similar plane from one of Yayo's *estancias*, or ranches, they called in the Screaming Eagles (a US-trained team of Bolivian chemists), who vacuum-searched the twin-engined aircraft and found traces of cocaine. For Gary Hale, this information constituted another piece of the puzzle which, when finally fitted together, would provide a picture of Yayo's organization and the intelligence to conduct a successful operation.

Following up the story of the missing pilots, a team of Brazilian policemen arrived in Trinidad, the capital of the Beni; they carried information about the stolen aircraft and the story was leaked to the Brazilian newspaper *El Global.* Under pressure from their powerful northern neighbour, the Bolivian government formed a commission to investigate the charges.

The copy of *Opinion* that Don was reading that Monday was dated a week earlier, 22 October. But this was the first time he had seen it. Shortly before its publication he had flown to Madrid to participate in the Trilateral Conference, a gathering of narcotics law enforcement officials from Spain, Italy and the United States.

He had been reluctant to leave La Paz in the midst of the last-minute planning of Operation Tandem but when he arrived in Spain, he realized that the meeting was more than an amiable get-together over glasses of sangria. It involved resources which he badly needed. Italy and Spain were particularly vulnerable to cocaine epidemics: Spain, because of its historical connections with Latin America, is a major port of entry for cocaine imports to Europe; Italy has the largest per capita population of heroin addicts. The two countries were now offering arms and equipment to help the war against narcotics. They had intended these resources should all go to Colombia until Don Ferrarone explained the dramatically changed situation in Latin America.

Bolivia was becoming a major battleground. In the last few years, largely as a result of over-production which had forced the trafficking organizations to streamline their operations, its strategic importance had increased substantially. For most of the 1980s Bolivia had been the second largest producer (after Peru) of coca leaf and a major producer of coca paste and base (a mash of coca leaves and various chemicals constituting the two first stages of cocaine manufacture). These had been sold to the Colombians to be converted into cocaine. While Colombia remained the world's leading producer of cocaine, exporting 566 metric tons in 1989, substantial amounts were now being processed within Bolivia in hundreds of laboratories scattered through the north and east of the country in the heavily forested Beni, Pando and Santa Cruz departments. Moreover, the traditionally provincial Bolivian trafficking organizations were in some cases bypassing the Colombians and distributing directly to the United States and Europe. The result was that Bolivia was now involved in cultivation, manufacturing and distribution.

Don succeeded in persuading the Europeans to give some of the resources to Bolivia, which had not been their intention because of the government of Bolivia's notorious inactivity in counter-narcotics. And although the amount of the aid was comparatively small, Don was running operations on a ludicrously tight budget.

Every additional radio, automatic weapon, magazine and pair of boots counted.

It was a twenty-hour flight from Madrid to La Paz and Don was tired when he got back to his desk on the Monday morning. As he walked into his office, he called to his secretary over his shoulder, 'Get in Gary and the rest of the guys.' The first item on his agenda was Operation Tandem.

The *Opinion* article caused his face to wrinkle in a grimace of disappointment. He pointed a finger at one of the pictures – a map of Bolivia with half a dozen arrows, all directed at San Ramon, the site of the proposed invasion. Shaking his head, half-humorously and half in despair, he asked his men, 'Can you believe this? It points out San Ramon, shows the aircraft, naming Yayo, saying he's stolen planes, saying he's got them stashed in San Ramon, saying he's been killing Brazilian pilots . . .' Then he turned to Gary and Jim Nims. 'You guys debriefed the CI – what's the latest?'

In Don's absence they had sent in an informant specifically to 'test the climate'. His report boded ill for the fate of Tandem. Two weeks earlier the town had been bustling – ten aeroplanes on the strip making half a dozen flights daily, drums of precursor chemicals (the commercial chemical used to process cocaine) arriving down the Rio Machupo, laboratories 'cooking' – processing paste and base – 600 kilos of coke ready for shipment. Now it was like a ghost town. Yayo had vanished. The Colombians (who in ever greater numbers were penetrating the Bolivian drug organizations) had also left. There were only two aeroplanes in the hangar and both were broken, one without wheels, the other missing its propeller.

It wasn't, however, the newspaper stories that had triggered everyone's departure. It was the Bolivian investigative commission wandering through the jungle searching for a mass grave containing the bodies of the murdered Brazilian pilots. Missing San Ramon, it had gone to San Joaquin, a village forty miles north and another traffickers' haven. One of the drug dealers in San Joaquin flew down to San Ramon and alerted Yayo Rodriguez. The trafficker left town the following day.

Don listened gloomily to Gary's report of the situation in San Ramon. There was, he realized, very little room to manoeuvre. He had three weeks at most in which to carry out the operation.

The date now was 30 October and the rainy season would begin in the middle of November – and when the rains began, they would transform the Beni, turn its dirt roads and airstrips into mud sinks and its low-lying areas into great lakes. It would be impossible to transport a battalion of men and their equipment. For six months, between late November and June, the region's main form of transport was by small boat.

Don went around the room, eliciting each man's opinion – 'Do you think the operation's blown? You tell me what you think is best.' This was his style, to draw everyone in, even if he reserved for himself the final decision. It was one of the reasons he was so well liked by his men, that and the feeling of calm and strength he conveyed.

Gary was eager to go ahead. 'Yeah,' Don told him, 'and all you're going to find is a couple of old ladies smoking their socks.' There was sarcasm in his voice but it was tempered by affection – he and Gary had much in common.

Then Don made his decision. They would postpone the operation, but for only a week. They should update their intelligence, send in another informant with instructions to probe gently. Maybe Yayo had moved to one of the outlying *estancias*; maybe they could attempt to raid a laboratory to break up production, although the results of such a helicopter sortie were always more problematical. Maybe, when the publicity subsided, Yayo would move back at least some of his business. In the meantime, the battle plan needed more work. Don did not like the idea of sending an advance team in through the jungle. There was too great a chance of being detected. How were they going to ford the river? There were houseboats docked at its edge, a pontoon ferry. It was too risky to have soldiers wading across, loaded down with equipment. What about barking dogs? Wouldn't they rouse the townspeople? Complete surprise was the key to success.

He set a new date for Operation Tandem: 7 November. The two critical go/no-go factors would be the weather and what the informant reported.

As his men filed out of the office, Don was gloomy. Much as he wanted the operation to happen – and he felt enormous pressure to produce substantial results quickly – he wasn't over-optimistic. Yayo was unlikely to return to San Ramon soon. The operation would probably have to be postponed until the following summer.

He stood up, stretched, rotated his neck and shoulders, feeling the stiffness in his body that was the result of so much tension. He hitched up his trousers; they were loose at the waist. He had lost twenty pounds in the four months that he had been in Bolivia. Partly it was the altitude – La Paz was 12,000 feet above sea-level, the highest capital city in the world – and the moment you stepped off the plane at El Alto Airport, you could smell, feel, almost taste, the atmosphere's thinness. Until your body adjusted, the lack of oxygen made you sick, caused headaches, dizziness and nausea. It killed your appetite.

But it was also the pressure that was causing Don's flesh to waste. He had been an agent for twenty years; he had had many tough assignments but he had never worked in such a stressful environment. At times the obstacles in Bolivia seemed almost insurmountable. The terrain was spectacularly beautiful but it was impossible to negotiate. One of his agents, Efrain De Jesus, regularly led a party of UMOPAR from La Paz south to Bolivia's border with Chile, attempting to grab the trucks smuggling in the chemicals needed to produce cocaine. These precursor chemicals, which were illegal in Bolivia, were manufactured in Europe and America, shipped to Chile (where they were legal), unloaded at the seaports of Santiago and Arica, then trucked to five checkpoints along the Bolivian border where the traffickers bribed the customs officers to wave the trucks through. It took De Jesus and his party a week to make a single expedition, even though the total distance was no more than five hundred miles. Only twenty-five miles of the road were paved (this part could be travelled in under five hours); the rest was dust and dry dirt, snaking higher and higher, strewn with chunks of rock, landslide rubble, until at last, 15,000 feet above sea-level, the Chilean border was reached. With all this effort, they probably succeeded in seizing only five per cent of the precursors coming into Bolivia from the Chilean ports, and this still left open Bolivia's border with Brazil (the other major source of chemicals), which the Bolivian government did not have the resources to patrol.

The communication infrastructure was similarly terrible. There was no telephone system outside the major cities. In the northern and eastern frontier areas, where the DEA and UMOPAR conducted most operations, they were completely dependent on HF radios, which often malfunctioned because of atmospheric conditions or because the sound waves were obstructed by natural obstacles – hills, trees, dense ground cover. To cover a country that was larger than California and Texas combined, the DEA and UMOPAR had a couple of aeroplanes – the Casa, a small troop transport manufactured in Spain, and an Aerocommander, an executive-style jet equipped as a flying command and control centre – and eight UH-1H Huey helicopters, Vietnam War vintage machines. Glancing through log repair sheets on one of the choppers, the American military adviser to the Bolivian pilots had spotted his name and a date in the 1960s; twenty years ago he had flown the same helicopter in South-east Asia.

Then there were all the security problems: the corruption, the uncertainty over who you could trust, the constant threats to agents, the knowledge that the phones were tapped. A few weeks earlier Don and a group of agents had been in the Beni capital of Trinidad, a rustic cattle town of adobe houses, red-tiled roofs, elegant colonnades and streets of hard-packed earth whose open gutters carried raw sewage. Dressed in camouflage clothes – they had just got back from a raid on a cocaine laboratory – they were unloading equipment outside the hotel where the DEA rented office space when Don spotted three men across the street with a video camera set on a tripod. He saw one of them step back, flick the switch. He saw the red light flashing. He had heard from a source that the Colombians were keeping the DEA under surveillance and were planning to sabotage the Casa. 'Quick, duck, get out of the way!' he ordered. He asked the UMOPAR to grab the camera (the DEA had no arrest powers; they were in Bolivia only as advisers), but by the time the UMOPAR got there the men had gone.

Only a few days earlier in La Paz a couple of drug dealers had tried to break into a DEA analyst's house. Charlie Vopat was testifying at a trial back in the States but his wife heard them trying to drill through a window. She jumped out of bed, created a racket, turned on all the lights and locked herself in the bathroom. The DEA had identified one of the men. He came from an old-time drug trafficking family who lived on the same street as Charlie's family. (One of the strange features of Bolivia was how traffickers and DEA agents lived cheek by jowl. Despite the country's huge territory, it had a population of only seven million and with its small middle class, anonymity was hard to preserve.)

The attempted break-in was the next item on Don's agenda. He picked up the telephone. 'This guy's going to regret having tried this,' he muttered and dialled the number of General Lucio Anez Rivera, the UMOPAR's commander.

But all these problems – corruption, security, limited resources, impossible terrain – did not really explain Don's stress. He had experienced all this in Burma and he had loved that posting. What made Bolivia different was the situation within the Embassy, the beaucratic infighting, the intensity of the Ambassador, as Don struggled to restore the DEA's stature within the Embassy. There were nights when he would go home to his wife and tell her, 'That's it, we're out of here, I can't stand this crap any more.' But then he would return to his desk the following morning, one of his agents would come in, all excited – 'Hey, look at this case' – and Don, who a moment before had been boiling with rage, would say, 'Oh, this looks great, let's go do it, let's go,' instantly caught up in the thrill of the chase. Sometimes he was reminded of a film clip he had seen years ago of a rhinoceros in Africa charging a petrified hunter. Abruptly, the rhino had stopped; he had spotted a swathe of green grass on the side on the path and happily he began to browse, oblivious of the hunter he had been about to kill. Whenever he recalled that image, Don would mock himself – 'I'm no better,' he would think, 'than that dumb beast.'

Don could not say he had not been warned – by his superiors at headquarters, testing his mettle, and later by some of his closest friends. He had been happy, very happy, when he had learned of his appointment. He fully endorsed the DEA's strategy of trying to choke off the flow of cocaine at source – in the countries where coca leaf was cultivated before the drugs reached US borders. If it had not been successful, this was not because the concept was flawed; it was because of inadequate resources and poor administration. He believed that he could make a great impact if, like a modern-day Lawrence of Arabia operating in the jungles, he was able to mobilize the Bolivians in the war against the traffickers.

Perhaps he was being naive. The day after his appointment his friends started calling. The first was Matty Mahor, the assistant head of the Denver office, an agent whom Don deeply respected. A New York City native with a thick local accent, Matty had learned fluent Cantonese so that he could work on heroin cases. Don would never forget Matty's reaction, it was so unexpected and so deflating. 'Do you know what you're getting into?' Matty had asked. 'Do you know the problems? Do you know what you're getting your family into? Do you know how much corruption there is and how dangerous it is? Do you know what the Embassy is like? Do you know how the Ambassador feels about the DEA?'

Forewarned, on 30 June 1989 Don had left Washington with his family. He was worried, more worried than if he were going out on an operation. He knew how difficult the move would be for his family and how his position as country attaché would make them vulnerable to kidnapping.

They flew from Washington to Miami, where there was a long stop-over. At 9.30 pm they boarded the Lloyd Aereo Boliviano flight for La Paz. The children were sleeping when it landed in Panama City at 3.30 am. The sun was rising as they reached Santa Cruz a few hours later. Although it was only just past dawn, the entire DEA office had turned out to greet them.

They took Don and his family to the VIP lounge, where his children sprawled on a couch, bleary-eyed, half asleep. Don and his wife shook hands with all the agents; he knew every name; he had read their personnel files in advance; he could see the nervousness behind their smiles. He knew what they were wondering – would this new boss be any better than the last?

Don was chatting with the men when he turned around and saw the light bulbs flashing, reporters shoving. One reporter pushed a microphone in his face; he spotted a television crew filming his children. Angrily, he cried out, 'What the hell is happening?' His men grabbed the film; they were very apologetic. They had no idea how the Santa Cruz press had learned that he and his family were on the flight from Miami.

They had left Washington in the middle of the hot, heady, green, fruitfully abundant southern summer. When they arrived in La Paz after the last leg of their journey from Santa Cruz, it was bitterly cold, the middle of winter. Never had Don seen such a god-forsaken landscape as the Altiplano (literally, the high plain) on which La Paz is sited. It was flat, barren, windswept, rocky; it appeared to be devoid of animals and people. Everything was brown. There were no trees, no vegetation to speak of, just a few bits of scrub that clung to the barely discernible soil.

One by one, his family descended the aircraft's metal staircase. He and his wife had not told their children about altitude sickness; they did not want to make them unduly anxious. His middle child, a seven-year-old girl, reached the tarmac and vomited. As Don helped her clean up, he could not help thinking that this was an inauspicious beginning for a two-year tour of duty.

But as they began the steep, twisting descent into the city, Don's spirits lifted. He had always loved this moment – the first sights, smells, sounds of a new country, everything so different. And La Paz was an extraordinary place, almost surreal, part Spanish, part Indian, primitive yet modern, its Prado lined with Indian pedlars, its baroque cathedral, San Francisco, both magnificent and brutal, its chaotic skyline, an unplanned mix of half-finished skyscrapers and crumbling colonial houses, and its university building on Avenida Mariscal Santa Cruz draped with white banners on which the students had painted anti-American slogans.

As Don Ferrarone was arriving in La Paz, one of the men who had helped to select him was sitting at his desk in DEA headquarters in Washington, DC. Chuck Gutensohn was the head of the cocaine section and his responsibilities included overseeing the DEA's much-criticized Andean 'source country' operations. Better perhaps than anyone else at headquarters, he appreciated the difficulties Don would be facing. But he was deeply committed to the concept of fighting the war against cocaine at its source and like Don, and so many other DEA agents, he was an unusual combination of cynic and idealist.

As explained by Gutensohn, the theory underlying the source country strategy is appealingly simple. 'If someone is shooting bullets at you, you don't try to run around and catch the bullets, you try to take the gun away. We have people shooting cocaine at our borders and we are running around the borders trying to catch the cocaine. Why not go down to the Chapare in Bolivia or to the Upper Huallaga Valley in Peru and take away the gun that is shooting the cocaine?'

Gutensohn's enthusiasm for the source country strategy was partly a reaction to the failure of border policing, the dominant law enforcement strategy of the 1980s. In 1982 the Reagan administration had responded to the politically important constituency of South Florida, whose citizens were outraged at the violence of the Colombian cocaine distribution gangs, by creating a task force to arrest and prosecute smugglers in the South Florida region. The South Florida Task Force, headed by Vice-President George Bush, was widely criticized in law enforcement circles as ineffective. Congressman Glenn English, Democratic Chairman of the House Committee on Government Operations, described it as 'a classic Reagan response to the narcotics problem, heavy on rhetoric, light on resources, flim-flam.' In fact it involved no additional resources – its agents were pulled from other equally troubled regions to work the politically more significant South Florida region; most of the equipment came from the Pentagon.[2]

The idea of attacking drug trafficking by sealing the borders had, however, widespread appeal to politicians and local law enforcement officials whose communities were suffering the effects of cocaine addiction and street trafficking – violence, property crime, infant mortality, child abuse, social decline. In the early 1980s Congress began a process (which continues today) of fortifying America's 3700-mile-long southern land and sea border, hoping to prevent the smugglers' easy access. The fortification consisted of a system of fixed, floating and mobile radars which would eventually stretch from Florida to California, the electronic equivalent of a Maginot line. Largely because of the expense of this equipment, by the end of the Reagan administration border policing had become the single largest component of the anti-drug budget, gobbling up thirty-eight per cent of the total resources devoted to the war against narcotics.[3]

The strategy was not only very expensive, it relied heavily on high technology military equipment which might be well adapted to conventional warfare but was much less successful in dealing with the guerrilla-like tactics of the drug traffickers. The radar shield had severe shortcomings, the chief of which was the inability to detect the small low-flying aircraft used by drug smugglers.[4] Equally important, the radar shield was directed mainly at air smuggling, which was how most cocaine was brought into the United States when the concept of the screen was first broached in the mid-1980s. But as drug traffickers realized the direction law enforcement was taking, they quickly diversified their routes and means of entry. They used faster, longer-range planes which could make air drops to boats in the outer Caribbean and return to their home bases without having to land for refuelling; they flew to Mexico instead of Florida, offloading cocaine for transport by trucks, cars, vans and 'mules' (human carriers) across the 2000-mile Mexican-American border; they hid cocaine inside legitimate cargo, transporting it on commercial aeroplanes and ships.[5] Indeed, motivated by the multi-million-dollar profits of the business and the undiminished demand for their product, the traffickers showed an extraordinary ability to adapt to the changing tactics of law enforcement.

Among the critics of the border policing strategy was the Drug Enforcement Administration. This was partly for jurisdictional reasons: Customs, the Coast Guard and the Immigration and Naturalization Service (INS) were primarily responsible for defending the border from smugglers and were the main beneficiaries of the increases in the anti-narcotics budget during the Reagan administration.[6] But the criticism was also because of the strategy's heavy reliance on high technology equipment, which the DEA tended to dismiss as 'hardware and toys', rather than on the human resources – undercover agents, informants – that the DEA was used to and good at manipulating. Moreover, it focused on the wrong levels of the trafficking organizations – the smugglers were usually low- and middle-level functionaries, easily replaceable – and perhaps most importantly, given the extreme porousness of the United States border, it seemed unlikely to be effective.

The DEA's alternative approach was to return to a strategy used by the Nixon administration during the heroin epidemic of the 1970s. Then, the US government, coupling threats to cut off foreign aid with promises of compensation, had managed to persuade Turkey, the main supplier of illegal opium, to curb the cultivation of opium poppies. (Turkey has since produced very little opium for the illicit market, although it is still a major transhipment country.)

No sooner had Turkey withdrawn from the illegal market,

however, than Mexico sprang up as a new source of supply. Unlike Turkey, Mexico had no tradition of poppy cultivation or opium use; it had been neither a consumer nor a producer of heroin. But in what seems to have been a purely entrepreneurial response to continuing demand, by 1974 its northern mountainous regions were planted with opium poppies and it was supplying eighty per cent of the American market. Following up on its success with Turkey, the United States had provided Mexico with the training and technology to eradicate its poppy plantations. Between 1976 and 1980 Mexico managed to cut its heroin production by seventy-five per cent.

This sustained, two-pronged attack seemed to have a temporary impact. For several years there was a significant decline, twenty per cent, in the number of heroin addicts as prices rose sharply and the purity of the drug fell. But by 1980 heroin consumption had returned to its original high levels as opium production shifted to countries less amenable to US pressure (and resumed in Mexico) and reduction of the supply of narcotics slipped to the bottom of successive presidential agendas.[7]

With the epidemic of 'crack' abuse that surfaced in 1985, the DEA decided to try once again a strategy that had seen at least some short-term success. This time the focus was the Andean countries where coca leaf was grown and manufactured into cocaine. The DEA decided to concentrate on Bolivia. Although Bolivia did not produce as much coca leaf as Peru (54,000 hectares vs. 120,000),[8] it was a major producer of coca paste and base. Equally important, the Bolivian government permitted the DEA to help plan and lead anti-narcotics operations. In Peru, the government was less open to US direction, and a Maoist-inspired insurgency group, the Sendero Luminoso, Shining Path, controlled much of the Huallaga Valley where most of Peru's coca leaf was produced. Here, the Sendero Luminoso had forcibly appointed themselves an 'armed union' for the coca growers. In exchange for a percentage of peasant coca production, they protected the peasants from anti-narcotics operations and exploitation by the cocaine trafficking organizations. They also levied a transit 'tax' on the Colombian coca paste buyers.[9]

The example of Turkey loomed large in the DEA's thinking but reliance on this model was perhaps misplaced. Turkey's central government was strong and the peasant producers were powerless;

nor was the Turkish economy dependent on opium production. Unhindered by notions of the due process of law or the threat of revolt, the Turkish government could afford to be ruthless. Its main technique for controlling illegal opium production was to threaten to destroy an entire village's legal poppy crop if even one person was found to be growing unauthorized poppies. This gave the peasants a strong incentive for self-policing.[10] But as Don Ferrarone was eventually to discover, the odds in Bolivia were not in the DEA's favour. The country was poor, its central government weak, its peasants were organized into a powerful political force and there was a history of government entanglement in the cocaine trade.

In the summer of 1986 the DEA, UMOPAR and United States Military had conducted Operation Blast Furnace, a four-month campaign against narcotics laboratories in Bolivia's Beni region and a seminal operation for the development of the DEA's Andean source country strategy. By traditional measures, Blast Furnace was probably a failure. The publicity inevitably attendant on the arrival in Trinidad of massive American troop transports, six Black Hawk helicopters and 160 uniformed military support personnel ensured that no active laboratories were encountered; there were few arrests and the amount of cocaine seized was negligible.

But by disrupting cocaine manufacturing, Blast Furnace forced the price of coca leaf to drop from $150 a carga (the peasants' unit of measure, representing 100 pounds of leaf) to $20, which was well below the estimated production cost of $30. Briefly, coca became an unprofitable crop. But as soon as Blast Furnace ended, the traffickers reactivated their laboratories and the price of coca leaf bounced back, although it was never to reach its pre-Blast Furnace high levels.

While Blast Furnace was taking place, the DEA was planning a follow-up programme, Operation Snowcap, a sustained campaign against the traffickers' organizations that would, it was hoped, permanently depress coca leaf prices, thereby forcing the peasants to switch crops. The key difference from Blast Furnace was the limit on US military involvement – the all too visible presence of the American Army was bruising to Bolivian nationalist feelings. The US Army would be confined to a training camp in the Chapare and operations would be conducted by the UMOPAR, financially supported by the State Department through its sub-agency, the Narcotics Assistance Unit (NAU) in La Paz, and advised and assisted by DEA agents.

In November 1986, with the start of the rainy season, Operation Blast Furnace ended. On the massive C5-A transport plane that arrived to withdraw Army personnel and equipment were six Vietnam vintage Huey helicopters. These helicopters, on loan from the US Military to the State Department and thence to the Bolivian Air Force, would provide the initial airlift for Operation Snowcap.

When Chuck Gutensohn was appointed head of the DEA cocaine section in the spring of 1988, his first priority was Operation Snowcap, which had already come under criticism from the State Department, specifically the NAU in the American Embassy in La Paz, which was actually charged with equipping, supplying and arming the UMOPAR. In the summer of 1988, and again a few months later, Gutensohn went to Bolivia on two tours of inspection. Much to his dismay, he discovered there were serious problems.

Bolivia's DEA operation consisted of four offices located in La Paz, Santa Cruz, Cochabamba and Trinidad. They were staffed by a dozen DEA agents on long-term assignments supplemented by three dozen agents drawn from the DEA and other federal law enforcement agencies (the Customs, Coast Guard, and Immigration and Naturalization Service) serving voluntary three-month tours of duty, all commanded and coordinated by the chief DEA agent in Bolivia, the country attaché.

Gutensohn realized that there was little communication between the regional offices. He saw a lack of leadership, a lack of direction. The intelligence chief, Gary Hale, had been baulked in his efforts to create an intelligence programme. There did not appear to be a battle plan. Poorly trained Snowcap agents were manning fixed road blocks, which the traffickers simply bypassed; they were breaking up *pozo* pits (which the peasants used to macerate coca leaf into paste, the first stage of cocaine processing) instead of attacking the trafficking organizations at the highest levels.

To make matters worse, the ire of Robert Gelbard, recently appointed Ambassador to Bolivia, had been evoked by the disarray. Gelbard was an abrasive New Yorker, the youngest Ambassador in the State Department and something of an *enfant terrible*, intelligent (with a Harvard degree in economics), demanding but temperamental. He had publicly criticized the DEA and his complaints, much to the agency's chagrin, were reported in the Congressional Record. Gelbard wanted to put an Army colonel, reporting directly to him, in charge of counter narcotics operations.

This prospect, which was anathema to every DEA agent, was especially repugnant to Chuck Gutensohn. He had fought in America's secret war in Laos and had experienced first hand the consequences of 'remote command'.

In 1970, when he was a twenty-five-year-old Green Beret and about to leave the Army after finishing his second tour in Vietnam, Gutensohn had been recruited by the CIA and sent to Laos as a civilian adviser to Laotian troops. Operating under conditions very similar to Bolivia – dense jungle terrain, makeshift equipment, little or no medical support, poor communications – he was under orders from an Army colonel. This colonel, who had no understanding of the terrain, would stick his finger on a map – 'Take one company and hit the Ho Chi Minh Trail here.' Gutensohn would tell him, 'You can't do that, you can't get them in and you can't get them out and how do I support them while they are there?' But the response would come back, 'The decision's made, we want the trail hit right there.' So Gutensohn would go out with 140 soldiers and come back with 28 including the wounded.

After Gutensohn had finished his stint in Laos and returned to the States, he joined the DEA. Nearly twenty years later, when, as chief of the Cocaine Desk, he assessed the problems in Bolivia, his experiences in Laos still loomed large in his thinking. He was determined that as long as DEA agents were the ones in harm's way, then it would be the DEA and not the Army who would command the troops. He also knew that his agency would have to act quickly if it was going to forestall Ambassador Gelbard, a formidable adversary, persistent, aggressive, and a potent figure in the execution of source country strategy because within the Embassy in Bolivia he was the President's stand-in *vis à vis* the other heads of agencies. These included the Narcotics Assistance Unit (NAU), the DEA, the CIA, Aid to International Development and the Army, making up what Embassy insiders called the Mission. The Ambassador had the power to eject the DEA from the country, an unthinkably humiliating prospect.

On his second trip to Latin America, Gutensohn met General Maxwell Thurman. The thin, ascetic-looking North Carolinian, whose thirty-five-year career in the Army was almost ended, was then Commander in Chief of Army Training and Doctrine Command. He listened sympathetically to the former Green Beret's exposé of Operation Snowcap's problems – how the agents' job was completely novel. On the one hand, they had to be big city detectives who could interview informants and work intelligence into 'target packages'. But they also had to act like military commanders, plan ambushes of laboratories and help lead the UMOPAR into battle, while always remembering that they were still policemen (although clothed in camouflage uniforms and carrying automatic rifles). If they were attacked, they were under orders to retreat; they could shoot to kill only if there was an imminent threat to their lives. Their job was to arrest, seize evidence, destroy precursor chemicals, not kill people. There was no prototype for this type of hybrid law enforcement agent – half policeman, half soldier.

Both Gutensohn and the General saw the connection between what the DEA was trying to achieve in Latin America and concepts being developed at the Center for Low Intensity Conflict at Langley Air Force Base in Virginia. Created in 1986 as a joint Army-Air Force institution, the Center studied what many soldiers thought would be the dominant form of warfare in the future – limited political and military conflicts usually confined to a specific geographical area, characterized by constraints on weaponry, tactics and the level of violence, and whose goals would be a complex mix of political, social, economic and psychological issues.[11] The war against narcotics seemed to fit this description exactly.

Thurman offered to help the DEA and when Gutensohn returned to Washington, he sat down with the Center for Low Intensity Conflict and General Downing from Thurman's command. Together, the Army and the DEA did an analysis which identified one thousand tasks required of Snowcap agents.

In the months that followed they created a very rigorous seven-month training programme: a week of psychological and physical testing, seven weeks of field training at the US Army Rangers camp in Fort Benning, Georgia, plus five months of Spanish language study at the Defense Language Institute in Monterey, California.

But the Snowcap agents needed more than training; they also needed a new commander. Finding the right man would not be easy. The DEA needed someone with experience overseas, who could restore morale and heal the divisions; someone with a strong will and clear focus who could stand up for the DEA yet win the Ambassador's approval. The new country attaché would be in charge of both the small group of agents and analysts permanently assigned to Bolivia as well as the Snowcap teams on six-month tours of duty. He would be responsible for developing a new DEA strategy, with new targets and operations that would effectively use the Snowcap people.

As Gutensohn and his bosses reviewed the candidates, one agent stood out among all the others. He was forty-one-year-old Italian-American Don Ferrarone, born and raised on a farm in Springfield, Massachusetts, a doctor's son, who looked more like a professor than a narcotics agent. The only renegade in a family of professionals, he had joined the DEA as a rebellious twenty-year-old in 1970. His career had been a succession of outstanding achievements. As a rookie undercover in New York City, he had managed to penetrate the Schiacca organized crime family; when he was shipped to France because the Mafia wanted to kill him, he had played a major role in dismantling the French laboratories supplying heroin to the United States in the 1970s. Returning to New York City a few years later, he had made the case that brought down 'Mr Untouchable', Nicky Barnes, the biggest heroin dealer of the 1970s. Out of nothing, he had created the DEA's first office in Burma.

But given this catalogue of successes, perhaps the most impressive thing about Don Ferrarone was the way he was assessed by his fellow agents. A few days after hearing of Don's appointment, Gary Hale called around the States to his DEA friends. From his cubbyhole office in the Embassy in La Paz, he asked, 'Hey, what do you know about Don Ferrarone? What's he like?' It was a question that deeply concerned him after his experiences with his last boss. So he was greatly relieved when he heard their response. To a man, they replied, 'Oh, he's energetic, a real go-getter and a real nice guy.'

3 Ready, Aim, Fire!

Six weeks after his arrival in Bolivia, in the middle of August 1989, Don Ferrarone had set in motion Operation Tandem. He told his men he wanted to do a big, bold, ambitious operation whose scope and success would conclusively demonstrate the DEA's resurrected competence. It was Gary Hale De Los Santos and Jim Nims, an agent from New Hampshire, fair-haired, blue-eyed with a sweet demeanour ('a real gentleman' was how Gary described him), who had pinpointed the little town of San Ramon as a potential target.

Every week Gary and his team of analysts processed a flood of intelligence – on the movement of aircraft, chemical precursors, the locations of laboratories, refuelling points, stashes, transportation routes. The list was lengthy, with probably thirty variables; some information was collected through classified sources, some from informants. It came into Gary's office in a random fashion. He might pick up something on aircraft traffic; then, fifteen minutes later, hear about a laboratory in the Beni; then learn of the seizure of a truckload of chemicals a thousand miles south on the Chilean border. The real trick was putting it together, taking the fragments and forming a picture. Sometimes this could be a slow and frustrating process, like working on a jigsaw puzzle with a thousand pieces and only a couple of colours. But with San Ramon, Gary was lucky. Everything fell into place very quickly.

He saw that in the area there was a high frequency of aircraft flights, reports of laboratories, reports of chemicals moving upriver, reports that San Ramon was a traffickers' haven, reports that Yayo Rodriguez was killing Brazilian pilots and using their planes to transport narcotics. Gary flew out to Santa Cruz and met with Jim Nims, who had four or five informants with direct access to San Ramon.

The town was small – its population was about four thousand – and primitive. The jungle began where its dirt roads ended. From the outside world there were only two ways to reach it. To the west, a road approached the town through the jungle, ending abruptly at the River Machupo. On the east side, there were two 1600-foot airstrips whose tower and hangar were controlled by Yayo Rodriguez. (These airstrips were not an anomaly. The main form of transport on the Bolivian frontier is small twin-engined aircraft and there are some three thousand private airstrips, or *pistas*, in the Department of the Beni, some built by trafficking organizations, others serving legitimate ranchers, most carved out of the jungle by men wielding machetes.)[1]

Although San Ramon was the headquarters for several traffickers, the most important was Yayo Rodriguez. His organization was based on some members of his extended family, middle-class ranchers of Spanish lineage who had diversified into cocaine when it became more lucrative than raising cattle. (Until the cocaine boom of the 1970s the region's chief industry was cattle ranching, which had been introduced by Jesuit missionaries in the nineteenth century.) Many of the assets they used in the cocaine business – *estancias*, airstrips, aeroplanes – were also still used in ranching. The aeroplanes, for instance, did double duty, carrying food to the hands, medicine to the cattle, slaughtered beef to La Paz, while at the same time moving chemicals, paste, base and cocaine around the country.

In many respects Yayo Rodriguez was a typical Bolivian drug trafficker. He was not involved in distribution, which required expertise in smuggling, marketing and international connections – skills that Bolivians, cut off from the mainstream by their country's geographical isolation, were often lacking. Instead, he concentrated on cocaine production.

The leaf that he used was grown in the Chapare, an area adjacent to the Beni but within the Cochabamba department. It was cultivated on small landholdings averaging a couple of hectares by *campesinos* – peasants – who harvested it three or our times yearly. Sometimes the *campesinos* themselves converted it to coca paste, a preliminary stage in the creation of cocaine. This was done in *pozo* pits, long troughs dug into the ground and lined with plastic, where the coca leaf is macerated. The pits are wide enough to allow the *campesinos* to march up and down them as they soak and stomp a mixture of coca leaves and chemicals, add more chemicals, then filter the residue to obtain the paste. At other times the *campesinos* would sell their harvest to wholesale leaf buyers who then produced the paste.

Once a week, Yayo's daughter, Maria, and her son, both fugitives from the Brazilian judicial system because of their involvement in an 87-kilogram cocaine deal in Corumba, Brazil, would fly into the Chapare, load up with paste, then fly back to the Beni. The paste was processed into cocaine in a network of small, mobile laboratories whose location could be easily shifted to elude anti-lab missions. Some of these laboratories were located within San Ramon, others on *estancias* within thirty miles of the town.

Under the supervision of a chemist, workers in the laboratories converted the paste to coca base (through the addition of sulphuric aid, aqueous potassium permanganate and ammonium hydroxide) and then mixed it with ether and hydrochloric acid to produce cocaine. The precursor chemicals were purchased in Brazil, smuggled to the laboratories via the River Machupo or flown into the region in twin-engined planes. Yayo's chemists, according to several informants, were Colombian.

His daughter Maria owned the chief hotel in San Ramon. In it lived the Mayor plus numerous Brazilians and Colombians. According to Jim Nims' informants, the Mayor, when he was not occupied with his official functions, worked as a paste buyer for a Brazilian narcotics trafficker who had recently arrived in San Ramon, bringing Yayo two tractors which would probably be used to build airstrips in the jungle. In fact the town was crawling with foreign traffickers. There had been a big influx of Colombians within the last year (resulting from stepped up counter-narcotics operations within Colombia) and a corresponding increase in narcotics-related assaults (two Colombians had been murdered six months earlier). Wherever the Colombian traffickers went, an increase in violence was predictable.

In addition to their properties in San Ramon and *estancias* in the Beni which housed laboratories, stash houses for processed drugs and storage places for chemicals, Yayo Rodriguez's organization had six houses in Santa Cruz which served as meeting places for illegal contacts, and rest and recreation spots for the Colombians. Yayo also had an extensive supply of HF radios which he used as a communication system. His organization was well protected. He had a radio link with Trinidad, where a corrupt officer kept him notified of the UMOPAR's movements. The traffickers code-named the UMOPAR '*los perros*' (the dogs), and called the DEA's Casa troop transport '*el pato*' (the duck).

As Don Ferrarone watched Gary putting together Operation Tandem, saw the hours he was working, he sometimes wondered if he was being fair to the analyst. But then Don realized that Gary was doing just what he wanted in a job that was everything to him, while his wife and children were back in the States.

Don would never forget his first meeting with the analyst, two days after he had arrived in Bolivia. The entire La Paz staff was crammed into his office. This was his maiden speech and Don was a little nervous, but their faces seemed respectful as he told them that he wanted to put more resources into intelligence – if he was going to make any mistake, it would be in that direction. They had to get absolutely right the wiring diagram of the country. Their strategy, if it could be called that, had been 'ready, shoot, aim'. He wanted to make it 'ready, aim, fire'. Instead of going after *pozo* pits, they were going to get the organizations. He wanted to identify the top twenty trafficking networks. He envisioned the Snowcap agents and the UMOPAR teams as a precision strike force who would arrest, seize and destroy these organizations' assets, the people and things without which they could not function: their chemists, chief paste buyers, accountants, pilots, their labs, aircraft, HF radio communication systems. The emphasis would be on crippling entire organizations, not just arresting major traffickers – which had limited effect because there was always someone in the wings waiting to take over.

Then Jesse Guttierez, a dark-skinned, slope-shouldered Mexican-American, burst into laughter. Mortified, Don felt the anger in him rising until he realized that Jesse was laughing from pleasure. (Don would come to admire Jesse, with his extraordinary street sense and velvety manner, as the classic example of a case agent.) Then Gary stood up and laid a stack of papers on his desk. When Don looked through them, he saw to his dismay that they were plans, good plans, but scrawled in their margins were comments like 'Stay out of this. ... This is none of your business ... too ambitious'.

In the next few days, as Don looked through the files, he realized that much of what he wanted was already in the office and as he got to know the men, he came to the conclusion that his little group were first-class agents. On their own, they had come up with imaginative programmes, such as Operation Screaming Eagle, which was Gary's idea, concocted over a bottle of beer with Joe DelaCruz, the head of the Cochabamba office. This programme was based on a statute authorizing the forfeiture of assets used in narcotics trafficking. It took advantage of the fact that the Bolivian legal system, based on the Napoleonic Code, permits the seizure and retention of evidence without proof that a crime has been committed for twenty-one days pending investigation. The DEA had brought in a team of chemists and trained the Bolivians to vacuum-search aeroplanes and test the dust for drugs (cocaine can be detected in microscopic amounts). The programme was first tried in 1986, when the UMOPAR and DEA went into Trompillo Airport in Santa Cruz where many traffickers kept their planes. They vaccuum-searched twelve aircraft and found traces of cocaine in six. Following this success, the programme was institutionalized and the Bolivian chemists became known as the Screaming Eagles team.

Another programme, Pretty Chilly, was directed at the precursor chemicals which were smuggled into Bolivia over its border with Chile. (Pretty Chilly was Gary's name for the operation – it's quite cold on the Chilean–Bolivian border, 15,000 feet above sea-level.)

As Don went out on anti-lab missions, he saw that many of the criticisms of Snowcap were unfounded. For instance, he had read statements in the Congressional Record that the DEA was wasting aircraft time looking for laboratories by flying over the jungle. But the first time out, he understood the difficulties; the DEA had the intelligence, information, identifiable targets, but the helicopters were getting lost, not through any fault of the Bolivian Air Force pilots but because whole sections of the aerial maps were marked 'no information'. The frontier regions had never been properly charted and even informants, who knew how to reach the laboratories through the jungle, could not guide them in by helicopter because looking down from the air all that could be seen was a blanket of green threaded with silver. There were no roads, cities, towns, airports, no distinguishing features, just mile upon mile of thickly canopied jungle.

Four weeks after Don had suggestd they mount a big operation, Jim Nims typed up a five-page report. Dated 13 September 1989, it was a summary of what he and Gary Hale had learned about the Yayo Rodriguez organization.

As Don read through it, he grew excited. San Ramon had everything he wanted – a major trafficker, his key people, many of his assets, aeroplanes, laboratories, HF radios, chemical stashes, all in one place. He envisioned destroying an entire organization in one knock-out blow. He told Gary and Jim Nims to work out the details.

He had no difficulty obtaining approval from headquarters. As for the Ambassador, although he was still pressing for an Army colonel to take over direction of counter-narcotics operations, his enthusiasm for Don's plan was undiluted. It was just what he wanted: resolute, militaristic action in the war against narcotics which would send a strong signal to the *narcotraficante* who only six months earlier had inflicted a humiliating defeat on the Bolivian anti-narcotics police.

In June 1989 the UMOPAR had gone into the town just south of San Ramon, Santa Ana de Yacuma, which was the stronghold of Roberto Suarez, Bolivia's most powerful and notorious *narcotraficante*. The head of one of Bolivia's traditional *latifundista* families of Santa Cruz – the elite estate owners of Spanish descent – who also had vast landholdings in the Beni, Roberto Suarez Gomez was the cousin of Luis Arce Gomez, Minister of the Interior during the notoriously corrupt 'Cocaine Dictatorship' of 1980–81. After years of eluding law enforcement, Suarez had finally been captured by the UMOPAR in 1988. He was travelling by horse from one *estancia* to another, communicating with his wife by HF radio, when an informant learned of his whereabouts and tipped off the UMOPAR, who crept up on the ranch after marching through the jungle. He was imprisoned in the Panoptico prison in La Paz (where his cell was promptly upgraded with a carpet and television). But his repeated attempts to escape from prison were a constant irritant to the Bolivian government. Only a few days earlier Don had learned through an informant that Suarez was allegedly offering $40,000 to a Supreme Court judge (the highest court in the land, seated in the ancient city of Sucre) to arrange his transfer on health grounds to a clinic in Trinidad – where the notoriously corrupt infrastructure could make an escape more feasible. Don relayed this to the Ambassador, who alerted the government.

On 22 June 1989, a week before Don arrived in Bolivia, the UMOPAR had decided to go into Suarez's stronghold of Santa Ana de Yacuma in an attempt to arrest Hugo Rivero Villavicancio, another of Bolivia's top *narcotraficantes*. In the early hours of the morning, after marching eight hours from a forward operating base, thirty UMOPAR forded the river (they had carried an inflatable boat through the jungle) and went into the town. When they entered Rivero's house, his guards opened fire. They managed to arrest his Colombian chemist but Rivero escaped – he leapt over a fence clothed only in his underwear. Then the townspeople joined in, throwing rocks at the anti-narcotic police and firing weapons; the Navy, which was garrisoned in the town, entered the fray on the side of the townspeople. Civilians were killed, caught in the cross-fire. For the UMOPAR, the operation was a disaster.

A few weeks later the indignant American Ambassador, angered by the Bolivians' ineffectual efforts to stop cocaine trafficking, had criticized the government for not having its own territory under control. Although this was patently true, coming from the Ambassador's lips it had caused a furore.

Since the Santa Ana episode, a new Bolivian government – the sixth since 1980 – had come to power. It was a fragile coalition of the left and right. Its President was Jaime Paz Zamora, the leader of the left-wing MIR and a former sociology professor and student political activist. During the 1970s he had vigorously opposed the authoritarian regime of President Hugo Banzer Suarez, who had first imprisoned and then exiled Paz Zamora. Banzer (whose private secretary, nephew and cousin were arrested for cocaine trafficking in Canada and Florida during his presidency in the 1970s) was now leader of the rival right-wing party,

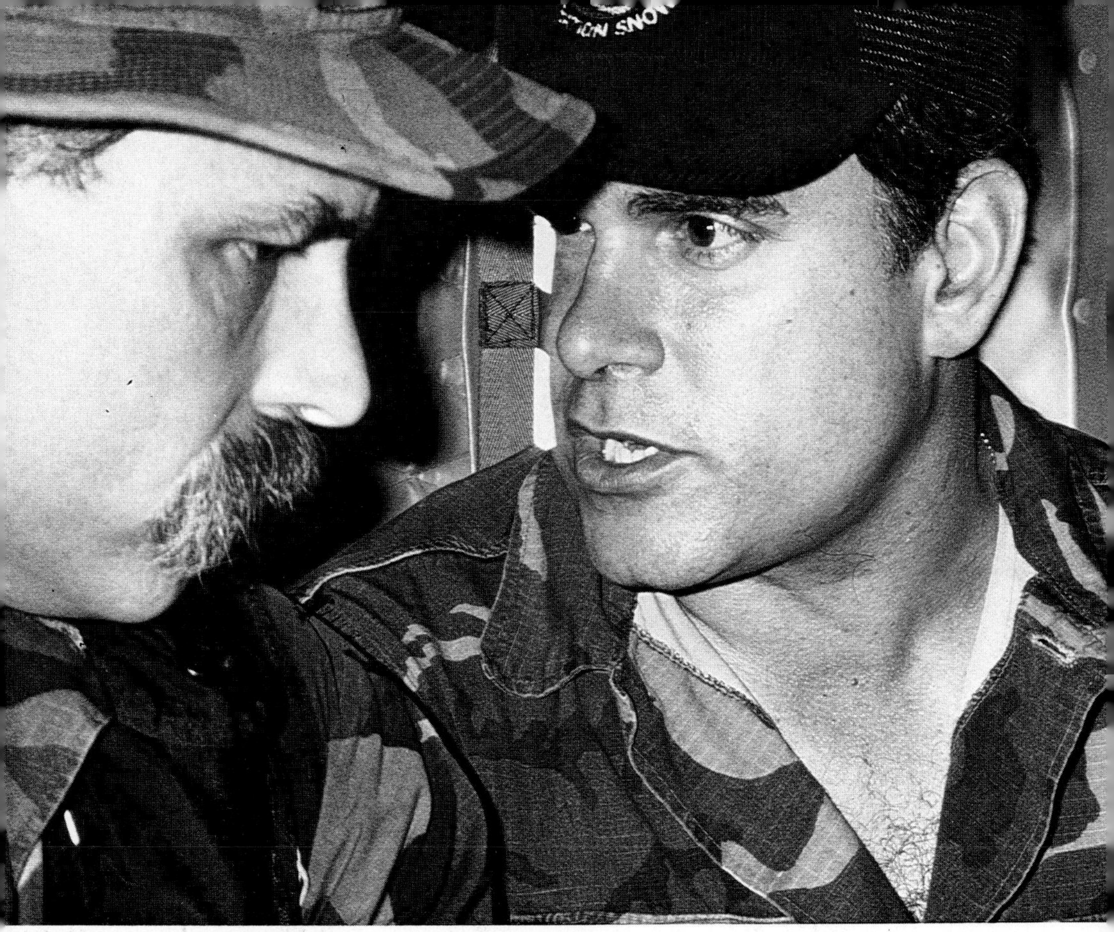

ABOVE Don Ferrarone, the DEA chief in Bolivia, briefing Special Agent Jim White as they fly to Las Vegas near the Brazilian border, the staging point for the assault on San Joaquin.

LEFT Sent by headquarters to Bolivia to create an intelligence division, analyst Gary Hale became one of the masterminds of Operation Tandem.

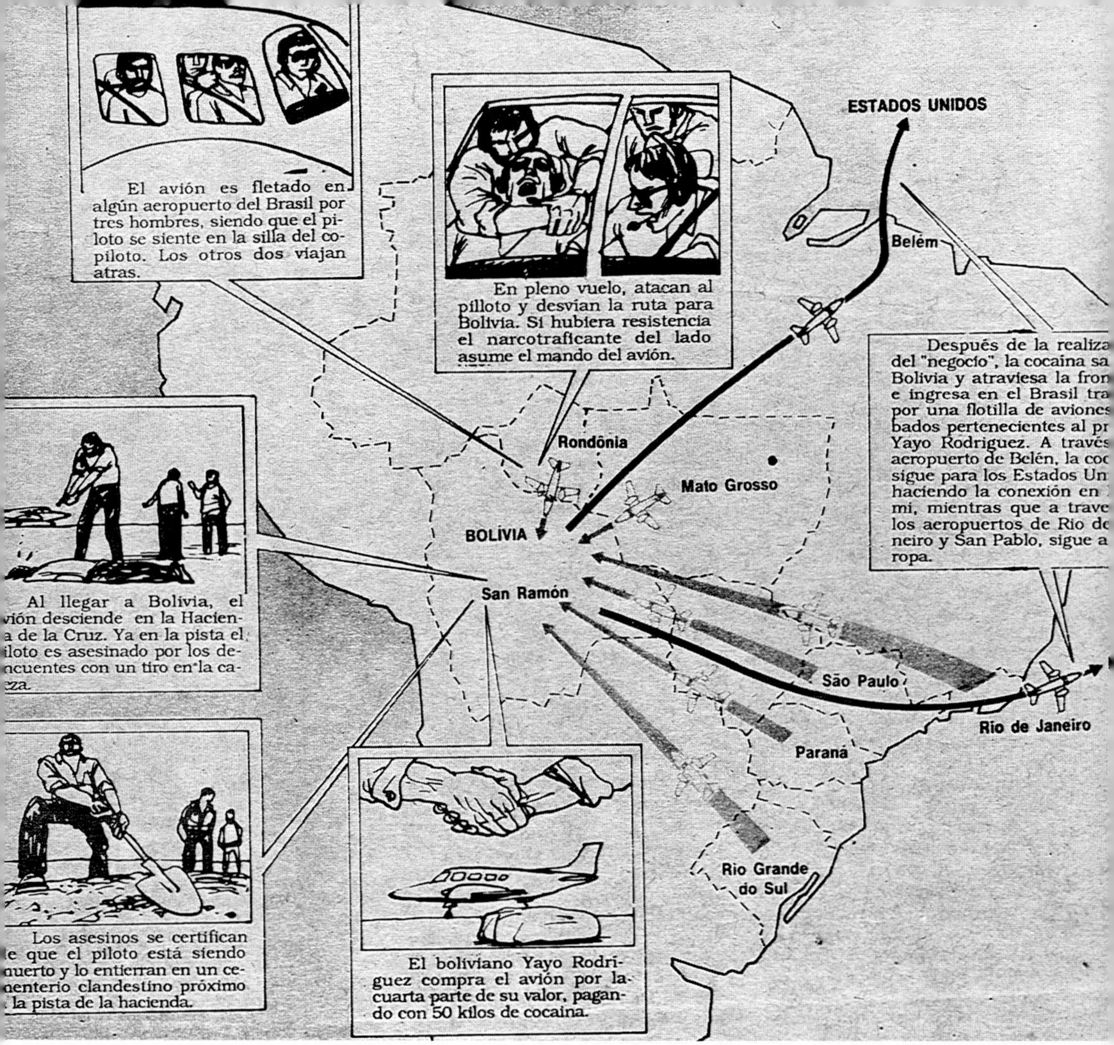

El avión es fletado en algún aeropuerto del Brasil por tres hombres, siendo que el piloto se siente en la silla del copiloto. Los otros dos viajan atras.
En pleno vuelo, atacan al pilloto y desvian la ruta para Bolivia. Si hubiera resistencia el narcotraficante del lado asume el mando del avión.
ESTADOS UNIDOS
Belém
Después de la realiza
del "negocio", la cocaina sa
Bolivia y atraviesa la fron
e ingresa en el Brasil tra
por una flotilla de aviones
bados pertenecientes al pr
Yayo Rodriguez. A través
aeropuerto de Belén, la coc
sigue para los Estados Un
haciendo la conexión en
mi, mientras que a trave
los aeropuertos de Rio de
neiro y San Pablo, sigue a
ropa.
Rondônia
Mato Grosso
BOLÍVIA
San Ramón
Al llegar a Bolivia, el
vión desciende en la Hacien-
a de la Cruz. Ya en la pista el
iloto es asesinado por los de-
ncuentes con un tiro en la ca-
eza.
São Paulo
Rio de Janeiro
Paraná
Rio Grande do Sul
Los asesinos se certifican
e que el piloto está siendo
nuerto y lo entierran en un ce-
nenterio clandestino próximo
la pista de la hacienda.
El boliviano Yayo Rodriguez compra el avión por la cuarta parte de su valor, pagando con 50 kilos de cocaina.

ABOVE The newspaper story that nearly killed off Operation Tandem with an artist's rendition of how Yayo Rodriguez, one of Bolivia's top-ranking traffickers, kidnapped and murdered Brazilian pilots, and seized their aeroplanes. All arrows point to the DEA's top secret target, Yayo's safe haven, the town of San Ramon.

RIGHT ABOVE Two of the stolen Brazilian planes seized by the UMOPAR and DEA in San Ramon. The bodies of their pilots were never found.

RIGHT BELOW Yayo Rodriguez, the cattle rancher who has become Bolivia's third-ranking cocaine trafficker, a rare portrait from the DEA files.

ABOVE A Bolivian *campesino* chewing coca leaves, a traditional custom which the Spanish encouraged when they enslaved the Indians. Coca stimulates activity and wards off cold and hunger.

RIGHT ABOVE In the first stage of processing coca leaf into cocaine, the *campesinos* mix it with chemicals in pozo pits, long troughs dug into the ground and lined with plastic, wide enough to allow the *campesinos* to march up and down, stomping the leaf until it becomes a paste. The chemicals eat into the paste stompers' skin and many of them have severe ulcerations on their feet.

RIGHT BELOW This *campesino* is drying coca leaves. On her two-hectare plot she also grows subsistence crops like carrots and yucca, but it is coca that brings in cash: the modest sum of $600 a year.

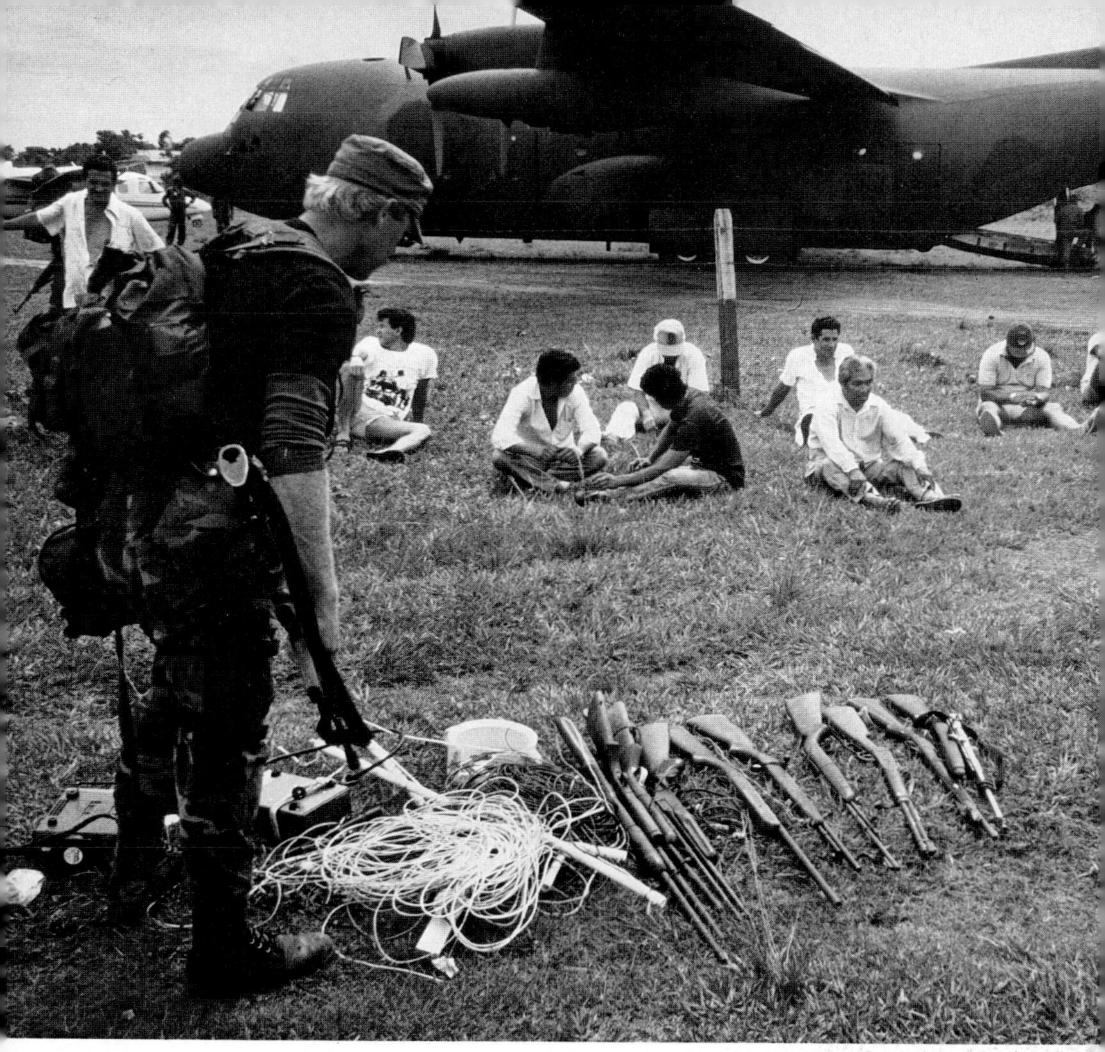

LEFT ABOVE The UMOPAR burning chemicals and equipment from a cocaine lab in San Ramon.

LEFT BELOW A band of UMOPAR securing a street corner in San Ramon while the rest of the force rounds up traffickers.

ABOVE A DEA agent inspects a haul of weapons and shortwave radios while traffickers wait to be boarded on to the C-130.

ABOVE The DEA agents in Bolivia are half policemen, half soldiers. They dress in camouflage, are armed with automatic rifles, and they lead the UMOPAR into battle. But their job is to help to arrest, seize evidence, destroy labs, not to kill.

LEFT Flying to Las Vegas, the staging post for the assault on San Joaquin, DEA agent Victor Cortez is worried that a corrupt Bolivian Army colonel may have compromised the operation.

ADN.[2] Under the terms of the coalition government, he ceded the presidency to the man he had once imprisoned in exchange for chairmanship of the powerful National Political Council and half the cabinet seats for members of his party.

On 6 August, only five weeks after Don Ferrarone arrived in Bolivia, the new President was sworn into office. As was the custom, he and Banzer proceeded to make sweeping changes in personnel, including appointing to sensitive command positions in the UMOPAR individuals whom the DEA suspected of involvement in drug trafficking.

The new government's attitude towards the cocaine industry was ambivalent. On the one hand, it was under great pressure from the United States to curb coca cultivation and drug trafficking. Bolivia's own addict population was increasing, particularly in Cochabamba where maceration pit workers smoked *pistillos* (crack-like cigarettes) as an antidote to the tedium and fatigue of stomping coca. (This is a familiar phenomenon – Thailand, Pakistan and Turkey all experienced dramatic increases in their addict populations after they became major heroin producers.) More frightening was the escalation of narcotics-related violence, which seemed to have been triggered by the arrival of the Colombians. The Bolivians found this especially repugnant because it ran totally counter to their pacific culture. (The Bolivian ethos is passive, non-confrontational; violent crime is almost unheard of.)

On the other hand, coca was an intrinsic part of Bolivian culture, used for centuries by the Indians in religious and social rituals. (Approximately fifty per cent of the Bolivian people are Indians, descendants of the Aymara and Quechua pre-Colombian indigenous cultures; twenty-five per cent are '*mestizo*', a racial mixture; and twenty-five per cent are of Spanish descent.) Coca leaves, openly sold in markets alongside stacks of bananas, were chewed to ward off cold and hunger, and brewed into a tea to cure altitude sickness. Until the enactment of the 1989 anti-narcotics law, coca cultivation had been legal throughout Bolivia.

But more importantly in explaining the government's attitude, during the 1980s production of cocaine had become the economy's mainstay. Bolivia has always been heavily reliant on a single commodity whose nature – silver, rubber, tin, cotton – has shifted with demand and the world market. As recently as 1971 its production of coca leaf (which then occurred almost entirely in the Yungas, the semi-tropical mountain valleys on the eastern edge of the Andes) was actually dropping as the traditional consumers, the *campesinos* and *mineros* (miners), became incorporated into the culture and the production of cash crops like citrus and coffee became more feasible.[3]

But in the late 1970s the demand for cocaine increased in North America, growing by leaps and bounds during the 1980s. This spurt in demand coincided with a succession of disasters that caused Bolivia to fasten on cocaine as its economy's life preserver.

First, there was a terrible drought in the Altiplano, the worst in a century, caused by freak weather conditions resulting from shifts in 'El Nino', the warm-water current that is the Pacific's equivalent of the Gulf Stream. The drought proved a catastrophe for highland agriculture because it took many acres out of cultivation for a decade, forcing thousands of Indians off their traditional lands. This disaster was followed by the collapse of the world tin market which, combined with the government's closure of unprofitable mines, left 27,000 miners unemployed.

Then, to control hyper-inflation, which reached 12,000 per cent in 1985, the government adopted strict monetarist policies. In the months following 'Decree 21060', the International Monetary Fund's emergency stabilization plan imposed in 1985, twenty per cent of Bolivian workers lost full-time employment and another sixty per cent were under-employed.[4] Jobless miners, *campesinos*, government employees, emigrated to Cochabamba to find work in the one sector of the economy that was booming – coca leaf cultivation and cocaine manufacture. According to President Paz Zamora, one out of five Bolivians was now working in this industry and although the figure may have been inflated, even the American Embassy conceded that the industry had become Bolivia's largest employer. For an estimated 300,000 Bolivian workers, it provided employment which could literally mean the difference between life and death.

A poll commissioned by one of the political parties during the 1989 presidential election campaign showed that out of a list of forty problems Bolivians ranked cocaine second from the bottom; thirty-eight other issues were more important. The country's number one problem, Bolivians agreed, was its abysmal poverty. Given these circumstances, it is hardly surprising that there was little popular support for strong anti-cocaine measures. This was evidenced by Bolivia's weak coca crop eradication record.

The cornerstone of the US State Department's anti-narcotics policy in Bolivia was reduction of coca plantations through crop eradication. In 1983 President Reagan's first Attorney General, William French Smith, persuaded the Bolivians to agree to reduce their coca crop to the level of 'legitimate demand' – measured by traditional consumption. But in succeeding years there was little government action. Propelled by powerful economic motives, the *campesinos* resisted, blockading roads, taking over government offices, holding Bolivian and American public officials hostage. There were bloody confrontations with the anti-narcotics police, resulting in the deaths of a dozen coca farmers.[5]

In 1987, a year after Operation Blast Furnace, the government of Bolivia caved in to the demands of the coca farmers' lobbies. It agreed not to use force to eradicate plantations and it banned the use of herbicides to destroy coca bushes. This was a big set-back for the State Department. The ban on herbicides was especially irritating. It not only made the process much more laborious (coca bushes have to be dug out by the roots – unlike opium poppies, annual flowers, which can be killed by slashing through their stems) but it also seemed illogical. The herbicides involved, according to the State Department, were much less environmentally damaging than the precursor chemicals, such as sulphuric acid, with which the cocaine manufacturers were indiscriminately polluting Bolivia's streams, rivers and jungle, or than the slash and burn techniques used to clear the jungle for new plantations.

In 1987 the US government took the unusual step of freezing foreign aid to Bolivia.[6] Despite this measure, in 1988 the government succeeded in eradicating only 200 hectares of coca bushes. In 1989 only 2500 out of 54,000 hectares were eradicated, while thousands more hectares were brought under cultivation.[7] As the Bolivian Ambassador, Fernando Illanes, explained to the American Congress, since the cocaine trade represented for Bolivia an estimated $600 million in income – only slightly less than its legal export income – the loss of $8.7 million in foreign assistance 'constituted a minor blow, a drop in the bucket'. Moreover, economic sanctions were politically counter-productive. They played into the traffickers' hands by inflaming anti-American sentiment. For extremists and even moderate factions, sanctions crystallized the Bolivians' image of America as a bullying imperialist power and made it difficult for the government to cooperate on anti-narcotic measures.[8]

In January 1989, under diplomatic pressure from the United States, Bolivia's comprehensive anti-narcotics law came into effect. It had been passed in the summer of 1988 over the vigorous objection of the coca lobby, the political organization representing the 35,000 *campesinos* engaged in coca cultivation, and to the acclaim of the American Embassy whose political counsel, Jim Cason, had attended as an observer every legislative session. Under the new law, coca cultivation became illegal except in the Yungas, the traditional area of cultivation which produced for local consumption; it maintained the ban on herbicides but empowered the government forcibly to eradicate plantations in the Chapare which produced coca leaf for the illicit market.

But seven months later, when Don Ferrarone arrived in Bolivia, the government was still equivocating on whether to forcibly eradicate coca.

In the middle of October 1989 Don Ferrarone asked his secretary to arrange a meeting with General Anez, the UMOPAR's commander. Before going any further with Operation Tandem (whose code-name Don had chosen from a list prepared by Gary; he liked the symbolism, Bolivians and Americans working together), he needed the approval of the Bolivian government. He approached the meeting with trepidation. The day before, he and Gary had discussed their tactics. How much could Don, should Don, tell the General?

The UMOPAR had a chequered history. Shortly after the unit's creation in the early 1980s, its then commander had led a coup against the democratically elected government of Siles Zuazo (1982–85). This coup, which resulted in the kidnapping of the President, was aborted after the US Ambassador's intervention.[9] The NAU had tried to improve the UMOPAR's professionalism, establishing a basic training camp in the Chapare run by the US Army. But corruption persisted within the officer corps. In its systematized form, it was called '*la cobertura*' which in Bolivian slang meant 'I'm covered, I've paid a bribe, I don't have to worry about law enforcement.'

The trafficking organizations each had an employee specifically charged with managing '*cobertura*'. Whenever there was a change in the officer corps, which happened frequently, these employees would descend on the Chapare. Like dozens of sperm making for an egg, they would try to contact and reach an understanding with the officers. Whoever first succeeded would negotiate a deal to cover the rest of the organizations. It was officers, not the enlisted men, who were the beneficiaries of corruption since they controlled the movement of troops.

The Americans were aware of the problem – there were frequent enough complaints from the coca lobby, which seized on any UMOPAR infraction to discredit the government's anti-narcotics efforts. The NAU had adopted a rule that no officer could be assigned to the Chapare unless he had successfully passed an officer's screening, training and indoctrination programme. But in the first weeks of the Paz Zamora–Banzer administration, a crew of officers who had not participated in the programme appeared in the NAU office, waving their orders and demanding that they be assigned to the Chapare – only to be roughly dismissed by the NAU chief.

The UMOPAR's latest Commander in Chief, General Lucio Anez Rivera, had just been appointed. He was a new man brought in by Paz Zamora, a native of Santa Cruz like former President Banzer. Don Ferrarone had never met him, knew no more of him than what his official résumé reported. Suppose Anez should want to know the name of the target? Gary vehemently argued they could not yet reveal it. Just as strongly, Don disagreed. He had had a complaint from Major Barriga, the head of the UMOPAR contingent stationed in Trinidad, who had called Don a few days earlier. Don reported to Gary the major's angry outburst – 'A bunch of your Snowcap guys came in, said they had a case. They wouldn't tell me about it. They kicked my guys off a helicopter and I had to go out there and tell them, "No, you get off. It's my country."'

This whole issue, Don pointed out, of the DEA's relationship to the UMOPAR, American aggressiveness and Bolivia's sovereignty was very sensitive. He had been surprised the first time he went to the regular meeting in the Embassy attended by every agency. He had not realized how deeply involved the Americans were in Bolivian internal affairs. He knew that if the DEA was to accomplish anything inside Bolivia, it had to treat its hosts with dignity. General Anez was the former Chief of Staff of the Bolivian Army, a patriot who had been exiled briefly after he attempted to overthrow the 'Cocaine Dictatorship'; as one of the leaders of the 'Dignidad Nacional' movement he had called for a campaign against cocaine and restoration of democratic rights. Don could hardly tell this man, his senior in age, rank and military experience, 'We want 320 of your guys, all your assets, but we don't want to tell you what we're going to do with them because you guys are all corrupt and we're afraid you'll leak it.'

There were other concerns. Anez's predecessor had not been aggressive – the UMOPAR's new commander be any different? The assault on San Ramon was a risky proposition. It might be too big, too controversial, for the President. Paz Zamora favoured alternative development, creating new sources of income for the impoverished Bolivians, which was a difficult prospect as long as the demand for cocaine made coca leaf more profitable than other crops. He was not enthusiastic about law enforcement. Bolivia's democracy was very fragile; he feared aggressive action that could lead to violence.

However, when Don actually met his Bolivian counterpart, some of his fears immediately receded. Anez's dark face, furrowed with creases, radiated warmth and good nature. He listened attentively. Without mentioning the name of the target except to say that it was in the Beni, the DEA agent laid out in detail the operational concept. He explained that they would need all their joint assets, nearly every UMOPAR soldier, every helicopter; they would have to rent three C-130s from the Bolivian Air Force. Of course, the operation would be run by the Bolivians. As always, the DEA's role would be to provide assistance.

Then Don said, gently he hoped, 'If you want to know the name of the target, I'll tell you. Sometimes people don't want to know but it's your call and whatever you decide, I can live with – I trust you one hundred per cent.'

Without hesitation, the General replied, 'I don't want to know,' and there on the spot without consulting anyone (which greatly impressed Don and Gary) he said, 'You have my blessings.' He would keep their plans secret – from his own staff, his superiors, even the President. He would notify Paz Zamora only after they had landed. Then, as Don and Gary were about to leave, he warned them, 'Watch out for the Army garrison at San Joaquin.' It was corrupt and if it learned of the operation it might come to the assistance of the traffickers, which could mean a repeat of Santa Ana. Don nodded and thanked the General. It was a very important factor, one they would have to account for in their planning. Don left the meeting feeling greatly relieved.

Gary and Jim Nims now stepped up their intelligence gathering, instructing informants to bring back specific information. They needed photographs of Yayo Rodriguez, his brothers, sister, nephew, pilots, chemists, accountants and other known traffickers. They needed photographs showing the exact location of homes, stash houses, chemical deposits, laboratories, weapons caches. But Don was taken aback by the first set of photographs. They were perfectly composed; the informants must have walked up to the front of each building and just stood there as they took the picture. Gary rolled his eyes, shrugged his shoulders. What could he do? The next set that came back was even worse. The CI had taken his own family members, posed them in front of the targets' houses, then snapped the pictures. Don warned Gary and Jim, 'You've got to talk to these guys; these informants have got to use a lot more caution, we've really got to get a grip on this.'

Tight security was absolutely essential. He did not want a repeat of Blast Furnace where, for six months, they had hit empty lab sites. Or of Santa Ana where the forewarned town organized its resistance. Nor did he want the San Joaquin garrison alerted. In no uncertain terms, he warned his agents, whose casual attitude he sometimes found irritating, 'This will make somebody a ton of money. I said it before and I really mean it. This is not bull shit. Nobody is to mention the name of the target, not to your wives, not to anybody, period.'

Don wanted to minimize the risk of stirring up the townspeople. He wanted a surgical operation with precisely identified targets. He wanted the UMOPAR in and out as quickly as possible. He wanted to squash any thought of resistance by using heavy manpower.

Two days before D-Day, they would pull in the UMOPAR from bases all over the country, by bus, truck and plane. They would convene at three places: the majority would go to El Alto

Airport; a contingent of sixty would gather at Trinidad; and the remaining twenty were destined for Santa Cruz. This massive movement of troops could not go unnoticed, not with the traffickers monitoring the UMOPAR's movements. To deceive them, Anez would tell officers and informants that he intended to mount a major patrol operation searching for precursor chemicals on the Chilean border – the DEA and anti-narcotics police had seized five tons two weeks earlier. Over the UMOPAR radios, he would transmit orders that the troops reporting to La Paz should bring cold-weather gear (which they would anyway need for sleeping rough at El Alto Airport). The UMOPAR troops in Trinidad would engage in anti-lab sorties to explain the unusual presence of all eight helicopters.

Don turned his attention to obtaining equipment. Enough rations and water were needed to support four hundred troops for three days, two days at the airport, one day in the field, plus guns, bullets, tear gas canisters. ... Radios were especially important. They were the only means of communicating in the jungle and if anything happened – if the townspeople counter-attacked, assaulted the airstrip, and his men had to flee, dispersing through the jungle – without radios they could be lost for ever in the jungle's suffocating thickness with no food, water, no means of making contact.

But as Don reviewed the resources available, he realized that they only had forty-two radios in the country, some of which were lost and some broken. When he went over the plan (which he did again and again to try to anticipate every possible problem), he saw that the operation was a logistical nightmare. He had to move men and equipment from points all over Bolivia to La Paz and Trinidad, then hit San Ramon just at daybreak before the first plane loaded with drugs flew out of the airport and while the townspeople still slept and the noise of the helicopters was less likely to rouse them; all this while simultaneously a small task force raided Yayo Rodriguez's houses in Santa Cruz. Everything had to be perfectly coordinated (although the aircraft – the three C-130s, the Casa, the Aerocommander and the eight helicopters – would be travelling at different speeds from different points of departure) because the success of the plan was based on complete surprise.

Although Don did not like to admit it, he realized that even though he and his agents had a hundred years of law enforcement experience among them (as he liked to tell Ambassador Gelbard in their running battle over the Army colonel), what he was trying to pull off was a battalion-sized military operation. He needed help from professional soldiers.

4 The Six-Thousand-Pound Gorilla

As Don was struggling to mount Operation Tandem, two events occurred in Washington which would ultimately determine the success of the operation and resolve who would command the source country war against narcotics – the DEA or the State Department.

On 18 September 1989 the Secretary of Defense, Richard Cheney, ordered military commanders to give greater priority to counter-narcotic activities. While refraining from direct involvement – arrests, seizures, interrogation of defendants (which would require the repeal of the Posse Comitatus Act, a century-old law prohibiting military involvement in police work) – the military was now to play a 'proactive role', providing equipment, training, intelligence and logistical support to the federal agencies involved in narcotics law enforcement.

This order, which was embodied in an internal Department of Defense memorandum, was a landmark in the history of the military's evolving role in the war against narcotics. It significantly broadened the military's involvement, which up to this point had been limited to helping the Coast Guard and Border Patrol track and identify suspect drug smuggling vessels. (In 1980 Congress had passed a rider to a defence authorization bill, permitting the Navy and Air Force to assist the Customs and Coast Guard by notifying them of sightings of suspected drug smuggling vessels. And in September 1988 Congress had made the Department of Defense the lead agency for detecting and monitoring smuggling vessels.)

Then, on 1 October 1989, General Max Thurman, who had helped the DEA organize the Snowcap training programme, was asked to postpone his intended retirement in order to serve as Commander in Chief of the Southern Command (Southcom) – which covered Central and Latin America. Unlike his predecessor and most professional soldiers, who resisted diverting resources from national security and entering the unfamiliar terrain of law enforcement, General Thurman was eager to join the war against narcotics.

Within three days of his promotion, he flew to Bolivia, where he was eagerly welcomed by Ambassador Gelbard. To the assembled heads of agencies, General Thurman explained how counter-narcotics would be an important factor in deciding how to deploy Department of Defense resources in Latin America. Fired by his own private store of enthusiasm, Thurman announced dramatically, 'I'm in the narcotics fight and I'm going to get you guys whatever you need.'

Don Ferrarone did not believe him. He looked at the gimlet-eyed General and his staff of lieutenant-colonels with their close-cropped hair and rigid faces, so different from the idiosyncratic narcotics agents. 'I've heard this before,' he said to himself and he was on the edge of being openly disrespectful. For years he had seen the DEA starved of resources; he had been in so many embassies around the world where the DEA had been the 'dirty little group' in the dark basement offices. In a couple of weeks he would have to suspend anti-lab missions because he had almost depleted the fund used to pay informants – and then there would be a series of frustrating calls as he tried to explain, without losing his temper, that if his headquarters had the appetite for more operations, then Washington would have to come up with more money.

The following day Don accompanied General Thurman to the Chapare. There, right in the middle of this wild region, one of Thurman's aides produced a black box and adjusted a parabolic aerial which automatically swivelled to fix on a satellite. 'Sir,' he said, 'it's Washington calling.'

Don watched, astonished and angry, for nothing could have brought home more sharply the plethora of resources available to the military and the impoverishment of his own operation. On some sorties he was using fifteen men where General Thurman would have deployed a hundred. His men were burned out – he could see it in their faces. He heard the complaints of some of his pilots; they had never flown so many flights or operated under such dangerous conditions. They were having to land on unknown jungle airstrips with no chance to size them up first; they were being told, 'You can't make a pass – we've got to surprise them.' Don's regular pilot, Robbie Robinson, had landed in one of the most inaccessible parts of Bolivia, in the north-west corner near the Brazilian border, only to tell Don, 'We're not going to get out, the strip's too short, we'll never make it.' But he managed. He lightened the plane, revving it hard at the end of the strip and rotating the tail, so the Casa went up like a rocket. He made this very dangerous trip three times, taking the UMOPAR out five men at a time. Don sat behind him on the last flight out; they hit the tree-tops as Robbie zoomed straight up. (He was a brilliant pilot if somewhat crazy; during his holiday he had flown upside down into the cone of an active volcano, Mount St Helens, in Washington state.)

Don had tried to explain to the Ambassador that the DEA's problem was not lack of leadership, it was lack of resources. 'We don't need more bosses, we need worker bees,' he had told him, 'not a colonel who will put the same three DEA agents under a microscope and say, "They've got their backpacks on wrong."' He had made the same point in a cable to the DEA Administrator, Jack Lawn (whom Don revered as the man who had brought heart to the agency, who knew the enormity of the task, the limitations on resources). Gelbard, who reviewed every cable, refused to send it. Don wanted to know why it hadn't been transmitted. When the Deputy Head of the Embassy explained, 'He tore it up; it's in his waste basket,' Don walked into the Ambassador's office, retrieved the pieces, taped them together and sent the cable to Lawn with an accompanying memo: 'This is the crap that I have to put up with but I want you to know my position.'

The Ambassador conceded the limitation of the military – 'They're either off or on' – but their power was almost intoxicating, with their high-tech equipment, the little black boxes with parabolic aerials. 'Toys for boys,' was the DEA agents' description.

Don partly appreciated the Ambassador's point; he saw that

Thurman's offer could prove a bonanza. Excepting soldiers (the host government would never permit US forces fighting on Bolivian soil), the military had everything he needed – aircraft, weapons, radios, high technology intelligence sources, planners. But the military was an unwieldy organization; it could be politically insensitive – 'the six-thousand-pound gorilla' was what Jack Lawn called it, and when a six-thousand-pound gorilla comes into a room, it is bound to break something even if it has the best of intentions.

Could Don accept Thurman's offer without losing control? Who would decide the deployment of resources? The DEA or an Army colonel? Don was as adamant as Gutensohn that it would not be the latter. Angrily, he had told the Ambassador, 'Even if you put him here, I won't talk to him, I won't let him in the office.'

And even if the bureaucratic dispute was resolved in his favour, there was another issue dividing him and his State Department colleagues. Before Don's appointment as country attaché, the NAU, DEA and UMOPAR had devised a strategy to break up Bolivia's cocaine industry which targeted the peasants' *pozo* pits. This strategy had been criticized by Chuck Gutensohn in his inspection review. It was, Don thought, a political time-bomb. The *campesinos* were as much victims of the narcotics trade as the ghetto drug addicts back in the United States. They were very poor, living in grass shacks on one- or two-hectare plots, on part of which they grew food for themselves such as carrots and yucca and the rest of which they turned over to the cultivation of coca leaf, their cash crop, which would bring in $600 or $700 a year. After converting the leaf into coca paste in *pozo* pits, they would sell it to the paste-buying organizations of the major traffickers. The attacks on the *pozo* pits were driving the *campesinos* to acts of terrorism, creating an alliance between them and the traffickers, and destabilizing the central government.

One of Don's first acts on arriving in Bolivia was to fly to the Chapare and meet with the Snowcap agents. 'No more *pozo* pits,' he told the men. 'No more operations against the farmers. Don't go after the bottom level of the pyramid, all we're doing is making generations of enemies and the results we're achieving aren't worth anything.'

In his conversations with the Ambassador, in his meetings with the other heads of agencies, Don urged them to rethink the strategy. They should break up the trafficking organizations through aggressive law enforcement, destroying their ability to manufacture cocaine. This would artificially depress the price of the raw product and when the price of a carga of coca leaf dropped below the cost of production (which the NAU estimated was $30 a carga), the *campesinos* would voluntarily switch to alternative crops.

In the middle of planning Operation Tandem, Don learned with dismay that a forcible eradication operation – the first since the enactment of the comprehensive anti-narcotics law ten months earlier – was planned for the end of October. Just when he needed every UMOPAR in the country, Anez was deploying thirty anti-narcotics police to protect the NAU's 'weed choppers'. Angry and frustrated, he went to the General. With his usual force, he said, 'I think this is a bullshit operation! These are the wrong people to be going after and the timing is bad. Every time you use the UMOPAR on eradication programmes, you stand a very strong chance of stirring up the local population and when that happens, they'll attack the UMOPAR and then we'll have to defend their camp.'

Anez, who was supremely courteous, listened patiently, giving no hint that Don might be unconsciously condescending. Didn't he know better than this recently arrived American the history of conflict between the peasants and UMOPAR? Twice, because of the *campesinos*' violent opposition, the government had been forced to withdraw the anti-narcotics police – from the Chapare in 1983, then five years later from Guayaramerin.[1] But this crop eradication operation was not under his control; it was the Americans' idea, worked out between a different Bolivian government ministry and the NAU. 'Does your government want to postpone the operation?' he asked pointedly. 'We understood that it was your government that wanted us to do something.'

Two weeks after Don escorted General Thurman to the Chapare, as he and his agents were frantically mobilizing DEA's scarce assets, Don called his headquarters in Washington. He was desperate, he said, for radios and people to help plan the operation. Snowcap, he had heard, was getting Army technical advisers.

Could they assist him? But as much as headquarters wanted to help him, none of these resources was immediately available. Don couldn't wait. 'Ah screw it,' he said, 'I'll go to Southcom.'

Reluctantly, he approached the Deputy Head of the Embassy. Two people, Don emphasized, were all he needed. She happily cabled his request to Quarry Heights, Panama, the foreign base of the Southern Command. Within twenty-four hours, four colonels and a major arrived in La Paz.

Over the next three weeks Don, who had come of age in the Vietnam War era and studied the history of the conflict in South-east Asia – he was fearful of repeating the same mistakes – was forced to abandon some of his prejudices. He recognized that the military planners were very helpful. They responded enthusiastically to the DEA's draft plan; it was a perfect Army Ranger-type operation – a quick in and out mission with a specific objective – but with one small difference, noted Major Ray Levesque, a specialist in low-intensity conflict, who tried to damp down his colleagues' excitement – 'They're not supposed to kill anybody!'

Southcom supplied equipment (a hundred radios were produced overnight) and supportive intelligence: twice daily weather reports obtained by satellite, which were so precise they could pinpoint the weather in five-square-mile radiuses. This was very important because if it rained for one day, it took another twenty-four hours for an airstrip to dry out and if the C-130s landed on wet strips, they would sink in the mud and be unable to fly out (knowledge acquired the hard way in Blast Furnace where on one mission a C-130 had sunk up to its fuselage, closing the strip to further aircraft). Southcom also brought organizational skills; they had experience in moving large numbers of people and equipment, combining and synchronizing different elements, experience which was inevitably lacking in the DEA. Moreover, in hesitantly opening the door to Southcom, Don unexpectedly discovered a powerful ally.

The idea of an Army colonel had been broached with Thurman and he raised it with Don on his next trip to Bolivia. Sitting in Don's office (which, although not in the basement, was still on a lower floor than the rest of the Embassy and substantially less plush than the head of the NAU's), the General, a plain-spoken man with an acute intellect who clearly liked the DEA agent, privately solicited his opinion. Don told him bluntly, 'I don't want to see a repeat of what happened in Vietnam where the Army, Navy, Marine Corps, Air Force, were all in one building and the Viet Cong were out there – everyone with a different philosophy, all squabbling over how to do it. In Bolivia, there's going to be one general in the field and that's going to be me.' And to Don's great relief, Thurman (who had served as an intelligence officer in Vietnam from 1961 to 1963) agreed.

On Sunday, 5 November, the movement of UMOPAR began all over Bolivia. Operation Tandem was going forward. For the past week the Southcom satellite had showed thunderstorm activity in the east, west and south in the Beni – everywhere but in the vicinity of San Ramon. It was, Gary Hale thought exultantly, as if God had parted the clouds and said, 'Alright boys, it's ok to go down.'

But would they find what they wanted in San Ramon? The latest informant reported one laboratory 'cooking' and several twin-engined Cessnas parked on the *pista*. Yayo Rodriguez himself had not been sighted but most of the other traffickers were back in town, encouraged by newspaper reports that the DEA was temporarily insolvent and unable to run anti-lab operations. This story (which had made the front page on 31 October) had come from Major Barriga, the UMOPAR commander in Trinidad, a distant relation of General Anez. This was completely impolitic but Don had not been angry. 'He's a bad boy – but he's right,' he told Gary, adding affectionately – for he found Barriga's dedication and enthusiasm very appealing – 'He's as much of a pain in the ass as you guys are; in fact, he's just like having a DEA guy out there.'

By the afternoon of Monday, 6 November, the bulk of the combined American–Bolivian task force was assembled in the cavernous military hangar at El Alto Airport. Three hundred Umopar soldiers stood stiffly at attention while their DEA advisers tied around each man's sleeve a ribbon colour-coded to show his team – Foxtrot, Golf, Alpha, Delta, Echo. The advisers towered above them, looking incongruously fair-skinned next to the Indians with their dark, withdrawn and roughly planed faces.

Three big-bellied C-130 aeroplanes, troop transports, were parked on the strip, overshadowed by the Andes mountains whose jagged, snow-tipped peaks overlooked El Alto. Single file, the UMOPAR trotted towards the planes, their feet beating rhythmically on the tarmac as they chanted their war-cry, their hoarse voices rising into the thin air. They were short, squat, big-lunged, barrel-chested men, descendants of the Incas and Aymara Indians, adapted to live in this rarefied atmosphere.

This was the first time many of the men had flown. They practised embarking and disembarking. They checked to make sure they had their safety catches on their weapons; one of Don's nightmares was that a C-130 would explode in mid-air because an UMOPAR had accidentally discharged his carbine.

General Anex, impeccably dressed in a pale beige suit, made his way through the crowds of men. He was searching for Don, whom he found in a small office on one side of the hangar, the operation's command and control centre for the next twelve hours.

Don looked pale; although he had shaved that morning, he had a shadow of a beard and his hair, thinned by sweat, stuck close to his head. He had been up most of the night, sleepless with worry. In the last twenty-four hours there had been a succession of problems, all unanticipated; they were what Clausewitz would have called 'friction' – the infinity of petty obstacles which prevent the activity of war from moving forward.[2] Some of the MREs ('Meals Ready to Eat', manufactured in Texas) were found to be contaminated and at the last minute there was a scurrying around to find replacements. Then the air traffic controllers called a one-day strike, which the fuel handlers joined in a gesture of solidarity, effectively closing down El Alto Airport. The last-minute intervention of General Anez finally obtained an exemption for military flights.

Don was on the telephone talking to the Ambassador. He hung up and turned to Anez, who was looking worried. One of his teams had arrived at El Alto without any guns and this was the team which would be the first on the ground, flying in on the Casa, and would have to secure the airstrip and control tower!

Don called over to his second-in-command, Gene Castillo. 'Hey Gene, we're out of . . .'

'We're out of what?' Gene interrupted irritably. He was in the middle of counting the UMOPAR assigned to him. 'I've got sixteen people. I think I'm missing somebody ...'

'They need twenty-eight carbines. Go back to the Embassy, we can get them from the armoury.'

Gene started to protest but Don shook his head. 'It's alright, it's alright. We've got plenty of time.'

He checked his watch – four o'clock. He caught Jim Nims' eye, waved him over, and called the rest of the agents, the DEA pilots, the Southcom planners, together. They had gone over it many times but he wanted to review it again, the trickiest part of the operation, the order of aircraft – their take-off and arrival times – which was absolutely critical to preserving the element of surprise.

Once again, he explained, they would assault the town in thirteen aircraft – the Casa, the Aerocommander, three C-130s, eight helicopters. Robbie Robinson would be flying the Casa; Donnie McKeough was assigned the Aerocommander; Bolivian Air Force pilots would be flying the C-130s and the helicopters. They were to approach San Ramon from different locations. The C-130s were to leave from La Paz; the rest of the aircraft would launch from Trinidad.

As of this moment, only the DEA pilots knew their destination.The Bolivian Air Force pilots would not be told until the very last minute, when they were already flying close to their target. As an extra precaution Gary, whose command of dialect was perfect, was going to sit in the third C-130's cockpit and monitor the radio traffic. Of course, the pilots would not like it. ...

The lead aircraft would be the Casa. It would land at first nautical daylight (before the sun has risen but when there is sufficient light to see). Fifteen UMOPAR commanded by Major Barriga and Agents Jesse Guttierez and Jim White would secure the control tower and survey the strip, making sure it could hold the C-130s' weight. If it looked good, the signal was green smoke. The no-go signal was a red star cluster.

Ten minutes after the green smoke signal, one by one, the C-130s should descend, while simultaneously the helicopters, coming from Trinidad, should drop small groups of troops around the perimeter. Their job was to secure the fording site by the River Machupo and block any escape from San Ramon. The Aerocommander, containing Don and General Anez, would circle overhead until the troop planes and helicopters had landed.

This timing and sequence had to be maintained precisely. If the Casa was late – or the C-130s – every other flight had to be adjusted. This would be Don's responsibility; he would have radio contact with the other aircraft, flying overhead in the Aerocommander which would serve as a command and control centre.

'I want to make certain,' Don emphasized to his pilot Donnie McKeough, holding up the diagram which mapped the flight paths and times, 'that we understand this – if things aren't right on schedule, we're going to hold back the whole crew and wait for our people to catch up, or make space, whatever's necessary. You guys have got to understand this, because you're going to be telling me what's happening. Donnie, you're the lead pilot for communication up there, and I'm going to be up there right behind you.'

Donnie nodded his head and jabbed his finger at Trinidad on the diagram. 'We've got 4.59 am as the estimated time of arrival over Trinidad – that's the important thing.'

The agents shook hands, embraced. They would synchronize their watches later that night. The Casa and Aerocommander teams left for Trinidad.

Trinidad, 6 pm. In the main hotel, where the DEA rented an entire floor to provide living quarters for Snowcap agents and space for an office, Bob Johnstone, the supervisor covering the Trinidad area, briefed the agents advising the helicopter teams. He told the men firmly that this operation was organized military-style. Each team had a job, they were to do no other – 'I don't want to see anyone tearing down the streets, chasing after people.'

Then his voice became sharper. 'We can't afford what normally happens. Everything is structured in a very, very timely fashion. The helicopters are lifting off at four am and you'd damn well better be on them.'

No matter what the situation, at 12.30 pm sharp they were to withdraw to the airfield for evacuation. If they missed their plane, they should make for a friendly *estancia* – each team would have a map showing its location. It was a few miles up the River Machupo.

Don walked into the room in Trinidad as the agents were organizing equipment – evidence bags, labels, notebooks to record seizures, handcuffs, rolls of tape because there were not enough handcuffs. He picked up the phone and dialled the hangar at El Alto Airport. He wanted his second-in-command, Gene Castillo.

'Do you have a current weather report? Is there anything, anything, that's a no/go on this thing?'

Gene reassured him that everything was fine, the weather was holding.

'Exactly who out there knows what the target is?'

'Nobody.'

'Ok,' said Don. 'We're going to keep the information here as long as we can – until we get to the point where it's no return.'

The men finished putting together their equipment. They ate and returned to their rooms for a few hours sleep.

At 2 am Don conducted the final briefing. 'I want you guys in with the least exposure,' he said, looking directly at Robbie Robinson, the Casa pilot. 'We're going to want everyone stacked up – helicopters, C-130s, Casa – all in the right order. Then Robbie, you will key off. I want those helicopters in just immediately after you're down – in case the shit hits the fan and you guys have got to be pulled out.'

La Paz, 2 am. In the hangar at El Alto Airport, Jim Nims and Gary Hale briefed the C-130 pilots. 'If radio communications fail, the Aerocommander will indicate where the targets are as we approach the runway. The location of the runway is about 350 degrees. Green smoke, you land. Red smoke, you don't land.'

The pilots, officers in the Bolivian Air Force, dressed in thick, brown leather flight jackets, sat slumped in their chairs, eyes trained on the floor, looking like sullen schoolchildren. They were furious at not being trusted with the name of the target. They were highly trained professionals and here were these gringos, treating them like puppets!

'Are we talking about one target or several targets?' the lead pilot asked truculently.

'There is more than one target.' Gary lied unashamedly. 'But the Aerocommander will choose and then guide you there.'

At 4 am, exactly on target, the C-130s took off from El Alto on a north-east flight path – their first destination, Trinidad. In the third C-130's cockpit, Gary Hale listened to the pilots' conversation.

'You are too close to my right, too close to my right. The lead plane is on my left. You are too close to my right! Are you sure you are on the right flight path?'

'That jerk is real close. . . . Are our lights on?'

Trinidad, 4.30 am. The noisy chug-chug-chugging of eight helicopters lifting off broke the black stillness of the pre-dawn morning. They headed due east in the direction of San Ramon. A few minutes later the Casa and Aerocommander departed; their flight speed was faster, they would overtake the helicopers.

Inside the Aerocommander, Don sat directly behind Donnie McKeough, studying the flight plan with a flashlight, tracking the planes, trying to coordinate their arrival times. Where were the C-130s? Had they taken off on schedule? Donnie was trying to raise them but he hadn't been successful. He tried again and again, speaking in Spanish, 'Condor, Condor, can you hear me?' Finally, on another frequency, the lead pilot's voice burst through . . . 'Affirmative! I read you very well? Do you read me?'

'I want to know when you are over Trinidad.'

'Would you like to speak in English?'

'Er, *cualquier*,' Donnie replied, his nasal American accent flattening out the Spanish. 'Whatever you like. We got you.'

'The gringo's just said something,' taunted the lead C-130 pilot. 'He said he was going to speak English and then he said, "*Cualquier*".'

One of the pilots came to Donnie's defence. 'No . . . you asked if they wanted to speak English or Spanish and the gringo said, "Whatever you like, man."'

'Only Spanish, only Spanish, right?' another pilot joined in.

'Of course!'

'Not even the gringo wants to speak English!'

At 4.59 am, still exactly on target, the C-130s arrived at their first destination. In the third C-130 Gary suddenly saw Trinidad, due east, twenty miles in the distance, a cluster of pinpoint lights breaking the blackness of sky and jungle.

The lead C-130's pilot radioed the Aerocommander, 'What do we do now?' The Aerocommander came back with instructions, 'Go into five-minute orbits.' One by one, the massive planes peeled off, stacked up. Forming three circles, they orbited several miles apart.

San Ramon, 5.05 am. High in the sky at 20,000 feet, the Aerocommander, a tiny speck almost invisible from the ground, wheeled round and round. First nautical daylight had been predicted for just this moment but a heavy layer of cloud blanketed the town; for a few minutes more, it would be dark on the ground.

Peering anxiously out of his window, Don told his pilot, 'Tell Robbie he's got to hold up, we've got to maintain ten-minute intervals.'

'They're making their approach,' Donnie reported.

'Who is?' Don said and for a moment he felt panic.

'They're making their approach,' Donnie repeated.

'Robbie is? Robbie's going in too quick! He's not supposed to go in too early. Donnie, Robbie has to have ten-minute spacing. Don't let him go in. I don't want him going in. Where are the helicopters?'

But it was too late. Robbie had already swooped down. The rear of the Casa opened like a yawn. The UMOPAR and DEA agents jumped to the ground, dashed for the hangar, then the control tower. Startled awake by the commotion, two young men bolted. The UMOPAR grabbed them before they could get to the town, laid their trussed-up bodies on the ground, then walked the strip up and down.

'Tell the helicopters to hold up,' Don ordered, then asked urgently, 'How does the field look?'

'It looks fine – hard and dry.'

Cross-legged and taciturn, the UMOPAR sat on the edge of the field, silently awaiting the eruption of dawn.

'It's a sleepy little town,' Robbie radioed from the ground.

Craning his neck, studying the horizon, Don watched as a

splash of pink spread, flattened, melted, until gradually the blackness faded into a single expanse of pale grey.

Where were the C-130s? According to plan, they should have arrived already. Nervously, Don checked his watch; five, ten, fifteen minutes passed and still no sign of the C-130s.

'Damn, I knew Robbie would do this. I knew he'd try to go in on his own. Let's get in closer, guys.'

Trinidad, 5.30 am. Twenty miles short of the town, the C-130s circled obliviously. In the third plane's cockpit, Gary Hale was waiting, ticking off the minutes, thinking, 'It's taking too long! This isn't right!' Finally, he prodded the pilot, 'Something is wrong! Tell the leader to get a hold of the Aerocommander.' The pilot started to argue. Gary insisted, 'Something's wrong, I know! Tell the leader, get Mr Castillo, Gene Castillo, up to the cockpit. I want to talk to him.'

But just at that moment, Donnie's voice burst over the radio. 'Condor leader! This is Aerocommander! Where are you?'

'Where am I? Still in orbit!'

'What?!!'

'You gave me no further instructions.'

'But you were supposed to take a twelve degree heading after five minutes in orbit!'

'You didn't tell me what the heading was!'

'Oh my God! Take a twelve degree heading – your target is San Ramon.'

One by one the planes peeled off. The sky was now light and Gary was worried. In these little towns in the Beni where by noon the thermometer registers a hundred degrees Fahrenheit, the people wake when the cocks start crowing.

'We are a bit low on fuel,' he heard one of the pilots reporting, then, 'The San Ramon runway is too small. . . . How many metres is four thousand feet? Do you have a calculator? It's too small.'

Gary thought anxiously, why were they saying that? It couldn't be too small! He had checked the length of the runway through so many different sources.

Suddenly he shivered. There, in the early grey light, he spotted in the distance a break in the jungle; then, in another few seconds a great snaking loop of a river winding back alongside a town; then, getting closer and closer, through wisps of cloud, the grid-patterned streets, the airstrip, the hangar, the plaza, even the church tower – San Ramon! It was instantly recognizable from the maps drawn by his informants, everything positioned exactly as they had said. After all those weeks of labour, Gary thought jubilantly, 'Everything, everything, is coming together!'

'Four minutes away from San Ramon,' reported the lead pilot to the Aerocommander.

'Do you want smoke signals?'

'Yes, please.'

'When do you want them?'

'Right now!'

'I can see the smoke! Tra-la-la-la,' the lead pilot sang as he depressed the joy stick and headed down.

From high above in the Aerocommander, Don watched as the first C-130, reflecting brilliant silver in the sun, shaped like a crucifix, glided in. His voice rang out loud, 'Perfect! Just what I wanted to see! One C-130 ... Here comes number two! Here comes three!'

The first C-130 rolled slowly to a stop. Its gate opened, the UMOPAR jumped out and dashed for their targets – a series of houses clustered round the main plaza, only a few blocks from the end of the runway. They fanned through the empty streets, cradling their weapons, nervously glancing over their shoulders. Backs to the walls, they stood against the red-tiled and colonnaded houses lining the plaza while other teams of UMOPAR and agents raced into the targeted houses. The townspeople, roused by the clatter of the helicopters' engines, opened their doors, peeped out of windows. A few women and children straggled out on to the street, started moving together; it was the first familiar sign of trouble. They would form a human barricade behind which the men would shelter, lobbing rocks, then sticks of dynamite as their courage gathered. This was what had happened at Santa Ana de Yacuma.

But the UMOPAR knew better now and just as quickly as the crowd gathered, the fierce-looking soldiers moved in with their carbines thrust forward. Seeing how many UMOPAR there were – almost as many anti-narcotics police as adult men in the town – the people scattered like fragmented beads of oil. As the morning wore on, an extraordinary tranquillity descended over San Ramon.

Twenty minutes behind the last C-130, the Aerocommander landed and Don laughed exultantly when he reached the hangar. 'This is good . . . this is good, good, good – just what I wanted to see,' as he spotted three small aeroplanes, one with a Brazilian tail number that had been painted over.

'How we doing?' he asked Gary, who stood with a radio to one ear.

'They've already rounded up six people. They got two guys, Argentinians, on a motorcycle with an Uzi machine-gun and hand grenades.'

'Is that right? Six already? Six prisoners already. That's good.'

The prisoners were marched single file down the street. They were mostly men, clothed in thin white shirts, wearing rubber sandals on sunburnt feet, their hands bound behind them. Don saw with delight that the grab had netted chemists, pilots, Colombians, Brazilians, several of Yayo's family members, every trafficker in town according to some of the townspeople (whose level of cooperation Don found unexpected and very interesting). Every trafficker except their main target, Yayo Rodriguez. They had just missed him. He had been in town the night before but only for a couple of hours. This was his new pattern – frequent visits to San Ramon but rarely staying twenty-four hours.

From the airstrip, Don saw black smoke billowing above the houses. The UMOPAR had found the one working hydrochloride laboratory and were burning its contents. The place did not look like much: odd bits and pieces – chemicals, plastic buckets, tape, brick moulds, microwave ovens – in a ramshackle yard. There were probably dozens of similar crude laboratories scattered around the town. This pattern of small decentralized laboratories was very troubling; it was impossible to search every house and yard.

In the distance, Don heard a series of explosions – the men had discovered four safes and one of the DEA agents was blowing off their hinges – then the thin whine of a Cessna's engine, jump-started by a Bolivian Air Force mechanic. Don watched the little plane teeter down the runway on stork-like legs and lift off, its small wheels dangling like delicate feet. A pilot was taking it to Trinidad to be searched by the Screaming Eagles team.

As he surveyed the results of the raid – scores of weapons laid out on the airstrip, dozens of HF radios, costing between $1500 and $2500 a piece, many brand new, and twenty-three prisoners sitting cross-legged on the ground – he thought with satisfaction, 'We've broken up this little rat's nest.' This was probably more a reflection of his emotional state than a realistic assessment of the operation's impact.

At 12.30 pm sharp the evacuation began and it was perfectly executed, all according to plan. One by one, the C-130s lifted off. The last C-130 was overloaded; the team guarding the northern perimeter had missed its helicopter and the third C-130 picked up every straggler. The UMOPAR squatted on the floor, shoulder to shoulder; they were young men, eighteen, nineteen, twenty, but with no bloom of youth – they had straggly teeth and prematurely aged faces. They handed around bits of chocolate, giggling like children as each time the plane banked they tumbled on top of one another.

Last to leave was the Aerocommander. General Anez turned and smiled at Don over his shoulder, made a thumbs up gesture – the operation could not have gone better. Then, soothed by the droning noise of the engine, he closed his eyes and his head dropped to his shoulder.

Don felt a rush of warmth towards the UMOPAR's commander. The General had come through on everything he had promised, keeping quiet about the operation until the last moment and then speaking directly to President Paz Zamora. He had guessed the target after reading the story in *Opinion*. He had pointed it out, smiling, to Don, and Don, unable to lie to him, had had to confirm it. He hoped, for Anez's sake, there would be no recriminations. Not having told his superiors beforehand put him in a vulnerable position.

Pen in hand, Don sat thinking, making occasional notes in the margins of the battle plan – what had gone wrong, the unexpected. He felt pride in the operation; its execution had been close to flawless – no injuries, not a shot fired, no property damage, no unnecessary violence. The UMOPAR had been thoroughly professional. Before the operation, Anez had warned them, 'No rough-housing of anybody.' Don had expected them to go in grumbling but instead they had been tough, quiet, cheerful and disciplined, even to the way they ate their lunches, sitting back to back on the edge of the strip, jumping up when they were summoned – 'We need blue group; we've got a new target.' Of course, he did not expect the townspeople to be happy about their town being invaded by a battalion of soldiers with gringos mixed in amongst them, but he felt no group of soldiers could have done better.

In many respects the operation had been successful, even if they had missed their main target. Although the safes had not contained drugs or money, they had yielded something more valuable – information, a treasure trove of intelligence. There were documents showing aeronautical maps going into Mexico, laying out how the drugs were being brought into the States and hinting that Bolivian Air Force pilots were flying the planes. There was also a cache of hand grenades which, luckily, had not exploded.

They had captured a major chunk of Yayo Rodriguez's communications system. They had broken up the Colombian side of his organization, arresting in Santa Cruz a very significant Colombian chemist and a very important Colombian pilot, although unfortunately just missing two Colombian hit men, who had come back to their house when the UMOPAR were inside. The UMOPAR couldn't pursue them because they didn't have enough vehicles.

The security for San Ramon had been perfect – in itself a major achievement – although in Santz Cruz, where they had gone into six of Yayo's houses, there had been a leak – from whom, he wasn't certain. In a number of houses when the agents arrived, they found suitcases packed; the targets had told them that they had heard the UMOPAR were coming.

Of course, missing Yayo was disappointing but Don wouldn't give up. Eventually he would get him, he would put out the word that there was big, big money in it for somebody. He would make Yayo Rodriguez a man without a country.

But Don's sense of elation was tempered by realism. He knew that the success of the operation was largely symbolic. It had boosted the UMOPAR's morale, squashed after Santa Ana. Temporarily, it would throw the traffickers off-balance. But San Ramon would soon return to normal, resume its status as a traffickers' haven. To have an impact, he would have to sustain operations – do several San Ramons simultaneously. But that was presently impossible: this single operation had drained their resources. (A measure of the challenge he faced was an incident that occurred the day of the raid, which Don only learned of several days later. An informant reported that the traffickers took advantage of the UMOPAR's absence to land and offload shipments of coca paste and base at Andrade Gutierrez, the landing strip for the UMOPAR's Chapare base camp.)

In the spring Don wanted to mount a new offensive. He wanted to blockade the Chapare, stop the movement of paste into the Beni, crater the airstrips, cut off the roads (there weren't very many), perhaps use a portable radar, increase operations on the Chilean border and create a chemical-free zone on the Brazilian border, similar to what had been done in South-east Asia when he had persuaded the Thais to block the trails into Burma. He wanted to maintain the pressure on San Ramon and renew the assault on Santa Ana, which, unlike San Ramon, would not be a soft target: according to reports brought back by informants since the last operation, truckloads of automatic rifles had been passed out to the townspeople.

Of course, he could not do this with the manpower available – it would take a thousand men to close down the Chapare. He needed help from the Bolivian Army, whose involvement in counter-narcotics the US government was seeking.

Under President Bush's National Drug Control Strategy, which had been announced in September 1989, two months after Don's arrival in Bolivia, the US was offering Bolivia $100 million in economic assistance and another $40 million in military aid with one major proviso: it had to bring the Bolivian Army into counter-narcotics operations. This was a controversial proposal within Bolivia, resisted by the civilian government, which was frightened of the military's power and reluctant to strengthen an institution from whose totalitarian grip democracy had only recently been wrested. (For twenty-two of the past thirty years, the military had dominated Bolivia's government. Full electoral democracy was only restored in 1982.) Moreover, the Army's helpfulness was uncertain at best. Under the Arce Gomez dictatorship in 1980–81, it had been deeply entangled in the narcotics trade and its officer corps had never been purged.

These were, however, the Ambassador's problems. It was his job to push America's interests, to persuade, bully, cajole the Bolivians, and he was good at this job, relentlessly persistent, and since the leadership issue in anti-drug operations had been resolved, very supportive of Don. Gelbard believed in law enforcement solutions. 'They give more bang for the buck,' was how he described them. And Don was giving the Ambassador what he wanted, someone to lead in the war against narcotics. Gelbard could not have found a better commander, one more committed, energetic, thoughtful, pragmatic. But whether Don would succeed was another matter.

5 The Surprise Party

Just as Don had predicted, Yayo Rodriguez returned to San Ramon a few weeks after Operation Tandem. There he could be secure as long as the rains persisted and from his bolt hole he challenged the UMOPAR. 'I'm here,' one informant reported him as saying. 'Come and get me if you want me, I'm not afraid.' Don dismissed the taunt as 'the usual macho chest-thumping', a face-saving gesture, a spectacle for the townspeople, but he had not forgotten his vow to get Yayo when the opportunity arose a few months later.

In the middle of March 1990 Don learned that a party was planned in the town of San Joaquin, the traffickers' haven forty miles north of San Ramon where the Bolivian investigative commission had searched for the grave of the murdered Brazilian pilots. The guest list included some of the country's top traffickers – Erwin Guzman, a fugitive whom the UMOPAR were actively seeking, Hugo Rivero, the target of the Santa Ana de Yacuma fiasco, and, most importantly, Yayo Rodriguez. The occasion was the birthday of Cain Daza Richter, a corpulent, middle-aged *narcotraficante*, who was one of the leading citizens of San Joaquin and lived in an elegant house on the town's little plaza.

It was General Anez who first learned of the party. He passed the news to Don, who asked the Santa Cruz office to verify it by sending into the town a couple of informants. They confirmed that the party was scheduled for 22 March. As was the custom in this part of Bolivia where birthdays, like christenings, were major festivities, the traffickers would fly into San Joaquin early in the morning, pass the day visiting and begin the real celebrating in the early evening. When that happened, Don decided grimly, he would surprise Yayo Rodriguez with his own little party.

It was only a week until Cain Daza's birthday, so Don had to act quickly. A repeat of San Ramon was out of the question: he did not have the resources or the favourable weather. Although the city of La Paz was gripped by drought, daily thunderstorms lashed the Beni in the flat tropical lands beyond the foothills of the Andes.

He reviewed the disposal of men and aircraft. He could not use the Aerocommander; he had stretched its flying hours to the limit and it had to be flown back to the States for repairs and service. But he had the Casa and three helicopters. And for the first time since he came to Bolivia, he had the flexibility of doing night-time operations because the NAU had recently supplied night vision goggles to the helicopter pilots.

As to manpower, in Primavera, an *estancia* on the Brazilian border only fifteen minutes' flight time from San Joaquin, a team of UMOPAR and DEA agents were running anti-lab missions along the swollen tributaries of the Amazon river. They were using rubber Zodiac boats propelled by outboard motors, supplied by a 'mother ship', a large wooden-hulled river-boat with a low-slung cabin. Only a week earlier they had destroyed a big laboratory, comprising fifteen buildings, the largest since Don had come to Bolivia. Grossly outnumbered, they had floated in with silenced motors, then whooping and hollering, and firing their carbines into the air, they had rushed the laboratory. They arrested four people, then burnt the buildings and destroyed seventy-five cases of precursor chemicals; the two brand-new three-bladed propeller aircraft they had seized were now the property of the Bolivian Air Force (which had acquired thirty-one planes in this fashion since the beginning of January).

Unfortunately, Don no longer had Gary Hale and Jesse Gutierez, both of whom had been transferred at the end of November. Jesse was now in El Paso, Texas, and Gary had been assigned to Washington headquarters. But from Santa Cruz Don could pull in Bob Johnstone. Solid, experienced, an old Bolivia hand, excellent at organizing men and equipment, Johnstone handled all of Snowcap's logistical problems and he was good with the agents, firm but supportive. In fact, now that Gene Castillo was talking of retiring, Don wanted Johnstone to become his second-in-command.

He decided to take most of the men from his Santa Cruz office. They could meet up in Trinidad, fly to Primavera and meld with the river operation. This would give him a force of forty. It would be more a guerrilla attack than a Ranger-style operation. They would grab Yayo Rodriguez, Erwin Guzman and Hugo Rivero if they could get their hands on him, but leave Cain Daza – although they had hit one of his laboratories a year earlier, he had been tried and acquitted *in absentia*.

It was a risky operation and Gene Castillo was pessimistic. They were venturing into hostile territory with not enough men and not enough aircraft, the weather was bad, the terrain unfamiliar and there was no guarantee that Yayo Rodriguez would be there. All these objections merely stimulated Don. 'Nothing risked, nothing gained,' summed up his approach to law enforcement.

He drew strength from the knowledge that he would be surrounded by good men – Bob Johnstone, for one, and Major Carlos Barriga, who had made a spectacular arrest a few weeks earlier when he had seized Luis Arce Gomez, the Minister of the Interior during the 'Cocaine Dictatorship'. A man who had collected together a bizarre gang of former Nazis and neo-fascists and inflicted on the docile Bolivian people all the horrors of Argentinian-style repression – murder, torture, disappearances – Arce Gomez had been indicted by a Florida Grand Jury in 1983 for conspiracy to import and distribute cocaine in the United States while he was Interior Minister. This case was still pending when Barriga arrested him in Santa Cruz in December 1989. Although there was no extradition treaty between the US and Bolivia, President Paz Zamora ordered that Arce Gomez (who wept when he learnt he was being sent to Miami) be put on a DEA plane, while Ambassador Gelbard called the US Attorney to stress the importance of the case. (Almost a year to the day after the raid on San Joaquin, on 23 March 1991, in a federal district court in Fort Lauderdale, Florida, the fifty-eight-year-old former Interior Minister was sentenced to a prison term of thirty years. According to evidence developed during his trial, Arce Gomez protected traffickers who paid him and had those who refused to pay arrested. He then sold cocaine, including some from police vaults, to cooperative traffickers.)

In addition to Johnstone and Berriga, Don had Jesse Guttierez's replacement, a new agent in Bolivia, Victor Cortez. A short, very muscular Mexican-American, Victor had sombre black eyes and a serious mien. Although he was Don's age, he looked older.

He had grown up in Brownsville, Texas, and joined the Army as soon as he graduated from high school, serving in Vietnam. At the age of twenty he became a policeman in Brownsville. Eventually (over the opposition of his parents, who were illegal immigrants from Mexico) he joined the Border Patrol; since he was mostly involved in narcotics cases, joining the DEA was a natural evolution. He was soft-spoken and self-effacing, but commanded Don's almost reverential respect for he had endured what every DEA agent dreaded and had shown remarkable fortitude.

In 1986 Victor Cortez had been assigned to Guadalajara, Mexico, to investigate the murder of DEA agent Kiki Camarena and had been kidnapped by the local Mexican police. They wanted to know about the investigation's course, where was it leading, what did the DEA know? He was brutally tortured, blindfolded, stripped naked, kicked and beaten; his interrogators forced water down his throat and nose so that he felt he was drowning and applied electrical currents to his body. He would have suffered Camarena's fate were it not for his fortuitous rescue by DEA agents.

After the incident in Guadalajara, Victor's wife had tried to persuade him to leave law enforcement. But Victor knew that he would eventually forget the torture. After Vietnam he had gone through a period of nightmare flashbacks; he would leap out of bed, crouch on the floor, cradle an imaginary weapon as he relived the terror. But these nightmares had gradually faded (although his eyes still filled with tears as he recalled them) and he knew the same process would happen over Guadalajara. Time, he trusted, would numb his psyche. And, as he said to his wife with quiet resignation, 'What else can I do? This is all I know and hopefully, I'm doing a good job. I'll stick with it until I retire. Sooner or later, we all have to die and if I die doing this job, so be it.'

Within a few weeks of his arrival in Bolivia, Victor became friends with a Bolivian Army captain who had been assigned to the UMOPAR's intelligence division. Dedicated police often form strong bonds quickly, whatever their backgrounds, and this is what had happened with the Captain and Victor.

When the Captain was a young lieutenant, he had been assigned to the San Joaquin garrison; now he warned Victor that its command structure had been significantly corrupted. Ostensibly guarding against a Brazilian invasion, the garrison was more a bulwark against an UMOPAR incursion. What had happened at San Joaquin was probably inevitable; it was certainly a common pattern throughout Bolivia. The garrison was a force of five hundred men in a frontier town of two thousand people; inevitably, officers socialized with the leading citizens and accepted the *narcotraficantes*' offers of gifts and money.

This doubled the risk of an already dangerous operation but General Anez thought he could handle the problem. He would go to General Moises Shiriqui, the Army's Commander in Chief, and explain the problem: they needed a trustworthy officer to take control of the garrison and prevent the soldiers from running to the traffickers' assistance; perhaps the Army could help by securing the plaza?

Despite the Army's traditional hostility to the UMOPAR, which posed a counterweight to military power, Don was hoping for a favourable response. The Army, he thought, should be eager to cooperate because Gelbard was in the middle of sensitive negotiations, offering $40 million in military assistance if the Army would join in counter-narcotics operations. Although the civilian government was debating whether to accept it, the Army was already licking its lips at the prospect of more arms and equipment. But, to Don's disappointment, when General Anez met with the Army's Commander in Chief, although General Shiriqui agreed to neutralize the garrison, he would not authorize the army to actively assist the operation.

On the morning of 21 March, Don, Victor Cortez and Victor's Bolivian Army captain friend drove from the Embassy to El Alto Airport. Don zipped up his jacket as he stepped on to the tarmac. It was the first day of autumn below the equator and a cold wind swept over the bleak Altiplano, whipping around the Indians' isolated tumble-down stone settlements scattered between the mountain peaks and the airport.

They could not leave immediately. Colonel Valesquez, the officer personally selected by General Shiriqui to take command of the San Joaquin garrison, had not yet arrived. As he waited for the Colonel, Don was brooding. The General had given orders which were not to his liking. He had told Colonel Valesquez that when he reached Trinidad he was to report to the commander of the Beni, brief him on the plan, then take a colonel from Trinidad into San Joaquin. This was a serious blow to operational security – the government of the Beni was notoriously corrupt – and Don had wanted to protest. But this was his first experience of joint military-UMOPAR ventures; he felt constrained to be polite, although he realized he might be jeopardizing the operation out of his concern for diplomacy.

Finally the Colonel arrived and they boarded the Aero-commander – Don had managed to squeeze one last trip out of Washington. The Colonel had thin black hair brushed to one side, a wide face and long, hooded eyes. He kept to himself during the flight. Don's attempts to be pleasant were brushed aside.

They arrived in Trinidad around twelve o'clock and met up with the Santa Cruz contingent (who had flown in on the Casa) and Major Barriga. In the DEA's office in Trinidad's major hotel, they began to work through the details of the operational plan. They were troubled by their lack of hard information. They did not know the exact time the party was starting – their informants' best guess was between 3 and 6.30 – nor its exact location, which could be either Cain Daza's house or a social club diagonally across the plaza. They studied the map of San Joaquin, memorizing the route from the air strip into town. It was a few minutes' trot – take the path to the main road, five blocks to the plaza, turn left, go one block, turn right again, hit Cain Daza's house, then the club across the plaza.

They had equipped both informants with HF radios but attempts to contact them had so far been unsuccessful. The HF operator now tried again.

'Pata, pata, pata, pata ... Goldo, Goldo.'

'Pata, pata, pata, pata ... Goldo, Goldo.'

Jim White, the agent assigned to the case who was stationed in Santa Cruz, was watching. 'Better use another antenna – see if that's any better.'

But there was still no response, only crackling static. They would try again when they reached Las Vegas, the forward operating base where they could refuel the helicopters. It was a handsome *estancia* confiscated several years earlier from Bolivia's most notorious trafficker, Roberto Suarez, who was now in prison in La Paz.

By early evening they had worked out many of the details. Although they still had not been able to reach either informant, they decided to send in a third CI the following morning who would travel to San Joaquin on a commercial flight. The plan was to meet him at an agreed location 12 miles outside San Joaquin; they would fly in by helicopter and quickly debrief him – he would, it was hoped, know by then the exact location of their targets.

At 8 pm Don was feeling optimistic. Then the telephone rang. Johnstone answered it and Don, who was joking with Major Barriga, paid no attention until he noticed that the room, swelled moments before by the sound of policemen's voices, had suddenly gone quiet. Johnstone looked worried as he explained that it was his wife on the phone, calling from Santa Cruz. She was alone with his mother; their house had just been attacked. Two men were involved; they were driving a white Mitsubishi, one armed with a submachine gun, the other with a pistol. They had put the gun to the head of the UMOPAR guard and told him if he kept guarding the place, he would be dead. They had fired shots through the door but no one was injured. His wife did not know who they were, whether they were coming back, or if any of the other DEA agents' families had been attacked. She was afraid to call the local police.

The whole Santa Cruz contingent except the case agent, Jim White, would have to get back to Santa Cruz quickly. It was after dusk; the airport at Trinidad had closed for the night. But the local television station was very cooperative – Carlos Berriga called its owner – and alongside the nine o'clock news they flashed a message urging the airstrip staff to return to work for an emergency take-off. By eleven o'clock they were ready to go and in the middle of a thunderstorm the Casa flew out.

The following day the remainder of the force flew from Trinidad to Las Vegas. The mood on the plane was very sombre. Victor Cortez, ramrod erect, carbine gripped in his hand, muzzle pointed upward, was facing Don, who sat hunched over, eyes fixed on the floor, his chin resting on his hand. The expression on his face was dark and gloomy, in striking contrast to his usual self-confident good humour. So much had gone wrong in the last twenty hours.

Because of that unforeseeable incident at Santa Cruz, he had lost six UMOPAR and two of his key people, his logistics man and Angel Perez, who was in charge of the informants. He had spoken to Johnstone early that morning. They had identified one of the men who had attacked his house. He was Roberto Suarez Levy, Roberto Suarez's second son, who was known to become violent when he was high on cocaine. He had shot at two other houses – not DEA homes – then had gone to the airport and shot up some planes. Now he was dead, killed by the national police when he resisted arrest, and they were trying to play down the DEA's involvement.

It was bad to lose Johnstone but even worse to lose Angel Perez because now there was a problem with the third informant. He had missed his flight and had walked right on to the tarmac, in full public view, over to where the DEA and UMOPAR were boarding the Casa and helicopters. Don could not believe that anyone could be so stupid. They had hustled him off the strip as well as they could and hidden him under a blanket in one of their trucks. But they couldn't use him again; the traffickers had people watching the strip and were they to put him on another commercial flight, anyone could check where he was going.

So they had altered their plan. They put Victor's friend the Captain on the Bolivian Air Force Cessna which was taking the two Army colonels directly into San Joaquin. Hopefully, he could talk to some of the people he knew in San Joaquin and have some hard information by the time they landed so that they could grab their targets before they fled. The moment the traffickers heard the Hueys, their reaction would be to run: the only helicopters in Bolivia belonged to the UMOPAR and the sound of their engines was like the warning of a police car's siren.

Don had wanted to leave Trinidad early in the morning but that was out of the question after what had happened the previous evening. The pilots had not returned until midday and they needed to sleep. This was understandable but already Don sensed he was going to have problems. The Casa pilots were not his usual men. They were newly arrived and TDY – Temporary Duty men doing a three-month tour; these particular pilots were stiff, humourless, 'by the book' types.

The Casa landed in Las Vegas around one o'clock. They fuelled the helicopters, briefed the river crew, DEA agents and UMOPAR, then went over their equipment; out of ten radios, only three were working. Don was especially concerned about the

UMOPAR's rifles and he asked Barriga to make sure each man test-fired his carbine. There had been serious problems with defective weapons. Only a few days earlier an UMOPAR lieutenant had been killed and a sergeant wounded during a fire fight in which sixty per cent of the UMOPAR's guns malfunctioned.

The incident had been the unhappy conclusion to a series of successful raids. The UMOPAR had broken up a large storehouse, seized 700 kilograms of cocaine, then two very large laboratories, one producing 2600 kilograms a day. When, within the week, the UMOPAR stumbled on another laboratory, the Bolivian bodyguards (who had been trained by Colombians) let loose a barrage from their .45 calibre machine-guns.

A political furore had followed, whipping up anti-American feeling. The incident had made the front pages of the papers for five days running, causing red faces in the US Embassy. The NAU, responsible for supplying the UMOPAR's weapons, said it was the UMOPAR's fault for taking poor care of their weapons. But Don had warned the NAU about the quality of the guns and the complaints the UMOPAR voiced about their equipment. He knew that they kept their arms in as good a condition as could be expected. The problem was the guns the NAU gave them. The UMOPAR, who were front-line soldiers, were being sent into battle with Second World War vintage carbines when the DEA agents, who were merely advisers, had modern M-16 carbines and the option of flak jackets. (They did not wear them because they were ashamed to go into the field more securely protected.)

Inside the ranch house at Las Vegas, Jim White briefed the river crew. But Don was too anxious to sit still. He left the house and walked towards the airstrip, stopping to watch the DEA medic who was examining a child, the son of the Indian couple who looked after the *estancia*. The boy looked about seven but might have been several years older; so many Bolivian children were stunted by malnutrition. His wasted body was covered with sores, some the size of a jam jar lid, and the medic, sounding sadly resigned – he treated the child every time he came through – was patiently explaining to the boy's mother, 'It won't do any good unless you keep the child clean, you have to keep him clean even if you have to clean him up three or four times a day,' as he handed her some antibiotic tablets and cream. But how do you keep children clean with no sanitation and no access to fresh water?

Don saw the two TDY pilots walking up and down the strip. They were pacing out its length, weighing equipment, and Don, aghast, thought, 'There can't be a problem! Robbie's flown in and out of this base dozens of times!' But they came over to him and said the strip was too short; he would have to reduce his load by fifty per cent, which meant that instead of going in with twenty men on the Casa he could only take ten. Then Barriga came up and Don saw from the troubled look on his face that their problems were multiplying, there was to be no relief. The NAU had sent only one pair of night vision goggles for three helicopters. They would have to spend the night in San Joaquin.

Don walked over to a thatched-roofed shelter where Victor sat crouched on the ground with a couple of UMOPAR soldiers. With a nod of his head, he pulled Victor aside. What should they do? Their chances at this point were no better than fifty-fifty. From a force of forty, they were whittled down to twenty. What if the Colonel failed to secure the garrison? From the moment they left La Paz, he had been acting strangely. On the flight to Trinidad he had barely spoken; his hooded eyes were restless, wary. That morning in Trinidad when they were waiting to fly to Las Vegas, he had disappeared for a couple of hours, walking off the airstrip with an unknown civilian, and when he reappeared, he was much more cordial, even offering to supply troops to secure the aircraft and plaza.

Don was ready to shut down the operation but Victor persuaded him that they should go forward. They had just received word from one of the informants. They had climbed two high trees and strung an aerial wire between them, hoping to project the radio waves above the jungle, and when this had not worked, they had sent up the Casa. The pilot had radioed through to Angel Perez in Santa Cruz. Amazingly, one of the informants had managed to get through to the agent, sending the latest intelligence in a coded message. The party was on and he had seen Yayo Rodriguez!

They modified the plan. Victor would go in first with a couple of UMOPAR. The Bolivian Air Force Cessna could serve as their transport. They would sneak in, find the Colonel and ask him to secure the plaza. Jim White and the bulk of the troops would follow in the Casa, Don and Barriga could use the helicopters. They would give the Casa a ten-minute lead. But the Casa pilots had to stick to this schedule because there was no radio contact between the aeroplane and the helicopters.

At six o'clock Victor and the UMOPAR landed at San Joaquin. They managed to reach the garrison unnoticed but Colonel Valesquez was not there. Victor borrowed a vehicle from the local commander and set off through the town in search of him. He spotted Valesquez driving a pick-up truck, heading towards the garrison from the direction of the plaza; in the passenger seat was the Trinidadian Colonel. Victor pulled alongside the pick-up truck, rolled open his window and shot out a series of questions. What news did he have? Was the party on? What time would it be? Where were the targets?

Valesquez said, 'Oh, the party has already taken place. There will be another, tonight at eight o'clock, but none of the people you are looking for will be there.'

Victor hesitated a moment. His dark piercing eyes were riveted on the Colonel's face. What did he mean? None of the people they were looking for would be there? That wasn't what the CI had said . . . But he didn't have the time to puzzle this out. 'Look,' he said urgently, 'things have changed. We don't have that many people, only a small group. We really need your assistance, just twenty men to stand by at the plaza.'

'Oh, I'll have men at the fort in case you need them.'

'No! We need them by the plaza where they can respond right away.'

'I'll put some men in two blocks away.'

'I don't need them two blocks away,' Victor said, and now he was almost pleading. 'I need them right here, right by Cain Daza's!'

They went back and forth, the Colonel equivocating, Victor's usually soft voice angrily rising. Finally, Valesquez said, 'I'll see what I can do.' He drove off to the fort. Victor decided to follow; he did not understand what was going on with the Colonel. He walked straight into the commander's office and found him together with Valesquez and the colonel from Trinidad. They seemed surprised to see him.

In the distance, Victor heard the hum of the Casa's engines. He and the UMOPAR ran back towards the airstrip where they met Jim White and a group of UMOPAR. What should they do? 'We're not going to get any help from the military,' Victor explained. They were vastly outnumbered. Should they retreat to the airstrip? No, they had come this far, they would take their chances. There was no time to waste; in a few minutes they would hear the helicopters' clatter. The Casa had landed ten minutes behind schedule. As so often happened, they had overshot their target, this time because their navigation charts were in error. They had gone as far as San Ramon before realizing their mistake, then turned round and headed north towards San Joaquin.

They ran back towards the town. As they reached the plaza, Victor noticed a little girl. She was wearing a thin white dress, her feet were bare and her hair was bound in thick black plaits; she was playing peacefully in the dusty street. Suddenly, he saw her point to the sky and heard her voice, high and thin, crying, 'Helicopters! Helicopters!' In the darkness, Victor made out the image of his friend the Captain, small and gaunt, stepping from the shadows. He was pointing towards a fleeing motor scooter. There were two men on the back. 'Cain Daza!' he was screaming, 'There's Cain Daza!' Bang! Bang-bang-bang! Gun fire erupted. Victor threw himself to the ground, saw the townspeople scatter and in the confusion, in the gloom, he did not know who was shooting – the Army, traffickers, Yayo Rodriguez? As he drew himself up on to his knees, he saw it was the UMOPAR, firing their guns into the air in a futile gesture to stop the motor scooter.

They split into two teams. One dashed into Cain Daza's house, the other raced for the social club across the plaza.

As Victor entered Cain Daza's house, he saw what had happened. There was food in the kitchen, dozens of clean glasses, a banquet table, band equipment in one corner. But the house was empty except for an elderly woman. He glanced around the room. A wedding portrait hung on the wall. The bride was beautiful – was that Cain Daza's daughter? But what really caught his eye was the bridegroom's uniform – it was a military cadet's, one of the UMOPAR told him. Ruffling through a stack of photos, Victor found a snapshot of the garrison's commander, probably taken to commemorate some important civic event. He was dressed in full military regalia and was handing the flag of Bolivia to Cain Daza Richter, who was smiling benignly, dressed in a tight-fitting white suit.

A small safe sat on top of a cupboard; reluctantly, the elderly woman produced a set of keys. Methodically, Victor tried each key until finally the door swung open. He pulled out a pistol, a wallet, Brazilian money, papers relating to Cain Daza's last court case and a document prepared by the Ministry of Aeronautics: a list of every aeroplane registered in Bolivia and passed to one of the country's major *narcotraficantes*.

They were searching Cain Daza's house when the Hueys – which had circled three times waiting for the Casa – landed. Don jumped from the helicopter and ran towards the Casa. 'What's happening?' he called to the pilots. 'What did you guys pick up on the radio?'

'We picked up that there was a party last night,' one of the pilots told him. 'There was probably going to be a party tonight at somebody's house and I've forgotten the guy's name, it's a Spanish name.'

'Cain Daza?'

'That sounds right.'

'Did they get the confirmation on the other guys?'

'No, they were unaware as to who was left in town.'

Don and Barriga headed towards the plaza. The air was warm, thick with the heady smell of vegetation raised by the evening dew, and the road in the darkness was a slash of brown bordered by the purple and green shadows of the jungle. It was deserted. There were no trucks, no people, no stray dogs, not even a chicken, and the only sound was the thump-thump of their feet. Why was it so quiet? Don was glistening with sweat; tiny beads dripped from his cheeks, lips, chest.

'I can't hear any guns,' he told Barriga. 'The thing I don't like is not seeing more aircraft on the *pista*.' There was only one Cessna and he had been expecting several – the planes of Cain Daza's guests, Yayo Rodriguez and the other traffickers, who would have flown into San Joaquin from San Ramon and Santa Ana.

They were at the edge of the town when they spotted Colonel Valesquez coming towards them. Barriga explained, 'Colonel, our other people are in, we need your cooperation, we need a team of soldiers to cover the plaza.'

'They won't have to intervene?'

'No, they only have to cover the plaza and the four streets that lead into it and make sure that no one comes in or out of the plaza.'

The Colonel assured him that that would be no problem. He shook Barriga's hand, almost effusive. Don, not knowing how Valesquez had equivocated with Victor Cortez, was delighted. 'We are getting great cooperation from the Army, great cooperation. We're in good shape. Now all we need is the right people here.' What a delusion!

He went directly to Cain Daza's, pushed open the door. The UMOPAR and DEA agents milled about, searching each room, opening drawers, closets. 'Look,' said one agent, holding up an Austrian AUG submachine-gun, 'It's the same sort of gun magazine that killed the UMOPAR lieutenant.'

Victor pulled him aside. 'The Captain we put in,' Victor whispered tensely, 'was surveilling this place. The Colonel who we brought in, he came in here.'

At first Don looked blankly at Victor. 'The Colonel we brought in from Trinidad...'

'The Colonel was here,' Victor interrupted.

'... and the Colonel from La Paz?' Don put up two fingers as he finished the question.

'Si!' Victor lapsed into Spanish. 'The Captain came and surveilled the place.'

'Is that right?'

'Yes, and he noted it down in his notebook that they came in here.'

'Which ones – the one from here?' Don couldn't believe it.

'The one that we brought,' Victor patiently explained again.

'The one we brought from La Paz and the one that we brought from Trinidad, both came in here or one?'

'Both! The Colonel had no reason to be in here. Those were not his orders.'

Don still could not believe it. Had they been betrayed by Colonel Valesquez, General Shiriqui's hand-picked person. Had he sold them out! Don exclaimed to Victor, 'But you should have seen the act that went on with Valesquez. He came up to me, he was telling me he was going to give us all kinds of cooperation, surrounding the place!'

Just then Barriga, who had been mixing with the soldiers outside on the street, touched Victor's shoulder. Their targets had been in town – at least, Yayo Rodriguez had – but he had fled. 'You understand Spanish well – I want you to translate this for Don. It seems that the army officers outside don't want to cooperate. They are very angry about this operation. They are upset, they are saying about Don, "This bugger wants it all done for him . . ." The cooperation they are giving is not sincere.'

What could they do? They were outnumbered five hundred to twenty. Don told Victor, 'We're just going to have to get out and fight another day.'

They walked back to the strip in the dark, silent evening. Despite all that had happened, his disappointment, anger, his desire for revenge – he felt he had been made to look a fool – Don was aware of the little town's beauty, the ancient church, the peaceful symmetry of the plaza, the colonnaded buildings of pale stucco and red tile; in the distance, he heard a sleepy infant crying and the exquisite night-time trill of a bird in the jungle.

That night they slept on earth; at dawn they took off for Las Vegas, leaving behind a team of UMOPAR and the helicopters to await the Screaming Eagles – they would seize and vacuum-search the one plane on the the airstrip, which belonged to Cain Daza. It was mid-afternoon before Don arrived in La Paz. Still dressed in combat clothes, dirty, unshaven, he cleaned up at the sink in the Embassy bathroom and changed into a clean suit which his wife had brought to him. Then he hurried off to a meeting with General Thurman, who was in La Paz for the day to discuss additional assistance.

Later that afternoon Don studied the huge map of Bolivia that hung on the wall in his intelligence unit. Since Gary Hale had left, this unit had expanded. It was now the biggest intelligence operation outside America. Most of the analysts were US Army personnel seconded to help the DEA; they were under the command of Major Ray Levesque, who had helped to plan Operation Tandem. They had put pins on the map to show all their targets, mostly lab sites, some fifty of which were confirmed and another 130 of which they had not positively identified because there were not enough agents to debrief informants. As Don looked at the way the red pin-heads were scattered and clustered, he saw a big circle around Trinidad that was empty of pins. With his thumb and middle finger, he measured its diameter, then checked the scale and computed the miles – the circle was exactly the distance a Huey could fly without refuelling. The traffickers were moving beyond the range of the helicopters, which meant the UMOPAR had to stage operations from a forward operating base with huts, cots, food, supplies of water and, most importantly, an airstrip big enough to take the Casa, which carried fuel for the helicopters in huge rubber bladders.

There was no doubt that they were having more success – Don could see it in his statistics, the number of lab sites hit, the quality of seizures, the reaction of the traffickers – they were fighting back, they were becoming more aggressive. And for the last six months the price of coca leaf had been dropping, although Don was not yet ready to claim this a triumph for law enforcement. The price of coca leaf was very erratic and it might be the result of over-production, so many *campesinos* had been lured into growing the crop.

He looked again at the map and this time noticed a string of lab sites along the Brazilian border, many more than there had previously been. He thought, 'If they move into Brazil, it will be a nightmare,' for Brazil's wildness and vastness surpassed even Bolivia's and its government would never give the DEA as much leeway.

The following afternoon was a Saturday. Don sat in his garden, an oasis of green in one of La Paz's parched canyons, surrounded by high walls and barbed wire but overlooked by a house from whose windows Don's chest and head presented a perfect target.

He was preoccupied by the events of the last forty-eight hours. What had gone wrong? What had been his error? He had no doubt that they had been betrayed by the military, he had interviewed Victor's friend the Captain.

The Captain had flown into San Joaquin with the two colonels and had taken up a post on the plaza in the 'Whiskeria' bar. At about 3 pm he saw the garrison commander drive by in a blue station wagon. In it were Colonel Valesquez and the Trinidadian Colonel. They stopped in front of Cain Daza's house and knocked at the door but the person they were looking for was apparently not in. They drove over to the social club, stayed for about forty-five minutes, then returned to Cain Daza's. The Captain didn't see them go in but he saw them leaving, at about 6 pm, just about the time that Victor was landing. 'No wonder,' Don thought, 'that Valesquez seemed disconcerted.' A few minutes later the trafficker himself stepped out of his house, on to the plaza, and sat watching the square until the little girl shouted, 'Helicopters, helicopters!' Cain Daza looked up at the sky, almost puzzled – maybe he wasn't expecting the UMOPAR so early – then leapt on to the back of the motor scooter.

Don felt certain the Captain was telling the truth. His story, at least its thrust, was confirmed by a young army lieutenant – it was important to remember there were also honourable soldiers – who had promised to come down to Trinidad and talk to Barriga. Nevertheless, Don cross-examined the Captain. Was he sure it was Colonel Valesquez who left Cain Daza's? How was he dressed? Where were you standing?

It was important that the evidence be clear because this incident was bound to become a *cause célèbre*. The government, he knew, would be very embarrassed; the first defensive reaction would be, 'We won't do business with the gringos.' Relations would go two steps back and then hopefully forward because he had worked very hard and successfully, he thought, to improve US–Bolivian relations, to bridge the gap in the two cultures, even if the conflict of interests sometimes seemed irreconcilable. Recently, there had been a meeting with the Minister of the Interior, Guillermo Capobianco Rivera, a close friend of President Paz Zamora and no American lover (his children were being educated in Havana). It had been called to discuss a litany of complaints – defective weapons, sour meat, wormy rations. The Ambassador was there, the Deputy Chief of Mission, plus many of the host government ministers. Gelbard started to bristle when Capobianco announced, 'We want to talk about the DEA,' but then the Minister said, 'We get a lot of help from the DEA, we're happy with the relationship and I know there are problems but they are helping us to fix them.' And after the meeting, Capobianco had taken Don aside and said, 'Let's have lunch, I know you guys are on our side.'

In the background, Don heard his telephone ringing. It was the river crew at Primavera. Miraculously, they had been able to reach him; for once, their communication system was working properly. They had identified another big lab but they were short-handed. What did he think? Should they try to take it? He told them, 'It's your move, you've got to make the decision, I can't assess the risk from this distance. But whatever you decide, you know I'll back you.'

He returned to the garden. His children were playing, throwing a ball to their gangly German Shepherd, still a puppy, who raced excitedly into the wall, banging its shoulder. His thoughts reverted to San Joaquin. Maybe he had been too much of a nice guy. Next time round he would do it differently. He would tell the Colonel, 'We're going to run an operation, you come with me.' He would put the Colonel in the DEA's office in Trinidad, isolate him from any contact with the world, then tell him when they arrived at Las Vegas, 'Here's where you're going, to San Joaquin. We're going to come in sixty minutes behind you, you have one hour to get control of that garrison. And we're going to stick a captain with you who will pose as your aide . . .'

He wondered what would happen to the Colonel – would he lose his job? What would become of his family? Although he didn't sympathize with Valesquez, he could understand why he had behaved as he did. It was easy for Americans back in the States to say that the Colonel's behaviour was intolerable, that the Bolivians must put a stop to all this corruption. That was what the Snowcap agents thought – until they actually got to Bolivia. Then they were shocked by the living conditions, the mud-floored hovels of the *campesinos*, barren of furniture, with a few cooking implements and a crude stove; and their children covered with ulcers, stunted, dull-eyed, crying from hunger. Bolivia's infant mortality rate was among the worst in the world – in some rural areas half the children died before they reached the age of five, from dysentery, tetanus, acute respiratory infections, diseases which were preventable. But most Bolivians lacked access to doctors, medicines, toilets, running water; even in the capital city of La Paz, there were open sewers, people defecated in the gutters, cleansed themselves in polluted rivers.

The Bolivian Air Force pilots flying the Huey helicopters were highly trained professionals, among the best pilots in Latin America, and what did they make? Maybe $800 a year? Would it not be understandable if they succumbed to temptation, sold information, flew a plane-load of coke into Mexico. It would be so easy for them to say, 'Put whatever it is that you've got into the back, I don't want to see it, don't tell me anything about your business except where you want me to land,' and in return be paid $2000, earning in two days more than twice their annual salary.

And what could the Americans do about corruption? The Embassy staff talked of 'institution-building'; it was a favourite phrase among State Department people, meaning Americans working together with the Bolivians, planting, nurturing, bringing to maturity, a professional police force, army, judiciary. But the problem of corruption was deeply rooted in Bolivia's culture, in its underdevelopment, its lack of internal markets due to its small and static population, its abysmal infrastructure, its land-locked geography. The department of Cochabamba, where the Chapare was located, was as sunny and fertile as California or Florida but fruit fell from the trees and rotted on the ground because the *campesinos* had no way to transport it to market. At this very moment, young Bolivian men and women were dancing, singing, parading through the streets of La Paz. It was 24 March, 'El Dia del Mar' – the Day of the Sea – a national day of mourning to commemorate the War of the Pacific, disastrously concluded in 1880 when Bolivia lost to Chile its access to the sea.

Don was roused again, this time by his dog's frantic barking. 'Joey,' he called, 'don't be so rough with him,' and as he gently rebuked his son, he suddenly smiled for he had just recalled his first cable to Washington sent only a few days after he came to Bolivia. It was addressed to Terry Burke, the Deputy Administrator, and in it Don had declared, 'We're going to take over; instead of getting things, we're going to get the organizations.'

How naive he had been. How embarrassingly innocent. All the traffickers they had seized in San Ramon, all twenty-three of Yayo's people, whom they had flown by C-130 to La Paz because they were concerned about the corruption within Trinidad's judicial system, all were now free – released by judges sitting in La Paz.

Still, in modest ways he had been successful. He had restored morale, healed divisions, made peace with the Ambassador, won the leadership battle and, in the State Department's new Andean strategy, announced after President Bush's meeting with President Paz Zamora at Cartagena on 15 February 1990, he saw the imprint of some of his ideas. The emphasis was shifting – from forcible crop eradication to alternative development. He had forged a good relationship with General Thurman and gradually he was building up more resources – in another few months they would have two more helicopters – although he would never have sufficient men, aircraft or equipment.

But the problems that were left were the insurmountable ones of Bolivia and even if he were to succeed here, there was still Peru, Brazil, Ecuador, Colombia, in each of which coca leaf could be cultivated and cocaine manufactured.

He was fighting impossible odds, and in his heart he knew it, but if tomorrow General Anez were to call him and say, 'We've just learned from an informant that Yayo Rodriguez will be in Santa Ana de Yacuma on Monday,' he would drop everything else and scramble to arrest him. With Candide-like optimism, he could still vow, 'We will get him. We will make him ours. It's just a matter – it's just a matter of time now.'

PART II

The Cocaine Capitalists

NEW YORK CITY

UPSTATE NEW YORK
WESTCHESTER CO.
NEW JERSEY
George Washington Bridge
THE BRONX
Morningside Hts
Harlem
LONG ISLAND
Hudson River
NASSAU CO.
La Guardia Airport
Whitestone
Bayside
Central Park
East Elmhurst
Flushing
Long Island City
Jackson Hts
Pennsylvania Station
Grand Central Station
Woodside
Elmhurst
Corona
Flushing Meadow Corona Park
Rego Park
Forest Hills
MANHATTAN
Glendale
QUEENS
Ellis Island
Statue of Liberty
John F. Kennedy International Airport
Jamaica Bay
BROOKLYN
Coney Island
N
0
6 kilometres
0
4 miles
Key
major roads
parks
Colombian communities
ATLANTIC OCEAN

6 The Investigation without an End

Jerry McArdle was twenty-three years old when he became a New York State Trooper. In 1981, at the age of thirty-one, he was assigned to the New York Drug Enforcement Task Force, an amalgam of federal, state and local law enforcement agencies that, under the leadership of the DEA, targets major drug violators and trafficking organizations in New York City.[1] Five years later he gave up his rank as a state police sergeant and took a reduction in salary in order to become a DEA agent and continue the case he had been working on since 1981, the investigation into the Cali Cartel, the largest cocaine distribution organization in the world.

After Bogota and Medellin, Cali is Colombia's third biggest city, with a population of 1.3 million, and the economic, industrial and manufacturing centre of the south-east region. Known to Colombians as their nation's sugar capital, it is also the corporate headquarters of a consortium of drug traffickers – Jose SantaCruz Londono and Gilberto and Miguel Rodriguez Orejuela – all residents of Cali, who export to the United States approximately sixty per cent of the cocaine consumed by Americans.

On 25 February 1988, Jerry McArdle and the other members of Group 96, the team in the Task Force to which he was assigned, achieved one of their greatest successes against the Cali Cartel. But while the other members of his Group and especially his Division Chief, Bill Mockler (who in 1978 initiated the investigation into the Cartel) rejoiced, Jerry McArdle felt failure, sadness and, briefly, a loss of his faith.

Their target that day was Alvaro Ivan Neira, a forty-year-old Colombian citizen, an illegal alien, living in Queens, New York, under the alias Luis Ramos. He was the manager of one of the Cali Cartel's 'cells', the secretive subgroups responsible for distribution in the States. It was his job to deliver multi-kilo loads of cocaine to wholesale customers, then collect, count and ship the money to Colombia. He also kept a detailed business ledger in which he recorded each drug transaction, the code-name and contact number of his customer, the time that they met, the quantity distributed, how much money he had collected.

On 25 February Group 96 and Troop K, a team of state police officers who had been working on this aspect of the investigation with the Task Force for nearly two years, followed Ramos for most of the day. They watched him make a number of 'meets', all in locations that were difficult to watch – on quiet, middle-class residential streets; in the Flushing cemetery off 166th Street, fifty square acres crammed with graves with only the occasional mourner on its black-topped lanes; on the service road of Grand Central Parkway near La Guardia Airport, a one-way street with non-stop rushing traffic. All of these meets were 'car-to-car', brief transactions lasting a few seconds, two vehicles stopping, one in front of the other, a raised boot, a parcel passed over.

They decided that Ramos was collecting money for loads of cocaine that had been delivered on consignment the previous week. They waited until he was finished with his rounds, then followed him back to his house on 58th Road in Bayside, Queens, a quiet middle-class neighbourhood of detached three-bedroom houses and small lawns that had been developed in the 1950s. It was just one block from the Long Island Expressway, the main artery connecting Long Island's suburbs to New York City.

Ramos's house was set on a knoll and its short driveway led to a garage underneath so it was possible to shift money and drugs between his car and the house without being seen. They saw the garage doors close over his red Chevy Caprice. They watched and waited for a few minutes more.

When they entered the house, Ramos was coming out of the shower. Sitting on a coffee table in the sitting-room, which was to the left of the bathroom, was a 9 mm automatic pistol loaded with teflon-tipped rounds, the professional criminal's ammunition of choice, capable of cutting through a policeman's bullet-proof vest. But Ramos ran in the opposite direction, towards his bedroom where he kept the rest of his weapons, three .38 revolvers in the drawer of his bedside table, an AR15 automatic rifle and an Uzi machine-gun. Two state troopers tackled him, naked and wet, as he dived for the loaded Uzi that was hidden under the bed.

Then they began a systematic search of the house. They found some of the money in a safe in the garage, the rest in suitcases, boxes and dufflebags locked in a cupboard in the playroom downstairs.

They put the money in the grey 1987 Toyota van which had been parked in Ramos's garage next to his red Chevy Caprice and drove it to Manhattan, to the Task Force's office on 11th Avenue and West 57th Street. The block-wide office building, nineteen storeys high and designed like a child's toy-brick tower, was the only skyscraper in a district of warehouses and garages, crowded by day but deserted at this late hour.

They parked the van on the pavement, directly in front of the building's entrance, and quickly shifted the boxes, bags and suitcases inside, carrying them to the bank of public lifts. As the agents lugged this booty into Bill Mockler's office on the 17th floor, their heavy footsteps were muffled by the sound of raucous jokes and laughter.

During the day one could see the Hudson River from Mockler's office, a broad expanse of fast-flowing water carrying shoals of grey ice from Albany into New York Harbour; rising above it were wooded cliffs with a lingering feel of wilderness and a vast winter sky that beckoned to the west. Mockler sat with his back to this spectacular view. He had only one interest – the Cali Cartel. With delicate hands that contrasted strikingly with the coarse features of his face, he unpacked the money. The notes were stacked in bundles and tied with rubber bands, and on the top of each bundle there was a slip of paper on which Ramos had scrawled a two-digit figure – '75', which meant $75,000.

The Task Force's last major success against the Cali Cartel had been three years earlier, in 1985, when charges had been brought against seven of the Cartel's major New York customers. It was Jerry McArdle's case, which he had developed out of business records kept by Justo Guzman, a previous manager of a Cali Cartel cell whom the Task Force had arrested in 1984. Jerry and another officer, Dennis Casey, had spent eight months putting the 'seven customers' case together and they were justifiably proud of their accomplishment. It had encompassed an entire cell, including some of the most experienced members of the Cartel in New York.

But its conclusion was a great disappointment. Despite the Assistant US Attorney's strenuous arguments that the defendants were illegal aliens, had no roots in the community, had used many aliases, and that, as major narcotics violators, they were facing long prison terms, the judge released all the defendants after setting bail. The result was predictable. Two defendants were murdered before their trial, probably because the Cartel suspected them of informing. Four others, including Omar Sanchez, the head of the cell, fled to Colombia. This left Jairo Escobar, the cell's junior member, who was tried, convicted and sentenced to prison.

Now, like a starving man about to feast, Mockler savoured each note as he counted the bundles, one hundred, a thousand, ten thousand, one hundred thousand, five hundred thousand, one million... It was a couple of hours before he had the final tally. It was a record seizure, a total of 7.8 million dollars.

Meanwhile, Jerry, a junior DEA Agent named Robbie Michaelis and two senior investigators from Troop K looked through the papers, documents and records that had been seized that night. Jerry flipped through Ramos's business ledger, a black and red spiral notebook, as important in its own right as the $7.8 million, since it contained a wealth of intelligence. Jerry saw a pilot's name (who, he later learned, had stayed in a hotel in Queens during this time period) and, on a separate piece of paper, a reference to a private airline at Republic Airport in Farmingdale, Long Island. This, he speculated, was probably how they planned to move the money out of the States, by private plane to Florida, then maybe on to Panama. Or perhaps when the plane landed in Florida, they would conceal the money in a container of goods destined for Colombia or hide it in the cargo of a tractor-trailer and transport it by road over the border with Mexico. The men who ran the Cartel were ingenious smugglers; they had used all these ruses and many others.

It was now nearly two in the morning. One of the agents who was processing evidence – they had searched another house and apartment that night, arrested three other people and, in addition to the $7.8 million, seized smaller prizes: five vehicles, seven weapons, six kilos of cocaine – said, 'Let's chip in and get a pizza.'

Jerry suddenly remembered that he was hungry. He opened his wallet, saw that it was empty, reached into his pocket and found seventy-five cents, and said to himself, 'This is all the money I have tonight.'

Seventy-five cents, $7.8 million, the contrast triggered a wave of reflection. Not for the first time, he wondered whether it was really worth it. Was he being paid enough money to do this? He had spent the last seven years of his life – since joining the Task Force in 1981 – working on the Cali Cartel investigation and although he knew he was working for a just cause, increasingly he felt the personal sacrifice was too great. The long journey to and from work each day, innumerable nights spent on surveillance, an unpredictable work schedule, birthday parties missed, a lost family life, broken commitments. How many times had he told his wife and children, 'I don't know if I can get home in time.'

And what really had he achieved? His team and others in Miami, Chicago, Houston, Los Angeles, had seized tons of Cali Cartel cocaine and assets worth millions of dollars; they had arrested many lower echelon people, most of whom had been sentenced to prison. But the Cartel was still flourishing.

To the average person, the money they had seized tonight would seem a fortune. But he knew that $7.8 million was a pittance to the men who ran the Cartel. In 1984, when they had seized the Justo Guzman ledger, Jerry had asked an Internal Revenue Service agent to go through the books and carefully check the figures. Based on its own business records, the IRS agent concluded that between 1981 and 1983 Guzman's cell grossed $54 million from its sales of cocaine in the New York metropolitan area. And this was a single cell. The DEA suspected that there were other cells in New York City, the largest drug distribution nexus in the United States, plus cells in Chicago, Philadelphia, Boston, Washington DC, Miami, Houston, Los Angeles, San Francisco, Montreal and Ontario.

Since 1979, when the agents in Group Five (Bill Mockler's team that had uncovered the Cartel's existence) first learned their identities, the DEA had been tracking the Cali Cartel's three 'chairmen of the board'. Jerry McArdle had seen their names on intelligence reports, on organizational charts, on the backs of indictments. He knew the names by heart – Jose SantaCruz Londono, also called Chepe, the Cartel's criminal brain, who had the physiognomy of a peasant and a street person's cunning; Gilberto Rodriguez Orejuela and Miguel Rodriguez Orejuela, who were brothers, middle-class, sophisticated, urbane-looking men with organizational skills and business acumen.

But these were just names. He had seen their pictures, but never the men in person; they were safely ensconced in Cali, Colombia. Sometimes, Jerry McArdle wondered if they really existed; were they real flesh and blood people? Kenny Robinson, a former New York City Police Department detective turned DEA analyst, whose knowledge of the Cartel was as vast as Mockler's and who, more than Mockler, was Jerry's mentor, would say, 'Chepe's a figment of the imagination. I'm really Chepe.' Kenny, a tall, broad-shouldered, ruddy-faced Irishman whose heavy physique supposedly resembled Chepe's, could afford this little joke. He was one of three policemen in America who had actually seen Chepe. The others were Mockler and Richie Crawford, a former member of Group Five now working on Cartel cases in Tampa, Florida. In January 1979 – before Jerry joined the Task Force – they had tailed the trafficker from Kennedy Airport to an apartment in Queens, then later to Republic Airport in Farmingdale, Long Island.

That was nine years ago and it was their only sighting – and at the time they were not sure who it was they were following. It had taken the DEA several years to establish Chepe's true identity. He had first emerged in 1976, posing as a businessman, Victor Crespo, in a DEA investigation in Peru of a scheme to fly coca paste to a Colombian *estancia* belonging to fellow Cartel head Gilberto Rodriguez, then smuggle the converted cocaine to New York City where it was to be distributed by Chepe alias Crespo. A year later, in 1977, when Chepe was arrested by New York City police and charged with possession of a gun – a charge on which he promptly absconded – he was using the alias Ramon Palacios. He had adopted a host of other names and in travelling to and from the States used three different US passports as well as Colombian, Panamanian, Costa Rican and Guatemalan passports. Often he wore a beard to disguise the flaky skin on the lower part of his face. (A Philadelphia doctor, whom Kenny Robinson discovered and inverviewed in 1979, had treated him for psoriasis the year before.)

This issue of identity – who were they pursuing? who were their targets? – was a continuous stumbling block in the investigation. The people who worked for the Cartel – Bill Mockler thought there were probably a thousand – changed their identities as frequently as ordinary people change their clothes. The Task Force could arrest a target, execute a search warrant on his apartment; they would discover a passport in one name, a driver's licence in another, a car registered to a third person, the telephone listed to another; a fifth person's name would appear on the rent receipts for the apartment.

When Jerry McArdle first started working on the Cartel, he had found this hodgepodge of identities completely befuddling. As a trooper, he had been assigned to East Fishkill, a small town wedged into the rolling hills, pastures and woods of Dutchess County, a two-hour drive north of New York City. His investigative caseload was typical of the county: accidents, thefts, the occasional burglary; he could track a suspect to his home by checking the address on his vehicle registration; he could interview landlords, neighbours, the shopkeepers on the main street, all happy to answer questions to help the police.

It was a shock when he began working in New York City. The members of the Task Force didn't like talking to people. Who could they trust? The superintendent of a building, a target's neighbours, the Colombians running the local shops – any of these people might tip a suspect off.

In all the years that they had worked on this investigation, they had been able to develop only five decent informants. The Cartel's employees did not turn State's evidence. They had families in Cali – the Cartel would only deal with people it knew – and if they cooperated with the police, their mothers, wives, children, would be the first ones killed.

There were other reasons people didn't 'rat' on the Cartel. The Cartel's upper echelons consisted of family and friends; the lower echelons – its customers – were usually people from Cali. This was why it was able to distribute cocaine on consignment; the Cartel only dealt with customers it knew and before a customer was given a load of cocaine he had to hand over deeds to a substantial amount of property – ranches, homes, businesses that he had in Colombia – with a value equivalent to the cocaine he would be handling.

To guard against the one or two renegades with nothing to

lose, the Cartel's leaders had broken the organization into cells. Each cell contained maybe half a dozen people and the people in a cell knew only each other. They did not know who was in another cell or where the cells were located. It was a drug distribution ring structured like the IRA or the PLO. (In the search of an apartment in Queens in 1979, Kenny Robinson had found books on espionage and terrorism read by Chepe.)

The head people in Colombia tightly controlled their US cells. They chose the customers for their multi-kilo sales; they dictated the date, the place, the time of transactions. Within minutes of its occurrence, both cell-heads and customers were required to call Cali to confirm a transaction (either the receipt of cocaine or delivery of money); if a cell-head or customer failed to call, this immediately alerted the people in Cali that there had been an arrest. And once the Cartel knew that one of its people had been arrested, it would immediately send out an emergency signal. It would beep '911' (ironically, the police emergency code), '911', over and over again, and then, following that, an untraceable pay phone number.

The Task Force was always at work on one cell or another. Recently, Jerry's group and Troop K had identified a Cali group in Manhattan. They were following the cell head; they had a bug on his phone and they watched him oversee a delivery of cocaine. Two of his people moved it from a townhouse on Manhattan's east side to a delivery car driven by a third person in the cell. The head himself did not touch the cocaine. He stayed well away from the area, near a public phone, and from this command post he communicated with the customer and Colombia. Jerry saw that the delivery was about to leave and, afraid of losing the cocaine, decided they should move in. They stopped the car, seized 35 kilos, managed to arrest the two delivery men but, in the confusion, the cell-head escaped. Within minutes, the state troopers monitoring the bug overheard someone in Cali directing the cell-head. 'Change your car, your apartment, your phone numbers, grow a beard, change your ID, change everything.'

This was not a unique incident. Many times after they had made an arrest, Jerry, Kenny Robinson and Bill Mockler had forced their way into an empty apartment and discovered food still hot on the cooker, half-eaten meals on the table. After an arrest, the people in Cali would disperse a cell, transfer its people

Cali Cartel Organizational Structure

CARTEL PRINCIPALS

Jose Santacruz Londono

Gilberto Rodriguez Orejuela

Miguel Rodriguez Orejuela

Exercise ultimate control and authority of worldwide criminal enterprise

---

FINANCIAL ADVISORS

All Colombians

Handle/invest move/hide money

CELL DIRECTOR/HEAD

All Colombians

Reports directly to Cali principals

Could control more than one cell

Oversees operations throughout the city for his principal

CELL HEAD

Reports to director of cell

Oversees cocaine distribution

Oversees money collection

Delegates responsibility for business transactions

Maintains cell records

Responsible for 15–20 cell members

CELL MEMBERS

All Colombians

Functions: bookkeeper, money handler, stash house sitter, cocaine handler, motor pool, etc.

Utilizes: pay phones, 15–20 beepers, 10–15 apartments, 10–15 vehicles, aliases and code names, security procedures, accurate record systems.

Also: handles cocaine and money, and transactions with wholesale customers

---

TRANSPORTATION OPERATIONS

Usually non-Colombians

A transport/service industry

Transporters utilize: beepers, HF radios and mobile phones

to Chicago, Los Angeles, Houston or back to Colombia. They would send in a new group, with new apartments, new stash-houses, new cars, a new series of phoney names on their licences, vehicle registrations, on their telephones; and the agents in the Task Force would have to start again.

Investigating the Cartel was like wandering through a maze, following a series of parallel paths, obscurely connected, twisting and looping, which more often than not culminated in cul-de-sacs. Since they rarely had informants and they could not use undercover agents, one of their main investigative tools was electronic or physical surveillance.

Jerry could still recall his first day on surveillance, driving over the 59th Street bridge which links Manhattan to Queens. It was a trip he was to repeat thousands of times because the Colombians in New York are concentrated in the Jackson Heights, Forest Hills, Flushing and Bayside neighbourhoods of Queens. Their target that night was a Colombian from Cali. They knew her car and its plate number, and they wanted to know who she was meeting. She was a single thread in a larger tapestry and if they could watch her for long enough, she might lead them to something. They parked their cars in the block where she was staying, Jamaica Avenue near Northern Boulevard. They watched, they waited; the hours dragged by and Jerry wondered, 'How long do we have to stay here? When is something going to happen?' Finally, at 11 pm, she came out of her apartment and drove off; the unmarked police cars took off in pursuit, not the hot pursuit of 'made for television' movies but a stealthy following for fear of being detected. All they were doing at this stage was gathering intelligence and if their target became suspicious, she would change her car, her apartment, switch identities, and the thread would be snapped. They followed her over the bridge, into Manhattan, up the east side, then back to Forest Hills, Queens. She had been watched before; she was watched again; she led them nowhere; they could never fit her in.

This was typical. They had filing cabinets full of investigative reports, pieces of the puzzle that still did not make sense, although over the years the pattern had become clearer as they analysed records and gradually developed informants, and as reports came in from Colombia and Europe.

Once Jerry got over his initial sense of disorientation, like Bill

Mockler and Kenny Robinson before him, he fell in love with the case. Investigating the Cartel was the ultimate challenge: every scrap of information was obtained only with a struggle. Because the investigation was so complex, and based mainly on records – analysing documents seized after executing search warrants, painstakingly studying seemingly meaningless pieces of paper, checking scribbled nicknames, every garbled series of numbers, address books, ledgers, business cards, receipts – it appealed to his intellect. Jerry was not the macho-style policeman, turned on by guns and the street. When he had donned the uniform of the state police, the grey suit and purple tie, it symbolized for him respect for law, the constitution, respect for the individual's rights.

This bent to his personality was reflected in his gentle manner, in his quiet, light voice. He was a pleasant-looking man with thin brown hair and Celtic features, serious, too serious, he had been told many times by his wife, which perhaps explained why he was despondent that night.

This investigation into the Cali Cartel weighed on him heavily. The agents who worked on it were so few and so weak compared to their targets. Why couldn't they get more help from their government? Why didn't the government do more about the Cartel? The men who led it – Jose SantaCruz Londono, Gilberto Rodriguez Orejuela, Miguel Rodriguez Orejuela – had been indicted by Grand Juries in New York and New Orleans. They were criminals. Why couldn't the government persuade the Colombian government to arrest them? They had homes in Cali, banks, many businesses and interests in the local football team, the America de Cali. Of course, he knew they were protected by politicians, the police, the military in Colombia. He had been told they did not stay in any one place; they moved from office to office, house to house, communicating by cellular phones (they were under the impression these were hard to bug). Miguel owned many of the taxicabs in town: the cab drivers acted as his eyes and ears, reporting any strange policemen who came into the city. Jerry had heard that the three men were as closely guarded as the US President; they had teams of bodyguards like the Secret Service, who travelled in advance to check things out; they lived in mansions surrounded by fifteen-foot walls.

But a whole army had guarded the President of Libya and that had not stopped the US Air Force from bombing his Tripoli headquarters, and surely cocaine, crack, the Cali Cartel, were doing more damage to America than the isolated terrorist groups sponsored by Qaddafi?

Why did so few agents have to carry this weight? It was so heavy, Jerry felt crushed by its load. Was this a weakness in him? Did Kenny Robinson, Bill Mockler, the two investigators he admired most, suffer from this same sense of helplessness? Did they ever have doubts?

The investigation into the Cali Cartel is the longest-running investigation in the history of the DEA. It began a decade before the February 1988 seizure of the $7.8 million, with the routine debriefing of an obscure informant by Kenny Robinson, a New York City detective then assigned to the task Force's Group Five.

In September 1978 this informant came into the Task Force office and described a Colombian drug ring that was operating in Queens. It was, he said, a big organization that took in other parts of the country, had tons of cocaine, an unlimited supply, dealt only with other Colombians and did business on consignment. Kenny was used to informants embellishing and there was nothing to corroborate this CI's story. Moreover, some of his claims sounded incredible. A national organization, tons of cocaine, an unlimited supply? This was 1978, eight years before the crack epidemic, when cocaine was still a middle-class indulgence. Kenny told the informant, 'Yeah, well, why don't you let us know when something's happening.'

A few days later the informant called back with an urgent message. In an hour's time, at 5.30 pm, the organization would be delivering a package on Queens Boulevard in Jackson Heights, Queens. He described the customer, the customer's car, and said the dealer would be driving a red Chevrolet.

Kenny's supervisor, Bill Mockler, the head of Group Five, could not make the meet. He and another agent, Richie Crawford, were on their way to La Guardia Airport to catch a flight to testify at a heroin trial in Chicago. So it was Kenny Robinson accompanied by three other members of his group who went to Queens.

As they picked up their car from the garage near West Street,

LEFT Kenny Robinson, the New York City detective who began the investigation into the Cali Cartel, eating dinner after a late night of surveillance.

BELOW DEA agent Jerry McArdle who took over the investigation from Kenny. Jerry is initiating a new supervisor, Marty Maguire, into the intricacies of the Cali Cartel investigation.

RIGHT The Operation Calico logo worn by the Cali Cartel investigators. Designed by supervisor Felix Demicco to help foster *esprit de corps* among the agents, it shows the United States and Colombia, the DEA's automatic rifle, the coca leaf and the condor with which the Cali Cartel's cocaine bricks are sometimes branded.

BELOW Agents unloading 5000 lbs. of cocaine seized from an apartment in Jackson Heights, Queens, in 1988.

OPPOSITE ABOVE $7.8 million seized from a Cali Cartel cell-head, Luis Ramos, on 25 February 1988. Bill Mockler counted and stacked the notes on two tables in his office.

OPPOSITE BELOW Jose SantaCruz Londono's cocaine. Each kilo-brick was wrapped in tape, sealed and stamped with a condor.

Rubi

ABOVE Bill Mockler and Bill Snipes searching the stadium in Milan where West Germany played Colombia, hoping to spot Miguel Rodriguez.

BELOW A few days earlier, in a hotel room in Bologna, Bill Mockler painstakingly studied surveillance photographs taken when Colombia played the United Arab Emirates, searching for the heads of the Cali Cartel or one of their associates who might lead the DEA to them.

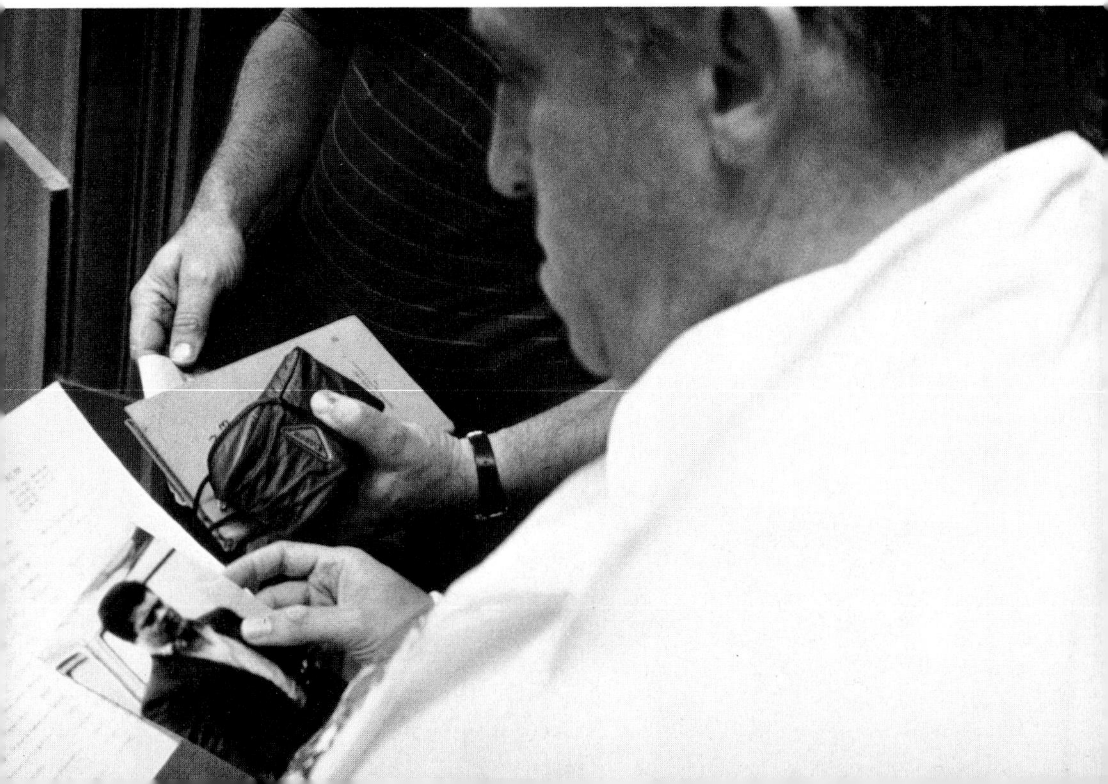

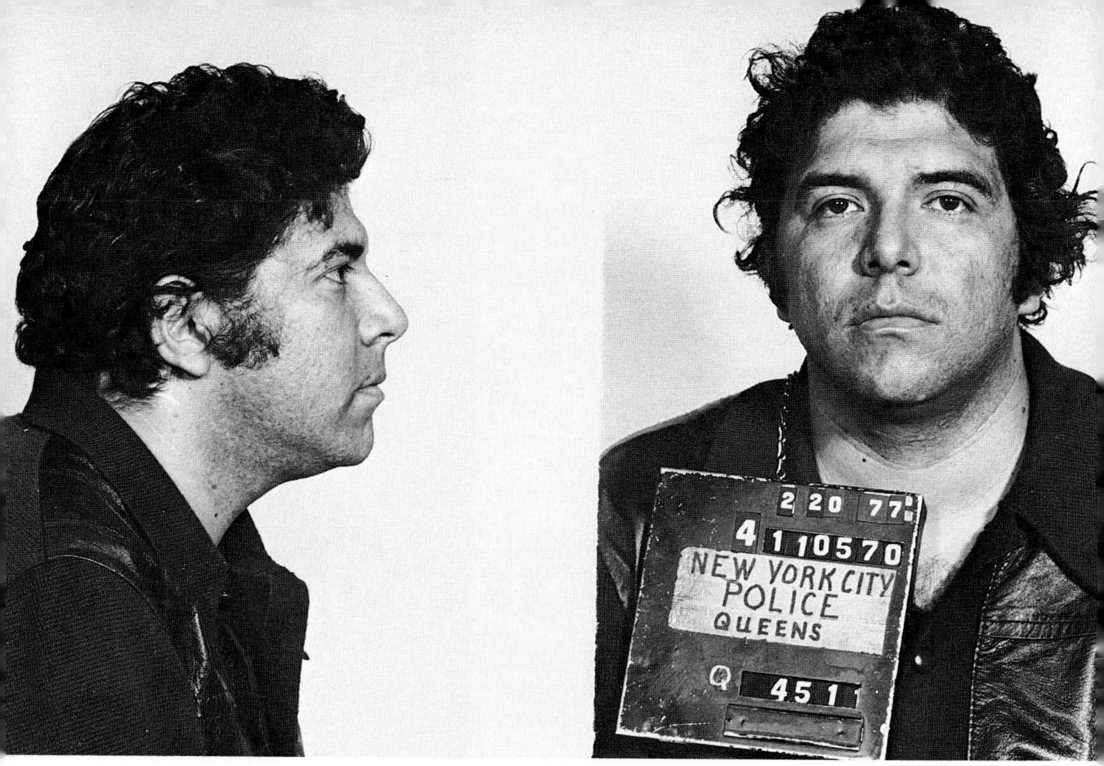

The three heads of the Cali Cartel, or as Bill Mockler calls them, 'chairmen of the board' – Jose SantaCruz Londono or Chepe (ABOVE); Gilberto José Rodriguez Orejuela (BELOW RIGHT); his brother, Miguel Angel Rodriguez Orejuela (BELOW LEFT).

The first game in Bologna yielded a handful of leads: one of Chepe's bodyguards (RIGHT) who was tailed to Rimini; the Luxembourg trio, Edgar Garcia, Jurado Rodriguez and Ricardo Mahecha Bustos (BELOW, circled, left to right), who were Chepe's money launderers.

OPPOSITE ABOVE At the last game in Bologna, Kenny Robinson and Richie Crawford, assisted by an Italian policewoman, scan the crowd for a familiar face.

OPPOSITE BELOW The head of the Italian anti-narcotics police force SCA, General B. Pietro Soggiu, in the observation booth in the Bologna stadium, explains to Frank Panessa, the DEA's chief in Italy, how they intend to monitor the crowd.

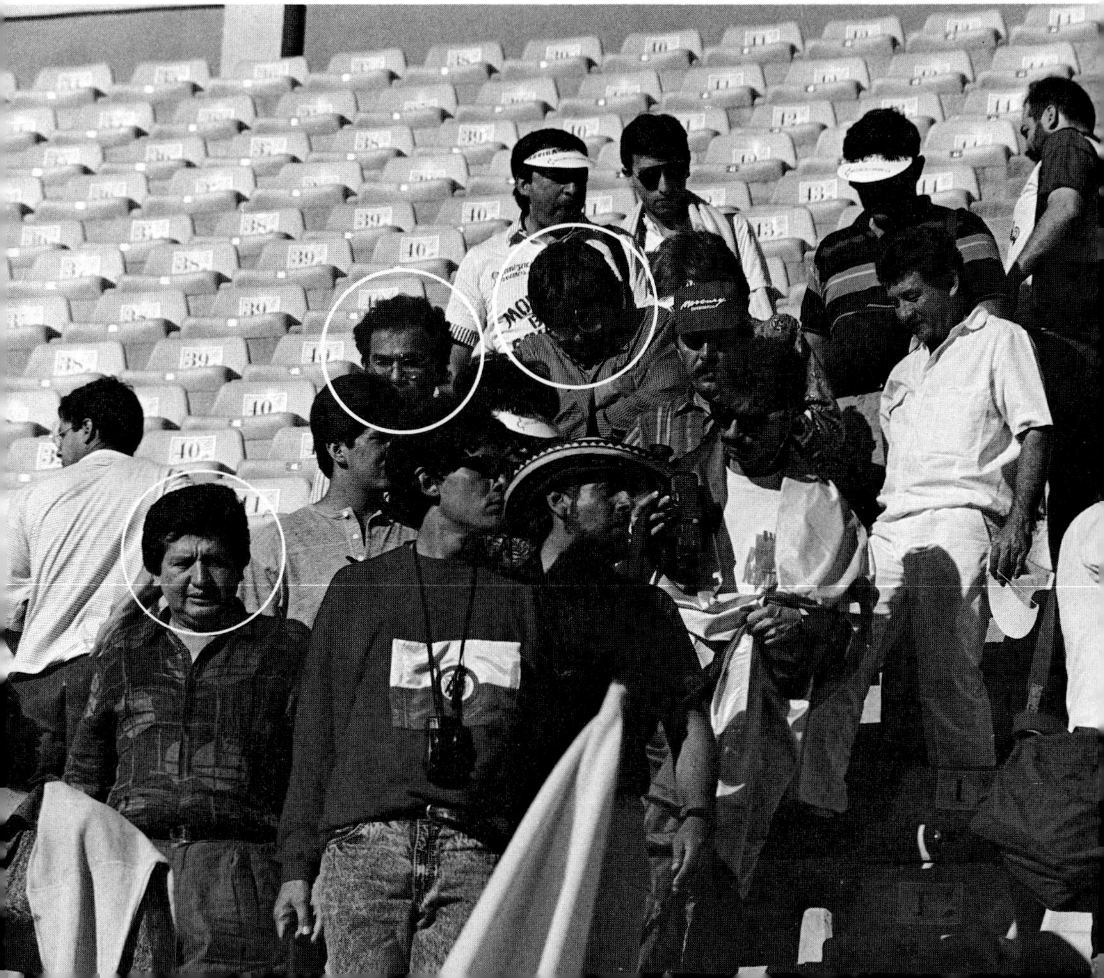

JUGOSL
COLOMB
VINI VITA

RIGHT Luis Echegarry – a Peruvian working for the Cali Cartel. His job was to rent stash-houses for guns, drugs and money.

BELOW Echegarry's boss, Luis Delio Lopez or Leto, a twenty-eight-year-old Colombian. In three years, Delio became a millionaire. With the DEA hot on his tail, he fled to Colombia where much of his money was invested in real estate and businesses. He has been charged in New York but Colombia will not extradite him.

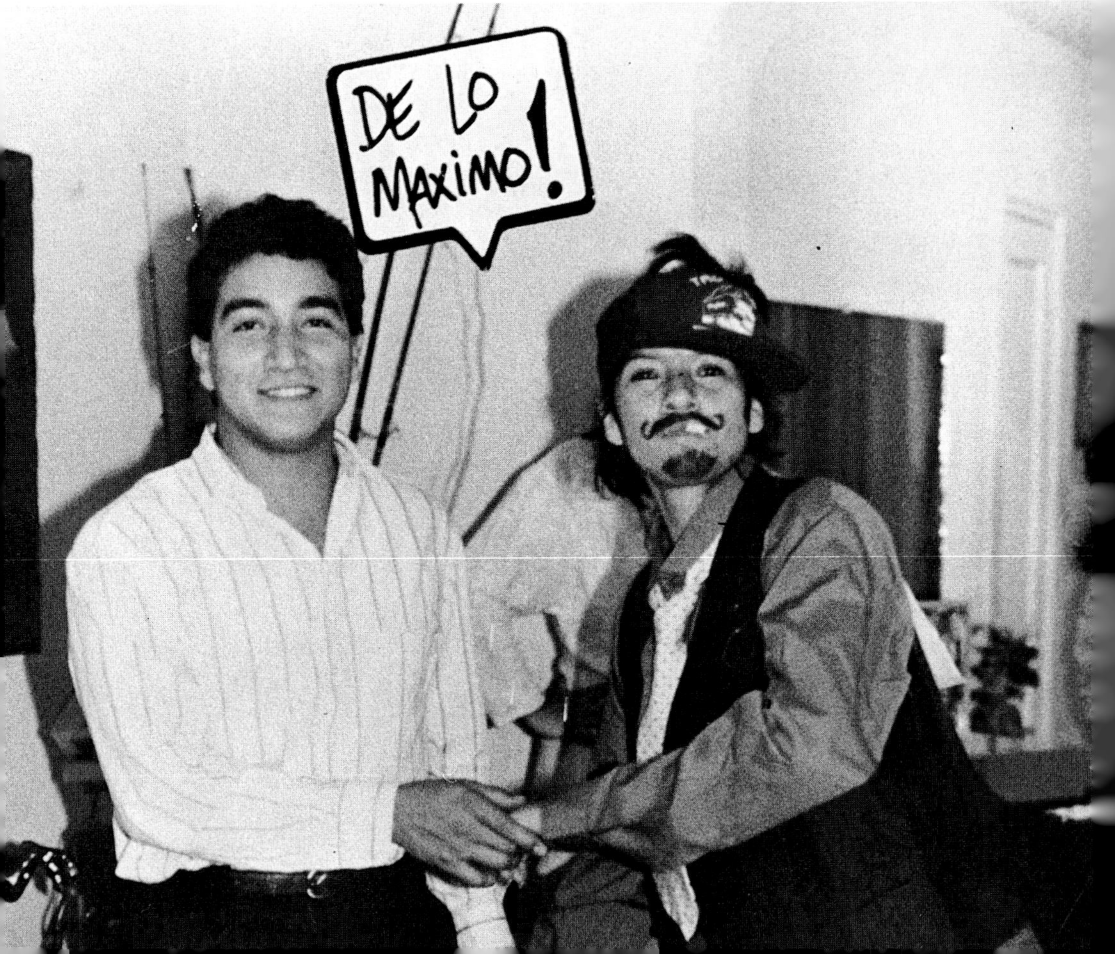

Kenny anxiously wondered, 'Will we get there in time?' The informant had called at the beginning of the rush hour when it could take forty-five minutes to drive across Manhattan. Why had he left his call to so late? What was his problem, was he getting cold feet?

But traffic that day was lighter than usual – which, in itself, Kenny considered a miracle – and they arrived at Queens Boulevard a few minutes before the scheduled delivery. They saw the customer, Nelson Gomez, standing on the street. Then they spotted the delivery car, the red Chevrolet, which pulled up and stopped just a few car-lengths in front of where they had parked.

It was the end of September, still balmy and warm, but Nelson Gomez was carrying a jacket draped over his arm. They watched him get in and out of the red Chevrolet. Then Kenny and his team emerged from their car. They were dressed in plain clothes but Gomez knew they were policemen. He turned on his heel, walking rapidly in the opposite direction. As he glanced back and saw them coming up quickly, he hurled his jacket over a low ironwork fence.

They grabbed him and picked up his jacket. It was wrapped around a brown paper bag and inside the bag was the cocaine: a one-kilo brick bound in white masking tape. But the key to the organization, the driver of the red Chevrolet, had escaped. There was, however, a single clue to his identity. Kenny had managed to obtain the red Chevrolet's licence plate number.

Later that night the informant told them, 'You'll never find the car, they ditched it after Nelson was arrested,' which, for ninety-five per cent of detectives, would have been sufficient discouragement. But not for Kenny Robinson – he was different.

Kenny ran the licence plate number through the state motor vehicle computer and, following a pattern with which he would soon become familiar, found that the car was registered to a fictitious address. Again, ninety-five per cent of detectives would have stopped there but again, Kenny Robinson was not so easily discouraged. He went to the Parking Violations Bureau, near the Criminal Court in downtown Manhattan, and asked one of the clerks if any summonses had been issued to the vehicle.

The clerk gave him fifty-odd tickets for parking violations. Kenny was looking for certain times – early in the morning and late at night – and certain addresses, locations in residential neighbourhoods. Some of the addresses he eliminated immediately, those on main thoroughfares or in commercial districts, and for the next few weeks, on his way to and from work – times when cars were most likely to be parked outside their owners' homes – he checked a dozen different addresses.

He never saw the red Chevrolet on the street but he did find another car, a blue Buick, which caught his attention because it was parked in one of the locations were the red Chevrolet had been given a ticket. It had a stack of parking violation tickets tucked under one of its windscreen wipers; like the red Chevrolet, it was parked illegally.

On the opposite side of the street there was a six-storey brick building whose tenants were bank clerks, secretaries, kindergarten teachers – respectable, law-abiding, middle-class New Yorkers who were not likely to be the blue Buick's 'scoff-law' owner. Kenny had a knack for obtaining information – he had an open face, a friendly manner and the benefit of six years experience as a street cop in Manhattan before joining narcotics. He found the building's superintendent.

'Do you know who it belongs to?' he asked, pointing to the blue Buick.

'A couple of Colombians,' the superintendent told him, 'and they've got another car that they keep in the garage in the basement.'

'Oh really?' said Kenny, 'Thanks. Do you mind if I check it?'

It didn't take long for Kenny to find the car. It was the right make, the right model, the right year and the right colour. There was only one problem – it had the wrong licence plate number. He decided to check the vehicle's' VIN number, a unique identification number affixed to the dashboard and the most reliable means of identifying a vehicle. It was the VIN number associated with the delivery car's plates. But if the VIN number was right, then the licence plates must be wrong and, if that was so, where did they come from?

Still puzzled, Kenny returned to the street and looked at the blue car again. Then he ran a check on its plates and the plates on the red Chevrolet in the garage. The mystery was solved. The plates on the Chevrolet were registered to the blue Buick on the street. The Buick's plates belonged to an unknown third car. Now Kenny understood what had happened. The red Chevrolet had not been ditched, as the informant had claimed. Its driver had got rid of its plates instead and rechristened it with the blue Buick's plates.

A long period of surveillance now began. For months, Bill Mockler, Kenny Robinson and the other members of Group Five watched the blue Buick and the red Chevrolet. During this period they identified their first cell-head, Jose Patino. In January 1979 they tailed him to Kennedy Airport and saw him meet a tall, heavy-set man with thick curly black hair and flaky patches on his skin, who had just arrived on a flight from Colombia. This was Jose SantaCruz Londono – Chepe – they later learned. They followed the two men for several days, to a penthouse apartment in Queens, then to Republic Airport in Farmingdale, Long Island, where Chepe took a private plane to Philadelphia.

Six months later, in July 1979, Kenny Robinson and Bill Mockler arrested Jose Patino. This incident proved to be a seminal event. Everything that has happened in the Cali Cartel investigation since – every arrest, every seizure, including even the indictments of Chepe and the Rodriguez Orejuela brothers – flowed from the evidence seized during the fortnight after Patino's arrest as the members of Group Five executed search warrants on four apartments in Queens and an apartment and warehouse in Baltimore, Maryland.

As is true of every successful law enforcement operation, the arrest of Patino was a blend of luck, diligence and cunning. Kenny Robinson had identified one of the apartments Patino was using in a building with an underground garage on Union Street in Flushing, Queens. (Its tenants, middle-class, professional people, included a Colombian doctor and his wife who would eventually help Kenny translate Spanish documents.) He befriended the superintendent, an East European immigrant who liberally supplied the detective with cups of coffee while letting him use an empty apartment facing Patino's for surveillance. From this vantage point, Kenny watched a window that was shuttered by blinds morning, noon and night. When it reached the point where he could no longer justify the surveillance – as always, Group Five had too few men and too many cases – Kenny gave the superintendent his card. 'Can you let me know,' he said, 'if you see him around?'

Kenny only half expected the superintendent to call but on 26 July the phone on his desk rang. It was the superintendent excitedly reporting, 'That Colombian you're looking for, he's in the building, he's here right now!'

Bill Mockler and Kenny Robinson caught Patino as he was coming out of the apartment with a black leather bag slung over his shoulder. They stopped him, questioned him, saw he was flustered. 'What do you have in that bag? Why do you need a beeper? Do you mind if we take a look at your apartment?'

If Patino had been a native-born trafficker, he probably would have said, 'Show me your warrant.' But as a Colombian he was not so conversant with the Fourth Amendment (the section of the Bill of Rights which limits the power of the police to search people, things or places) and, like many Colombians, he was under the impression that since the drugs and money belonged to the organization, he himself was not criminally liable. So he acceded, thereby legitimizing the search under the US Constitution.

They took Patino back to the apartment. They were looking though his bag – 'What's the money-counter for? Why all the rubber bands?' – when suddenly his beeper sounded. They heard an agitated voice, a man speaking Spanish. '*Pepe, qué pasa? Pepe, qué pasa? Llamame, llamame!*' (Bill Mockler had never forgotten those words, that voice – 'Pepe, what's happening? Call me! Call me!' It was the first, and last time, he heard Chepe speak.)

Then a call-back number appeared on the beeper's screen. If they had only known then what they learned much later, they would have dropped everything else to trace that call-back number. But they were just beginning to fill in the pieces so they inevitably concentrated on what they had found on Patino: a series of rent receipts for different apartments in Queens.

They took Patino first to an apartment on Roosevelt Avenue and 82nd Street. Here, Chepe was receiving mail, including a false passport under the name Victor Crespo. When they roused the superintendent, Patino was yelling, 'This is where I live, right? Tell them this is where I live!' The superintendent, who was confused and frightened, whispered to one of the agents, 'No, that's not right.'

Their next stop was an apartment on Burns Court. Patino turned pale and started sweating when they opened its door. It was a small apartment – a bathroom, bedroom, kitchen, living room – with a huge Mosler safe containing forty pounds of cocaine. There were hundreds of empty one-kilo bags strewn all over the place, traces of cocaine in the bathtub, sink, on the floors, in the kitchen, on the stove.

They lifted one of Chepe's fingerprints from a soda can in the refrigerator. Maybe it was him, maybe Patino – both had been going in and out of the apartment – who had sealed and barricaded the windows and hung deodorant sticks throughout the apartment, hoping to mask the drug's sickly smell. But the chemical residue was in the air, in the dust, and the stench was so potent that Kenny's head ached from it and as he searched through the apartment the realization sank in, 'Thousands and thousands of kilos of cocaine must have passed through this place!'

While Kenny and Mockler went through the stash-house, Richie Crawford and another agent drove to 'The Towers', a high-rise building overlooking Long Island Sound in Bayside, Queens. This was the apartment where Chepe was living. In it they found his original Colombian passport, an important find for a man so elusive, which showed his true name of Jose Santacruz Londono. (Up to this point, they had thought he was indeed Victor Crespo.) They also found bank statements and account books belonging to Gilberto and Miguel Rodriguez Orejuela that showed the proceeds of drug sales in New York flowing directly to them.

Ten days later, sorting through documents, Richie Crawford found an electricity bill for a fourth apartment, on 79th Street in Flushing, Queens. When they were finally able to get into the apartment – they reconnoitred it first, then obtained a search warrant – they saw from its contents that they were a fortnight too late. The cocaine was still there – two kilos in a safe – and there were plenty of guns lying around the place, but the bags and the shoe-boxes that had contained the money, each marked with a name and a number – 'Negra, 75' – they were all empty.

But it was not until they found the phone whose number Patino was supposed to have called, a pay phone in a Carvel ice-cream store a few minutes walk from the apartment on 79th Street in Flushing, that Mockler was able to fit the pieces together. As he stood by the phone and looked at its number, he realized that this was the telephone from which Chepe had dialled Patino's beeper. 'Pepe, what's happening? Call me! Call me!' Chepe had probably waited at that phone for many minutes, not knowing what had happened, imagining different scenarios – Pepe had been robbed, the police had grabbed him – before hurrying back to collect the money.

These were, of course, only Mockler's surmises but their accuracy was confirmed several years later when Group Five developed its first good Cali Cartel informant, Robert Lafferty III, an American pilot who had worked for Gilberto Rodriguez and Chepe. (The Cartel often employed 'gringo' pilots; they were less likely to arouse suspicion when flying into small American airports.)

After his arrest in Fort Lauderdale in 1981, Lafferty agreed to work for the DEA as an informant. He explained that it was he who had got Chepe out of New York the day after Patino's arrest. He was in Florida when Chepe called him and he had flown to New York the following morning. They had met at Republic Airport in Farmingdale, Long Island, and Chepe was carrying a suitcase stuffed with $2 million.

Chepe told Lafferty that he had been waiting for Pepe, who was supposed to help him count and bundle the money. ('Ah,' thought Mockler when he heard this part of the story. 'That's why Patino had the rubber bands and money-counter.') When Patino had failed to appear at the appointed hour or call Chepe at the pay phone by the Carvel, Chepe had run back to the apartment and cleaned out the money, called Lafferty and told him to fly up from Florida.

The evidence seized as a result of Patino's arrest proved to be an investigator's El Dorado. It took months for Group Five to go through every scrap of evidence, to decipher codes, to trace bank accounts, to connect the apartments in New York with the apartment and warehouse in Baltimore (which they succeeded in doing partly through the analysis of telephone records). But by the time they had finished, they had identified the men behind the organization, they had an idea of its scope, of its manner of operation.

The organization functioned at the highest level of the cocaine trade, buying paste in Peru and Bolivia, converting it to cocaine, then smuggling it into the United States. Its roots, they later discovered, were in a Colombian kidnapping organization called the Chemas gang, founded in the late 1960s by Chepe and Gilberto and Miguel Rodriguez Orejuela, who invested the capital accumulated from kidnapping in Colombia's newly developing cocaine industry.

By 1975 the organization was well established in the States, with Chepe managing the most profitable distribution network in New York. In 1976 he set up a phoney lumber company in Baltimore, Maryland, to bring in shipments of mahogany planks which had been milled in Brazil, hollowed out and stuffed with packages of cocaine, probably processed in Colombia, and shaped to fit the concave space. In the lumber company's warehouse near Baltimore's seaport, the members of Group Five discovered the car which the Cartel had used to move the cocaine north to New York. Although bought in New York, it was registered to a fictitious Maryland address. It had received parking tickets near the Burns Court apartment in Queens which the Cartel used as a stash-house.

Over the next three years, Kenny Robinson, Bill Mockler and the other members of Group Five followed a trail of evidence that led to Florida. On the back page of a spiral notebook they had found in Chepe's Bayside, Queens, apartment, they saw a name and an address for Hallandale Beach, Florida, which led them to a Florida apartment that Chepe had rented. (It had been vacated immediately after Patino's arrest in July 1979.) Then, going through a 'Dempsey Dumpster' loaded with trash, they discovered the carbon copy of a store receipt for furniture. The purchaser was listed as Fernando Gutierrez, one of the aliases Gilberto Rodriguez was using, and it gave his address as a luxury high-rise condominium building on a private island, Grove Isle, in the Coconut Grove area of Miami. They spent several days watching Rodriguez. From Florida, they hopscotched to Alabama, where the Cartel had bought a ranch and constructed an airstrip (presumably to land shipments of cocaine), then back to Florida and New York. They made more arrests, seized more cars, money, cocaine, guns, records and real estate, including the Alabama ranch. Then, in 1982, Bill Mockler was transferred to Miami.

The transfer was inevitable. No DEA agent stays in the same post for ever. But for the members of Group Five, particularly Kenny Robinson, the reassignment of Bill Mockler was a significant loss.

Kenny had been assigned to the Task Force in 1970, a reward for outstanding work in the New York Police Department's Brooklyn South Narcotics Division. Two years later Mockler had become his supervisor. Kenny's initial impression of his new boss was 'Wow! This guy is strange!' Mockler was very aggressive, very demanding, he had a wild streak and he drank excessively. He was moreover a very odd-looking man with a long jaw, protruding teeth and a gummy smile. But inside this ugly wrapping was a fine intellect, a charismatic personality, a man who commanded respect. Mockler had astonishing powers of observation, a photographic memory for licence plate numbers, makes and models of cars, names, faces, addresses, telephone numbers. Sometimes Kenny would think, 'One night, after a binge, he's not going to remember, everything's just going to drop out of his head.' But that wasn't the case. Then, in 1976, a doctor had told Mockler, 'If you keep drinking like this, I give you six months to live.' The following day, Mockler stopped drinking; he gave up alcohol without any cushioning, the way a drug addict goes 'cold turkey'. But the most remarkable thing, to Kenny at least, was that Mockler still loved hanging out in bars; he had just as good a time with a glass of water in his hand, although his main diversion now was looking at girls.

During the period of Mockler's leadership, Group Five had developed the reputation as the Task Force's best team. It led the other teams in the number of arrests, the assets and drugs seized, the quality of cases. This partly reflected the individual talents of the agents – Kenny Robinson, Jose Guzman, Richie Crawford, Ray Vallely, Tom Deignan, Mike Purpura, and Jerry McArdle in the last year of Mockler's regime – but it was also a tribute to Mockler's skill at managing people. He had the ability to pick out a person's talent, nurture it, let it develop.

Early on Mockler had recognized Kenny's patience, his stamina, his head for detail; he saw that Kenny could work with almost no supervision. When Kenny had come to him after the arrest of Nelson Gomez and said, 'They supposedly ditched the car but I know I can find it,' he didn't brush him aside or try to discourage him. 'Go ahead,' he told him. 'See what you can come up with.'

During the investigation's early years, 1978 to the early 1980s, no one imagined the size and scope of the Cartel. This was the period when cocaine was considered a middle-class diversion, harmless, inconsequential. Prosecutors from the Eastern District of New York (who were responsible for handling most of Group Five's cases) routinely declined to prosecute 'kiddie-dope' cases, even when a defendant was charged with a kilo sale of cocaine. But even though heroin cases consumed most of the DEA's resources, Mockler had encouraged Kenny Robinson to pursue the Cali Cartel investigation. Then when Kenny would come up with something definite, Mockler would shift the entire Group on to the Cartel.

Periodically, Mockler would be criticized by his bosses. They would say, 'The other Groups have more arrests, they're doing better.' And he would retort, 'When we make a seizure, when we make a case, we beat them all. We make the statistics for the year so why do you bother about how many bodies I have out on surveillance?' But Mockler, who was bureaucratically astute, would temporarily pull everyone off his favourite investigation and make a few 'buy and bust' cases (which on the streets of New York were as easy as shooting ducks in a farmyard) simply to satisfy his superiors' enthusiasm for statistics. 'Feeding the Wolves' is what he called this and when the wolves were sated, his group would resume their surveillance.

With Bill Mockler's departure, Group Five split up. By the end of 1983, of its original members, only Kenny Robinson was left. But he continued to work on the Cali Cartel, assisted by Jerry McArdle who had become his de facto partner. Together, they worked on the Justo Guzman investigation – Kenny's case which had resulted in the seizure of Guzman's ledger in 1984 and led to the indictment of the seven customers and ultimately to the seizure of the $7.8 million in 1988. They also uncovered a network of cocaine processing laboratories in isolated farm houses on Long Island, in Up-State New York, Virginia and North Carolina. (This, Kenny thinks, was the Cartel's solution when, at the DEA's urging, both the United States and Colombia cracked down on the export to Latin America of precursor chemicals manufactured in Germany and the US.)

It was when they were working together on the Justo Guzman case that Kenny realized Jerry McArdle could become his successor. This was very important, for the pressure was building on him to retire. Several times the New York Police Department had wanted to return him to the Narcotics Division to make room for others. (The Task Force was considered a plum assignment.) But Kenny's DEA bosses resisted. Kenny, they argued, had too much knowledge, he was a walking computer on the Cali Cartel and if he left, who would replace him?

But Kenny knew that eventually the pressure would prove irresistible and, with Mockler gone, Richie Crawford in Tampa, Florida, Tom Deignan promoted and Jose Guzman about to retire, he urgently needed to find a successor. And it was not the kind of case he could hand on to just anyone – few police had the intellect, the disposition, the stamina, the enthusiasm.

In 1986 the DEA offered Kenny Robinson a job as an intelligence analyst – his age disqualified him from joining as an agent – which he accepted. He retired from the New York City Police Department and moved two flights up to the Unified Intelligence Division.

Jerry McArdle, seeing that the State Police might reassign him, decided to transfer to the DEA as an agent while his age, thirty-six, still rendered him eligible. With Kenny gone, Jerry carried on the investigation but the work that he had once loved he now found a burden. When he told the other agents in his group, all new people and usually younger, what he was doing, he saw their eyelids droop, their pupils glaze over. He could hardly blame them. He knew he lived in a labyrinth of detail, of dates, documents, seizures, names, addresses, all significant to him but meaningless jumble when he tried to explain it to others.

Moreover, his new boss, Jerry Murphy, had another priority which Jerry McArdle conceded had to take precedence. Murphy was determined to charge one of the men involved in the torture and murder of DEA agent Kiki Camarena, Ramon Matta Ballesteros, whose cocaine organization was partly located in New York. Murphy let Jerry pursue the Cali Cartel investigation and even assigned an officer to help him but he put the rest of the group to work on Ballesteros, who was eventually convicted and sentenced to multiple life terms in prison.

In 1986, when he was about to be transferred from the Task Force to the Cocaine Desk in Washington, Murphy called Jerry McArdle into his office. 'Look,' he said, not unsympathetically, 'you've been working on this case since 1981. You have to put an end to it. Try to wrap it up. Every case has a beginning and an end.'

This, Jerry knew, was the conventional wisdom. But how could he close down the case when the Cartel was expanding? What the investigation needed was more, not less attention, and Kenny, to whom he talked daily, was in complete agreement. They had hundreds of documents, unexplored, unanalysed, they had active leads to half a dozen cities.

Then in 1987, at Kenny's instigation, they obtained their superiors' permission to seek help from DEA headquarters in Washington. There they met with Jerry Murphy, now a coordinator on the Cocaine Desk, and made a special plea to him, for more resources, more agents, more analysts, a computer, money to travel; for recognition of the investigation's importance – it should become one of the DEA's top priorities. They needed some mechanism for institutionalizing their knowledge so that if they were transferred, retired, or hit by a car the next day, the investigation could be carried on without them. They suggested a mini-police force exclusively devoted to the Cali Cartel, with the resources and power to move from coast to coast and beyond the borders of the United States. (Although Jerry did not say so, what he really wanted was to revive Group Five.)

They wanted the moon; they received substantially less. Headquarters would not agree to a mini-police force. This conflicted with the DEA's organizational structure of regional offices whose chiefs determined priorities and allocated resources accordingly. Instead, headquarters would create a Special Enforcement Operation, code-named Operation Calico. Its elements would include more analysts at headquarters, a budget to travel, a directive to regional offices to give greater priority to cases involving the Cartel. But, perhaps most importantly to Jerry McArdle and Kenny Robinson, in New York City, still the Cartel's centre, Operation Calico would be headed by their old boss, Bill Mockler, whom the DEA sent back to New York at the end of 1987.

7 'You Have to Wish and Dream and Hope'

In the months following the creation of Operation Calico and Bill Mockler's return to New York City, the DEA and other law enforcement agencies had a string of successes against the Cali Cartel. First came the arrest of Luis Ramos and the seizure of $7.8 million on 25 February 1988. Then a few weeks later in Tarpon Springs, Florida, Richie Crawford, one of the original members of Group Five, and a team of DEA agents seized 7200 pounds of Cali Cartel cocaine. It had been smuggled into Florida in hollowed-out mahogany timbers, the same ruse used by Chepe in Baltimore in 1979. Five months after this, in August 1988, Jerry's group, now headed by Felix Demicco, seized 5000 more pounds of cocaine in Jackson Heights, Queens. Some of the kilo-bricks were stamped with a rampant condor, one of Chepe's brand marks. (These brand marks, Jerry McArdle thought, identified the laboratory that produced the cocaine and served as an accounting link between the Cartel's manufacturing and transportation divisions.) Then, in November 1989, another load (this time five tons!) of Cali Cartel cocaine, sealed in plastic and concealed in drums of pesticide, was seized from a warehouse in Long Island City in Queens.

These successes vindicated Jerry McArdle, Kenny Robinson and Bill Mockler, proving to distant and sometimes still sceptical superiors both the magnitude of the Cartel and that Operation Calico was necessary. But they also underscored law enforcement's insufficiencies. Over the years Mockler and his men had shifted their tactics. They had started the investigation by arresting customers, then, when they realized their significance, they targeted the cell-heads. But the cell-heads were rapidly replaced, usually by the best customer on their list. Once the Task Force realized this, they embarked on a new strategy of arresting whole cells. After Mockler's return to New York City, their vision expanded by additional resources and their morale strengthened by the backing of headquarters, Mockler, Robinson and McArdle began to think of new tactics.

Why not attack the Cartel at its heart and its brain, why not go after its three 'chairmen of the Board'? They were, after all, wanted for charges in the States, which meant the DEA would not have to spend years building a case. If they succeeded in arresting and convicting these men, the biggest cocaine dealers in the world, what a victory for law enforcement! Was not this, after all, what the DEA should be doing – going for the heart of the world's largest cocaine distribution organization? But how could they reach SantaCruz and the Orejuela brothers? As long as they stayed in Cali, their base seemed impregnable.

Then in January 1990, during the course of one of their daily chats, Kenny Robinson mentioned to Jerry McArdle that four years ago, in 1986, Chepe had been seen at the World Cup soccer games in Mexico City. The Colombian emigrants to New York, Jerry knew, were avid soccer fans. They had formed neighbourhood soccer leagues in Jackson Heights which played every weekend in Flushing Meadow Park. (He had watched some of their games when he had been looking for targets.) Cali itself was a major sports centre and its football club, the America de Cali, was reputedly owned by the Rodriguez Orejuela brothers. Although Jerry had never seen the club's documentation, he had heard this from many informants, people who had lived in Cali, who personally knew Gilberto and Miguel. In 1987, when his team had gone into a Queens apartment during the course of a money laundering investigation, Jerry had seen a stack of magazines featuring the America de Cali. The apartment's tenant, a Colombian from Cali, had disarmingly asked him, 'Do you know Gilberto? I'm a big fan of his soccer team.'

(In this particular money laundering scheme, the Cartel had employed half a dozen 'smurfs', low-level employees who went from bank to bank, purchasing money orders for $9000 in cash – which was how the Cartel neutralized the legal requirement that banks notify the Treasury Department of cash deposits in excess of $10,000. Jerry had found a list in this apartment which showed every bank in Manhattan and Queens broken down by neighbourhoods and streets.)

As Kenny and Jerry discussed what they knew about the Colombians and soccer, Kenny said, 'Why don't we try to have a presence at the World Cup games in Italy in 1990?' As soon as he said this, they rose from their chairs and headed for Bill Mockler's office. There was always a line of young agents waiting to ask questions of Mockler but when he saw Kenny and Jerry he cleared his office, telling his secretary, 'Hold my calls.' He listened intently as Kenny explained the idea.

The tournament occurred only once every four years and in the world of soccer it was the greatest event, the ultimate expression of nationalism and sport. The last time Colombia had qualified for the World Cup was in 1962, when the games were held in Chile. Now that Colombia had qualified again – by defeating Israel – the Italian tournament was certain to attract some of the drug barons. They were responsible for the sport's renaissance in Colombia; they had invested heavily in its first division teams, offering generous contracts to players from Argentina, Uruguay and Paraguay. The traffickers were undoubtedly frustrated because their teams now could not play in Colombia: after the November 1989 murder of a referee, Alvaro Ortega (for a call favouring America de Cali over a Medellin team), the government had closed all stadiums and cancelled the national championship play-offs.

Moreover, as Mockler knew, there were close ties between the Cali Cartel and Europe. When Richie Crawford had searched Chepe's flat in Bayside, Queens, in 1979 after Jose Patino's arrest, he had found a drawer full of expensive shirts that were still in their original wrappings, with sales tags showing they had been purchased in Italy. In 1987 Chepe had spent several months in Milan, learning Italian and setting up a cell which was fed by a pipeline of shipments from Colombia to Spain. In that same year there had been a high-level meeting in Miami in which Cartel representatives discussed new methods of smuggling cocaine into Europe. In going through recently acquired Cartel business records, Kenny had seen payments to cell members in Paris. In fact, Kenny was convinced the Cartel was expanding its European networks. In Italy cocaine was selling for $60,000 a kilo, three times the price it commanded in New York City.

Still, the operation the agents were contemplating would be a long shot. They could not be sure their targets would go to Italy. It would also be complex and very expensive, involving the orchestration of resources and intelligence in New York, Washington, Italy, Colombia and Argentina, and the consent of headquarters and the Italian police. But notwithstanding these objections, Bill seized on Kenny's proposal. The opportunity was unique, the best they might ever have, and if they were successful, the kings would tumble. It would be the end of an era.

He told Kenny to write up a plan. This was sent to Washington and over the next few months shaped and refined. The DEA decided to expand the list of targets to include some twenty fugitives, traffickers who had fled to Colombia after being charged or convicted in the United States. Frank Panessa, the DEA's country attaché in Italy, obtained the cooperation of the Italian police.

Colombia's World Cup team could not prepare for the games at home because a group called Clean Football in Colombia had threatened to kill its coach, Francisco Maturana, unless he dismissed players from Atletico Nacional, America de Cali and Millonarios Bogota, teams linked to drug money.[1] But while it trained in Florida, Frank Panessa in Italy arranged for fax machines, computers, extra telephone lines, hotel space for analysts and agents. The SCA (Servizio Centrale Antidroga), the Italian anti-narcotics police force, mobilized its manpower. Kenny Robinson and Jerry McArdle put together photographs, fingerprints, indictments and arrest warrants for each target.

On Monday, 4 June 1990, six days before Colombia played its first game in Italy, a team of DEA agents and analysts arrived in the city of Bologna. They passed the next three days familiarizing themselves with the city, the location of its hotels, its railway station; they visited the stadium, which bristled with cameras, and the observation post, a small room in the bowels of the stadium where they would secretly scan the crowd through more than a dozen video monitors. They drove by the luxurious villa where the Colombian team was staying – it had arrived in Bologna on 25 May – but saw very little. The villa's long drive was concealed by a row of poplars.

In the lounge of the hotel which they were using as their headquarters, they set up a secure phone line so that they could call New York, Washington, Bogota, other countries in Europe and, most importantly, Rome where the DEA kept its link to NADDIS, its criminal investigations computer, the most extensive narcotics intelligence system in existence.

The agents and analysts studied files, films, photographs of their targets. With their Italian counterparts, they practised surveillance, breaking off to eat astoundingly large and long lunches. And while they bought World Cup footballs for their children and Colombian team sweatshirts for themselves they waited – for the day of the first game and for Bill Mockler.

On Wednesday, 6 June 1990, Bill Mockler took an evening flight from New York to Rome, arriving early on Thursday morning at Leonardo Da Vinci Airport. There he was met by an agent assigned to the Rome office who drove Mockler and Armando Marin, one of the administrators on the Cocaine Desk who would serve as the treasurer for Operation Offsides, to Bologna.

Mockler was never at his best early in the morning; with jet lag and fatigue, he was more irritable than usual. Accustomed to maximum road speeds of fifty miles per hour, he winced at his driver's heavy foot on the accelerator; they were speeding along the autostrada at a hundred miles an hour. 'My head feels like it's glued to the back of the seat,' he complained to his companion. 'What's wrong with the Bologna, airport? Why didn't we come in there? This is like landing in Miami and then driving to LA.'

It was the first day of the World Cup games and as they drove to Bologna, Cameroon was preparing to play the world champions, Argentina. Later that day, in an extraordinary upset victory, the tiny African nation defeated Latin America's giant, a victory tumultuously acclaimed by most of the Italian nation whose team needed to defeat Argentina to keep in the running for the cup.

But to the DEA agent from New York City, who won what game was a matter of indifference. He had come to Italy with a single purpose. More than Jerry McArdle or Kenny Robinson, whose steady disposition, strong family life and Catholic faith provided a counterweight, Mockler was obsessed with the Cali Cartel investigation. He had one consuming professional ambition: to confront Chepe and Gilberto Rodriguez, who had been indicted by a federal Grand Jury in New York City, in one of his native city's courtrooms; to reel off the volumes of evidence collected over a decade; to listen as the foreperson announced the jury's verdict, 'As to count one of the Indictment, we find the defendants guilty! As to counts two, three, four . . . guilty, guilty, guilty!'

He especially wanted to capture Jose SantaCruz Londono. He had spent so many years pursuing Chepe that sometimes he felt as though he knew the man personally and, in an odd sort of way, he respected his adversary. He admired his organizational skills, his energy and business sense, the forceful personality that had enabled him, starting from nothing, to build a multi-million-dollar business enterprise whose net profits surpassed those of most Fortune 500 companies. He often referred to him as 'my Professor Moriarty', for like Sherlock Holmes and his fictional adversary, Mockler had never been able to lay his hands on Chepe.

The closest he had come to capturing him was in 1979, nearly eleven years ago, when he and Kenny Robinson had arrested Jose Patino. But Chepe had been spirited out of New York by Robert Lafferty, who had flown him first to Miami, then back to Cali. Within two years, however, Chepe had returned to the States. Between 1981 and 1983 he lived in Manhattan at three different apartments, all in first-class neighbourhoods – around the Lincoln Center, the Upper East Side and Central Park West – and he used three different aliases. To explain his frequent trips to Houston, Miami and Los Angeles, he let it be known that he was in the vending machine business.

This was during a period when Group Five was particularly active; they made several important arrests, several large seizures. And ironically, Chepe's apartment near Lincoln Center was only a few blocks north and east from where the Task Force was located. His favourite hang-out, Martin's Bar, where he spent several hours every day, was on Broadway and 61st Street, only three blocks from the office where Mockler sat plotting his capture.

The source of much of this information was an informant,

developed. Alfredo Cervantes – now in the US Government's Federal Witness Protection Program, with a new name, new social security number, driver's licence, passport, and living at an address which is a closely guarded secret – worked for Chepe as a driver. He provided some of the details that, combined with other intelligence, helped flesh out a portrait of Mockler's master criminal. Chepe liked to party, he liked to drink, he was a ladies' man, he had more than one family. He was a multi-millionaire but he was also stingy: he paid his workers in coke rather than money, which meant that if they were arrested trying to convert it to cash, they had nothing to leave to take care of their families. Chepe liked American food, the dynamism and excitement of New York City and also its egalitarian society. He resented the way he was treated in Cali, where, because of his trade and low social status, he was despised by its upper-class families. When he was rejected for membership of Cali's best country club, he built a mansion that was its exact replica. He sent his legitimate daughter, Ana Milena, to a small private college in Boston, Massachusetts. His legal wife, Emparo Castro, and his mother lived in the United States.

Chepe loved money, he loved power but, even more, he loved excitement. He had a team of lawyers who represented the Cartel's people. He knew the names of the agents who were working against him. He studied their trial testimony to learn their tactics and adapted his organization to defeat their methods. He gleaned court documents to learn the names of informants. He enjoyed playing cat and mouse with the DEA agents. Sometimes, Mockler thought, 'he enjoys taunting me'.

Mockler had slightly more success with Chepe's partner, Gilberto Rodriguez Orejuela, the satisfaction, at least, of seeing him jailed for a year. In November 1984, after Mockler had left Group Five and was working in Miami, Gilberto was arrested in Madrid with Jorge Luis Ochoa, a major Colombian trafficker, one of the leaders of the Medellin Cartel. This association of drug dealers from Colombia's second largest city included the notorious Pablo Escobar, Carlos Lehder and Gonzalo Rodriguez Gacha. Like the Cali Cartel, the traffickers from Medellin manufactured and exported cocaine but they played this game by different rules. Whereas Chepe, Gilberto and Miguel Rodriguez eschewed unnecessary violence, the Medellin Cartel assassinated those who opposed their interests. Their victims included policemen, judges, politicians, nuns, clerics, journalists, union activists, peasant organizers and left-wing guerrillas.

By the end of the 1980s, the traffickers from Cali and Medellin were bitter enemies, engaged in a bloody territorial war that was partly precipitated by the Medellin Cartel's attempt to break into the lucrative New York market. This conflict had resulted in scores of murders in the States and Colombia. Teams of Cali hitmen raided Medellin; and Medellin '*sicarios*', professional assassins, had retaliated with attacks on Cali. (On 25 September 1990, a group of Medellin hitmen would gun down nineteen people on a farm near Cali. Their target, Francisco Herrera, one of the Cali Cartel's top people, escaped.)

But before this war, the two trafficking consortiums had worked together, sometimes making joint shipments of cocaine to the States, and in 1984 Gilberto Rodriguez and Jorge Ochoa had travelled to Spain to set up new air routes for the export of cocaine. There they indulged in a lifestyle that was bound to attract attention. Ochoa, posing as Moises Moreno Miranda, bought four Mercedes and an eight-thousand-square-foot mansion complete with swimming pool, tennis courts and discotheque in one of Madrid's most fashionable suburbs. Gilberto Rodriguez, using a Venezuelan passport and calling himself Gilberto Gonzalez Linares, lived in a fancy hotel in the centre of the city while he bought two huge apartments and two Mercedes. By 25 September 1984 the Madrid police had identified both men and were monitoring five 'wires'. On 17 October the U S Ambassador requested their arrest.

Bill Mockler was summoned to Spain to assist the investigation and late on 15 November 1984 he had looked through a one-way mirror at police headquarters in Madrid: he saw a small man, five foot six inches tall, with dark brown hair and eyes. Mockler had last seen him in 1980 when Group Five pursued the Cali Cartel's trail to Florida and had watched this man's condominium in Grove Isle. Mockler had no difficulty in identifying Fernando Gutierrez alias Roberto Antonio Matarraz alias Gilberto Rodriguez. He had, after all, tailed him for several days; they had come close to catching him with a shipment of cocaine.

Mockler had brought to Madrid a stack of files and in a short amount of time, he tried to explain the complex history of the case: Chepe's operation in New York; his relationship to Gilberto; the ledgers and bank books found in Chepe's Bayside apartment, which showed the profits from Chepe's drug sales flowing into bank accounts belonging to Gilberto and his brother Miguel; how Gilberto took over the Florida operation after Chepe fled to Colombia when they arrested Jose Patino . . .

Mockler taught the Spanish police how to read the ledgers they had seized in Rodriguez's hotel room. He warned the lieutenant who was in charge of the investigation ('a good cop' was Mockler's laudatory description), 'When you arrest him, be prepared to go directly to a judge because he'll have a battery of attorneys screaming to get him out.' Unlike Ochoa, his colleague from Medellin, Gilberto would not kill police or judges or bomb the police station – but he would use every other technique, bribery included, to manipulate the legal system.

Then Mockler described what had happened in Peru when Gilberto was there in 1981, arranging for a shipment of base to his Colombian laboratories. Within an hour of his arrest by the Peruvian anti-narcotics police, his lawyers appeared at the police station and had the charges dismissed, his records expunged, but fortunately not before a friendly policeman slipped the DEA agent who was in the police station a copy of Gilberto's fingerprints and his photograph.

After watching the Spanish police working on the case – 'two dozen cops crammed into a tiny room, manning seven wires, with one car at their disposal, up against the two biggest drug dealers in the world' – Mockler feared the outcome of a contest that seemed so depressingly unequal. His fears were justified. The arrest of Gilberto was the high point of the case; its course after this was like an invalid's slow decline.

On the basis of Mockler's evidence, the Spanish judge agreed to hold Gilberto for seventy-two hours while the US government filed an extradition request. This was followed by an indictment which charged SantaCruz and Gilberto Rodriguez with conspiracy to distribute narcotics and participation in a continuing criminal enterprise, crimes in America punishable by life prison terms. This move was countered with an indictment and extradition request that emanated from Cali. Mockler, of course, was very angry. Had the Colombians spent years on surveillance, seized drugs, money, property, painstakingly analysed ledgers and bank records, dusted for fingerprints, uncovered forged documents? The Colombian indictment was as convincing as the dummy corporations the traffickers used to launder their money.

Twice, in 1985 and 1986, Kenny Robinson had travelled to Madrid to help the Spanish prosecutor prepare for the extradition hearing. From a purely legal perspective, their prospects looked good. But there was the nationalism factor, the common culture, a Spanish court's sympathy for the argument that the Colombians should be allowed to try their citizen first in their own court system.

In 1986 the Spanish court ruled that, even though the American indictment had been filed first, the Colombian indictment should be given precedence.[2] A triumphant Gilberto Rodriguez was returned to Cali where in March 1987 he went through the form of a trial.

The prosecutor had asked the DEA to produce three witnesses: Bill Mockler, Kenny Robinson and Richie Crawford. DEA headquarters would not approve Kenny Robinson's going – he was an analyst, not an agent – but gave Mockler and Crawford the option of testifying. After his experiences in Spain, Mockler found this decision easy. The trial's outcome was a foregone conclusion; it was nothing more than a tactical manoeuvre to create a double jeopardy defence to forestall a future prosecution in the States. (The double jeopardy clause of the US Constitution bars a second prosecution for the same crime if a defendant has been previously tried and acquitted.) The trial would also provide the Cartel with an opportunity to probe the DEA's investigative techniques. (The Cartel could not believe that the DEA's cases were developed out of their own records. When Gilberto was arrested in Spain, the Spanish police found among his papers DEA reports released to the defence to help it prepare to cross-examine an agent. Gilberto had read these reports – they pertained to an associate's trial – and had underlined the names of people he thought might be informing.)

Despite all of this Richie Crawford, now in the DEA's Tampa office, wanted to testify in Colombia. He was more of a romantic than Mockler, for some of the reasons he gave for his decision – there were several phone calls between New York, Washington and Tampa – were symbolic rather than practical. His testimony, he said, would be a statement: of support for the Colombian government which had just extradited Carlos Lehder, an important Medellin trafficker whom the DEA badly wanted; of honour to the Colombian officials and police murdered by the *narcotraficante*; and of defiance to the heads of the Cartel – 'The DEA's not afraid to come into Cali and point the finger at you.'

So on 17 March 1987, Richie Crawford arrived in Cali. His testimony took two and a half days. When it concluded, the judge disallowed his evidence and acquitted Gilberto Rodriguez.

It was nearly one o'clock in the afternoon when Bill Mockler reached Bologna on 7 June 1990. With weary eyes, he briefly glimpsed the city's centre and, momentarily, was intrigued by its medieval splendour, its red-brown buildings and numerous colonnades – one of the city's unusual features – its churches and campaniles, the palaces that crowned the Piazza Maggiore, the cathedral, San Petronio, built at the turn of the fourteenth century, which seemed more monumental, more mysteriously overbearing than the tallest skyscraper of New York City.

His driver skimmed quickly round the city's central plaza, turned down a narrow cobblestoned street a few minutes walk from the Piazza Maggiore, and stopped the car in front of a small hotel called Al Cappello Rosso. For reasons Mockler never chose to probe – its situation, only three blocks from the police station, the charms of its waitresses, which Mockler appreciated, its obliging manager who did not object when the police upended his sofas to create more surfaces for their computers – the SCA had chosen this hotel as its headquarters for the week during which Colombia would be playing at the stadium in Bologna.

The late spring weather in Bologna can be cool and damp but when Mockler stepped out of the car, the day was bright and hot. He stretched his stiff limbs and blinked in the sunlight. As he walked towards the hotel, a tall middle-aged man, balding, with a double chin and beak nose, burst through its doors. He was Frank Panessa, the DEA's country attaché to Italy, who had been expecting Mockler. He embraced and kissed him.

'Here's the ugliest man in the world,' he said, laughing. 'How are you doing?' he asked, then added, 'Now that I've done all the god-damn work, you're here!'

An engaging smile transformed Mockler's lopsided face. 'Sure, pick on me when I'm tired. At least let me get a few hours sleep.'

Frank took Mockler's suitcase and walked him into the hotel. He put his arm round the other agent's shoulder. 'It's good to have you here,' he said.

As Mockler took the lift upstairs, he asked, 'Do you know where Kenny and the rest of the people are?'

'They went for a walk, they should be back any minute now.'

'Ok, I'm going to shower and change and then I'll come back down, we'll get something to eat.'

'Yeah, take your time.'

Panessa and Mockler were old friends and colleagues, part of the generation of agents who had joined the DEA in the late 1960s. Both were native New Yorkers, from ethnic working-class backgrounds, who had reaped the benefits of the educational and economic opportunities to be found in post-war metropolitan New York. They were roughly the same age, Mockler forty-seven, Panessa forty-nine, and they had worked together in the 1970s.

Panessa's career had taken a different turn from Mockler's. His forte was undercover work, specializing in heroin cases. He was almost perfectly typecast to play a mafioso: tall, paunchy, heavy-lidded and swarthy, he could be both foul-mouthed and courtly, and he spoke fluent Italian, knowing the customs, style and slang of Southern Italy. (His own family had come from.)

It was typical of Frank that on his arrival in Bologna he had commandeered the best room, the bridal suite, at the Al Cappello Rosso, for he liked in large proportions all of life's fine things and, on a DEA agent's salary, he was rarely able to indulge his taste. The exception had been the year he spent undercover, masquerading as a mafioso in the 'Pizza Connection' case – so-called because its chief target owned a string of pizzerias, 'fronts' for a thriving heroin import business. Posing as the owner of Prima Exports, a Philadelphia merchant whose sideline was heroin, Panessa played out some of his dearest fantasies – travelling to Germany and Italy. He had once walked into a restaurant in New York, ordered seven different pastas, taken a bite of each, and slipped the 'maître d.' a $50 bill for a bottle of wine that 'tasted like piss', smiling benignly while the waiter said, 'From your mother's village in Italy, Senor, it is the best!' It was the highlight of his career, an Oscar-winning performance, so credible that at the trial (he bought a million dollars' worth of heroin and nine defendants were charged), the aggrieved defendants told their lawyers, 'But he was like our brother!'

Panessa had a close relationship with his counterpart, General B. Pietro Soggiu, the director of the SCA, who had the difficult task of coordinating the three Italian police agencies with jurisdiction over narcotics crimes. These were the Polizia dello Stato, the civilian police force responsible for maintaining law and order; the Carabinieri, the military police responsible for counter-espionage who also help police rural areas; and the Guardia di Finanza, the customs and tax police force.

When Panessa first mooted the idea of Operation Offsides, it was immediately endorsed by General Soggiu. There was a history of joint DEA–SCA narcotics operations and the agencies frequently exchanged intelligence and resources. Moreover, there was nothing ambiguous about Italy's attitude to narcotics. After the assassination in Bogota of the Colombian Liberal Party politician, Luis Carlos Galan, by the Medellin Cartel in August 1989, and President Virgilio Barco's subsequent appeal for help, it was the first country in Europe to respond with resources. Italy provided aid valued at $13 million, which included helicopters, armoured Fiats and firearms training. It was helping the Colombians devise a plan to safeguard its judiciary based on the Italians' system for protecting the pool of magistrates in Sicily that handled Mafia cases. It had also helped organize the Trilateral Conference between the US, Spain and Italy which both Frank Panessa and Don Ferrarone attended in September 1989 in Madrid.

Italy's support for Colombia was not disinterested. More than any other country in Europe, it was vulnerable to an epidemic of cocaine abuse. Because of the Mafia, its proximity to Turkey, its thousands of ports and coves which made smuggling easy, it already had the worst heroin problem in Europe, with the largest heroin addict population and the highest rate of heroin overdose deaths per capita. General Soggiu's worst fear was a marriage between the Cartel and the Mafia because if the Colombians succeeded in bringing cocaine into Italy, there was already a sophisticated distribution system in place.

The afternoon that Mockler arrived in Bologna, Frank Panessa convened a meeting in the hotel lounge. The room had a colour scheme of dark chocolate brown: the fabric on the walls, the tables, chairs, carpets, even the sofas were brown. Mockler would pass most of his sojourn in the city within the lounge's four walls, or in his bedroom which was also decorated in brown, which led him to exclaim bitterly at the end of the week, 'If anyone asks me back home what I saw in Bologna, I'll say brown!'

To staff Operation Offsides, in addition to the agents resident in Italy the DEA had brought in fifteen people from the United States and Colombia. These analysts and agents had a combination of skills. Some had worked in Italy, knew the language, its cities, traffic patterns, driving habits (all very important when the time came to tail their targets). Others were experts on the Cartel. (This latter group included Sandy Smith, one of several analysts in Washington who worked on the Cartel, Kenny Robinson, Richie Crawford and Jerry McArdle.)

Although Bill Snipes, one of Frank Panessa's people stationed in Rome, was the operation's case agent, as long as Panessa and Mockler were present, its de facto direction lay with the senior agents. The operation, they now explained to the team, had essentially three phases.

First, they had developed hard intelligence from classified sources in Colombia and Argentina that Miguel Rodriguez would be coming to the games. Until Gilberto's arrest in Spain in 1984, Miguel had been a shadowy figure at the financial end of the business, involved in various schemes to launder money, such as the attempt to buy Miami's Northside Bank in 1979 and channel profits from the sale of cocaine into legitimate businesses. (Besides having interests in America de Cali and banks and radio stations at various times, the Rodriguez's had a chain of 250 drug stores called Las Drogas La Rebaja.) But Gilberto's arrest and his subsequent desire to keep a low profile had forced Miguel to take a more active role and, according to the DEA's latest intelligence, he was involved in the day-to-day management of the cocaine business.

Miguel's trip to Italy seemed to be a mixture of business and pleasure and ostensibly involved his interest in soccer. Two of the men on the Colombian team came from America de Cali. Miguel wanted to watch them play, observe the other teams' performances; at the games' conclusion, he would probably buy and sell players.

He would be working with an Argentinian soccer broker, who was a close associate and a friend of the family. The broker, whom the DEA referred to as 'Q', was handling the family's arrangements for travel. This was typical of the top three's *modus operandi*; they frequently sent a legitimate person ahead as an emissary, someone not connected with the narcotics trade, who could, without arousing suspicion, book hotel rooms or rent apartments, purchase furniture if that were necessary, stock them with food, even buy clothing.

'Q' himself was scheduled to arrive in Rome the day after the first Colombian game, on Sunday, 10 June. He would be travelling with two people, male Hispanics. Their names had been checked in the NADDIS computer; no evidence had been found of a narcotics connection. On the other hand, names meant nothing. ... They had other information, again from classified sources, that some of the family would be arriving in Rome on 18 June; that others were coming on the 21st.

But surrounding this pearl of hard fact, there were many uncertainties. They did not know exactly who was coming – Miguel's wife, his thirteen-year-old son, two teenage daughters? They had heard his wife had recently had a baby – should they be on the look-out for a woman carrying a six-month-old infant? There had been allusions to other family members travelling. Did that mean Miguel's sister, Gilberto, Gilberto's family? Other intelligence suggested this group might include Chepe. Nor did they know if the family would be travelling together or straggling in separately, flying directly from Bogota or coming through a city in Europe. Miguel's wife and children, they thought, would be travelling legitimately. They could not be so sure about the head of the family.

After the game on Saturday, Kenny Robinson would go back to Rome. Since he was one of the few agents who could identify the targets, he would work with the Italian police and help monitor Leonardo Da Vinci Airport.

The second phase of the operation was more complex. It was centred on the games in which Colombia was a participant. The first game would take place in two days time, on Saturday, 9 June, when Colombia would play the United Arab Emirates. The Colombians' second game was scheduled for the following Thursday, the 14th – Colombia versus Yugoslavia. If Colombia unexpectedly survived for a third round, it would be on 19 June against West Germany in Milan.

The agents were hoping for a repeat of what had happened in Mexico and to spot some of their fugitives in the stands – the top three of course, but also, hopefully, Jaime Orjuela, Chepe's right hand, whose mansion in Cali was located in the same exclusive neighbourhood. They would also be looking for Omar Sanchez, the lead defendant in the 1986 'seven customers' case who had been tried and convicted in absentia. There were sixteen other fugitives and by now everyone in the team should have reviewed the target packages.

The problem would be to identify and seize the traffickers. On the assumption that some of them would be travelling legitimately, the Italian police would be making the rounds of the first-class hotels, obtaining photostat copies of all Colombian passports which Mockler would review. At the games themselves, they would be searching for faces. The Italians had set up an excellent observation post. They could obtain close-up views of the crowd through more than a dozen video cameras. Here, they hoped, Kenny Robinson and Richie Crawford would prove helpful. Also, the agents from Bogota had brought over a Colombian CI who claimed to be close to Chepe's family.

The third phase of the operation was 'the Luxembourg connection'. This referred to the investigation initiated by the Luxembourg police with the help of Cheryl Holmes, a DEA analyst in Washington. She was the head of the DEA's Financial Intelligence Unit, who had fortuitously learned of a Cali Cartel link-up two months earlier, in April, when she had attended a money laundering conference organized by the DEA's Brussels office. There she had met Pierre Kohman, of the Sûreté Publique, the Luxembourg detective force whose jurisdiction includes drugs and white-collar crimes. Commissaire Kohman, the head of the money laundering division of the Sûreté Publique, had mentioned one of his cases to her. He had identified a Colombian, Jurado Rodriguez, who had opened up several bank accounts in Luxembourg. He was depositing large sums of money whose origin was Panama. Was it drug money and, if so, whose, and how could they prove it?

That same day Holmes called Sandy Smith in Washington and asked her to check out Jurado Rodriguez. Smith called back with good news. Jurado was a Colombian national, a graduate of the Harvard Business School and the former president of the Cali Stock Exchange, but, most significantly, he was an associate of Edgar Garcia – and Edgar Garcia was one of Chepe's closest people, his 'accountant', the man responsible for managing and laundering the profits of his drug business.

Edgar Garcia's name had first cropped up in 1984, when Jerry McArdle was working on the investigation into the InterAmericas Bank of Panama. InterAmericas was owned by Gilberto Rodriguez, Miguel was its vice-president and Edgar Garcia one of its directors. It was probably a misnomer to call this institution a bank since it did not look, feel or act like a bank. Its location was a private house in Panama City and its sole *raison d'être* was to launder drug money. Its list of clients read like a drug traffickers' Debrett – Gilberto Rodriguez, Miguel Rodriguez, Chepe's half-brother Lucho, and Gonzalo Rodriguez Gacha, the most prominent member of the Medellin Cartel who in 1989 had been killed in a shoot-out with the Colombian police.

Intermediaries, such as Alfredo Cervantes, Chepe's driver-turned-informant, were bringing the money into Panama and depositing it in the bank as cash. (Once when Cervantes was flying down to Panama, the engine malfunctioned and they crash-landed in Florida. He and the pilot escaped from the wreckage unscathed, ran into the brush to avoid the police, then returned after dark to retrieve the cash.)

To conceal the origins of the money, the traffickers had set up dummy companies. These businesses, which were empty ciphers, were registered in Panama, had officers, boards of directors, people, like Garcia, empowered to sign cheques, who set up accounts at legitimate banks. When an intermediary like Cervantes deposited cash into the InterAmericas Bank, it was credited to an account – Chepe's, his girlfriend's, his wife's, his half-brother's – then transferred to a dummy corporation's account in a legitimate bank; after a lapse of a few days, the money would be transferred back to the InterAmericas Bank. (As an extra service, the bank issued credit cards to its most prominent customers – Chepe, Miguel, Gilberto, Chepe's half-brother Lucho.)

When Pierre Kohman in Luxembourg realized who Jurado

Rodriguez was, his connection to Edgar Garcia and the Cali Cartel, the Sûreté Publique began monitoring his movements and his telephone calls. During the week before the World Cup games, Jurado had been very active, travelling to Spain where he met Edgar Garcia, who had come over from Panama with another Colombian, Ricardo Mahecha. At the moment, all three Colombians were in Italy. The Guardia di Finanza had them under surveillance. They were driving a car, a dark blue Opel Turbo. They had stopped in Milan and met with an Italian whose house was near the Piazza Buenos Aires; this unknown contact would from now on be a subject of interest to the Italian police. They would be staying overnight at a hotel in Milan and travelling to Bologna some time tomorrow, Friday, where they had reservations for two days at the Pullman–Excelsior near the railway station.

That night, Mockler and Panessa ate dinner together at a small restaurant which was a ten-minute walk from Al Cappello Rosso. On his arrival in Bologna, Frank had made its owner's acquaintance and negotiated a special fixed price for DEA agents – a four-course meal for 30,000 lire – but most of the agents, 'barbarians', Frank grumbled, preferred to eat at the McDonald's on the Via Rizzoli. The padrone enthusiastically greeted the agents, emerging a few minutes later with a large platter in his hands, offering the choice of two local specialities, gnocchi and penne all'arrabbiata, or linguini con vongole.

Mockler marvelled at how Frank inhaled the pasta. 'You sure like to eat,' he told his friend with the slightly sour tone of a man suffering from dyspepsia.

Frank laughed as he wiped his hands and mouth, and returned to his analysis of the unfolding developments in Operation Offsides. Why were the 'Luxembourg three' now in Italy? Who was this Italian they had met in Milan? A high roller clearly – there had been three luxury cars parked in his drive. Would Edgar Garcia be meeting Chepe? And if so, at some other place if not the games in Bologna?

It was too much of a coincidence, Frank thought, Miguel coming to Italy, this trio from Luxembourg. 'I don't think

Miguel's coming over just to buy and sell players. I think he's here to set up distribution networks and contacts. I honestly believe that Chepe will be coming. They know they are going to realize a lot of money and that they can't send it back to the Miami banks or the Caribbean because we've knocked the hell out of them with our money laundering stings. They want to be able to get it out by car. That's why they're setting up bank accounts in Europe.'

Mockler listened to Frank spinning his theories, nodding occasionally, not commenting on their validity. He had other concerns he wanted to air. The Italians, for one, did they understand the ground rules? That it was better to lose someone than expose the surveillance, not to scare off the big fish by arresting second-tier targets.

'As soon as we make a move we're going to tip off our hand, so we've got to be sure we're getting the right person. If we're close but wrong, that's going to defeat the whole purpose of the operation. It's extremely critical to get the individual pinpointed and then just grab him at the right time.'

Frank reassured him. Vincenzo Boncoraglio, the Vice-Director of the SCA, a very intelligent man, had been on the telephone that afternoon, talking to the head of the Carabinieri in Rome. 'I want you to put your very best people on the operation,' Vincenzo had explained. 'We have to weigh up carefully whether the people we are watching are "hares", whose capture or arrest could blow the whole operation, or whether they are people whose arrest suits our operation.'

Mockler, Frank said, should not be deceived by the appearance of chaos. The Italians, he would find, were good on surveillance and they had intelligence assets not available to the DEA. The hotels, for instance, were concerned to stay on the right side of the Guardia di Finanza and would give detailed acounts of the movements of their guests. And the SCA could 'throw a wire' on a phone within twenty-four hours, which would be a critical asset as the operation unfolded.

Look at the hundreds of men and women, the resources that SCA had committed, and not just in Bologna but in Rome, Genoa, Naples, Milan. It was the biggest anti-narcotic operation in their history and, to emphasize its importance, tomorrow, Friday, General Soggiu himself was coming to Bologna.

'We've both, SCA and DEA, put a lot of money into this operation,' Frank said. 'But I think it's going to pay some good dividends and, hopefully, we'll get some of the Italians who are involved in this thing too. And as for you and me,' Frank added, laughing, 'it'll be our swan song. We'll go out in a burst of glory . . .'

Mockler frowned – he had ten more years before he reached the DEA's mandatory retirement age and no intention of quitting prematurely. 'Speak for yourself because I'll be here for a while yet.'

They had finished eating. Frank dabbed with his napkin at a spot of sauce, a small blotch of red staining the white tablecloth. 'You know,' he said, 'I've got a good feeling. When you look at everything, at the intelligence we've got out of Argentina, at these three guys from Luxembourg – it has all the earmarks of being a success. My only fear is that there might be a compromise beforehand. That's my only concern, that somewhere along the line, there'll be a compromise. . . . But if that doesn't happen, they're going to be here. Maybe not all of them, maybe not Gilberto. But Miguel definitely, and I think we're going to get Chepe. I've just got this feeling and I've got good instincts. . . .

'Of course,' he added with a self-deprecating laugh, 'I've been wrong before.'

Then Frank sighed as he rose heavily from the table. 'But what are you going to do? You have to wish and dream and hope. . . . And maybe if I wish hard enough, who knows, it'll happen.'

The two agents walked back to their hotel beneath the colonnades of Bologna. Crossing the vast expanse of the Piazza Maggiore, they stopped to watch a group of Colombian musicians, exotically dressed in richly coloured peasants' clothing. They chatted briefly with a group of agents – with their blue jeans, sneakers and short jackets, so obviously American – who had also been attracted by the plaintive strains of the music.

And as Mockler listened to the bells of San Petronio chime, counting its eleven rings first, then the 'dong, dong, dong, dong, dong, dong . . .' of the town clock, he thought, 'Who knows? We might get lucky. Maybe on Saturday, we'll spot Chepe.' Oh, how he would love to return to New York with that trophy!

8 The Waiting Game

By the end of the first football game in Bologna, they had not found Chepe, nor did they find him at the second game on the following Thursday, 14 June. As the days passed by and more games were played, in Milan, in Florence, in Genoa and Naples, bringing them closer and closer to 8 July, the day of the World Cup final, the last day of the games, the participants in Operation Offsides began to relinquish their dream. In retrospect, from the very beginning the operation seemed cursed.

At three o'clock in the afternoon of Saturday, 9 June, the Colombian captain, Carlos Valderamma, had pranced on to the the field at the head of his team. He was an extraordinary-looking man with long twisted ruddy-gold hair and a ballet dancer's sinewy muscles, a Rudolf Nureyev from the Amazon jungle. He was a world-class player, a national hero to many Colombians, and as he raised his fist to salute the crowd, his compatriots jumped to their feet and burst into a roar. This was a moment of transcendent pride, a moment when they could forget their nation's murderous chaos, the bombings, the torture, the daily assassinations.

For Kenny Robinson, sitting in the airless observation booth filled with the acrid smell of cigarette smoke and sweat, it was the moment in which he almost despaired. Never in his life had he seen so many Colombians, ten thousand at a conservative estimate, and ninety per cent of them were probably legitimate, judging from the enormous banner, 'Cafe Si! Droga No!', they had draped across the stadium.

'This is going to be an impossible task,' he thought, before reminding himself that his strength was the meticulous search, which should be no more difficult today than scanning hundreds

ITALY

SWITZERLAND
ALPS
YUGOSLAVIA
Milan
Venice
Turin
R. Po
ITALY
Ferrara
Bologna
Genoa
Santa Margherita
Ligure
Portofino
Rimini
Adriatic Sea
FRANCE
Florence
SAN
MARINO
MONACO
Livorno
Ligurian Sea
Elba
R. Tiber
CORSICA
Rome
Naples
SARDINIA
MEDITERRANEAN SEA
N
0
50
100
150 kilometres
0
50
100 miles

of records for a name or a number or looking for a red Chevrolet that might have been ditched but might also be parked on one of two dozen streets in Queens, New York. He began to look through the stands, row by row, up and down each aisle, waiting for his eye to signal his brain, 'I know that guy.... That's a familiar face.'

By the time the game had finished at six o'clock – with a Colombian victory, 2 to 0 – the Offsides team had developed a couple of leads. The Luxembourg trio, Jurado Rodriguez, Edgar Garcia and Ricardo Mahecha Bustos, whom the Guardia di Finanza had followed from Milan to Bologna, had been seen, chatting with a couple of men. (Two days later these men were identified as journalists.) Even better (or so it seemed then, although everything was to shift in retrospect), the Colombian informant, who had been smuggled into the booth before the start of the game, identified one of Chepe's bodyguards.

A team of Italian police and agents undertook the surveillance. They followed the bodyguard out of the stadium and saw him board a bus, then tailed the bus to Rimini, a seaside resort on the Adriatic, an hour's drive from Bologna. And here they made an unexpected discovery. Most of the Colombians had settled in Rimini, preferring its honky-tonk atmosphere, its beaches and discos, to the monuments and museums of culturally rich Bologna. This was a discouraging development because it would stretch thin the resources available for surveillance.

On Sunday night Mockler drove to Rimini with Jerry McArdle and Brian Collier, an agent assigned to the Rome office, in search of the bodyguard they hoped would lead them to Chepe. Their first stop was the Hotel de Londre, where the bodyguard had been 'put' the previous night. The Italian police had already learned that one Colombian guest, but not Chepe, had deposited $40,000 and diamonds in the hotel safe.) Mockler, however, preferred the five-star hotel next door as Chepe's likely choice. 'He always stays in the best place in town,' he explained, 'and it would make sense him having his bodyguards living next door so they'd be close but not with him. He usually has three or four bodyguards when he travels.'

They crossed over the street and entered the Embassy night-club – the best disco in Rimini, according to Brian Collier – and here they experienced a brief burst of excitement. A tall heavy-set man with a full beard walked into the club with three attractive girls on his arm.

'Everything's right!' Jerry whispered to Mockler. 'He's the right size, he's got the right-shaped head, this is the right kind of place and he's acting right.'

But Mockler did not share Jerry's enthusiasm. 'I don't know.... Of course, the last time I saw him was about nine years ago but I don't think the nose is the same.'

Still, it was a lead and they had to pursue it. When a breakdown in communication between their team and the Italians, plus the difficulty of following their subject at three o'clock in the morning, caused them to lose their target, they spent many hours sniffing out his trail until, picking it up again, they were able to establish that their Chepe look-alike was a native Italian.

Mockler expected this sort of thing – he was used to panning in streams and coming up with 'fool's gold' – but the incident that Sunday morning was a lapse of security and potentially damaging. He had been woken by an early morning call from Richie Crawford.

'We have some bad news. Have you seen the newspapers?'

'My eyes are still shut, how the hell can I read a paper?'

One of the Italian police had shown Richie a small article, a couple of paragraphs, reporting that the DEA was in Bologna, watching the games and looking for drug dealers from the Medellin Cartel. Because of the absence of detail and the conspicuous error that the DEA was looking for Medellin not Cali Cartel traffickers, they assumed the story was based on speculation. Probably a reporter had noticed the Americans in the stadium and put two and two together: Colombians, cocaine, Americans, DEA. But although it was a tiny bomb, it might very well be lethal because the story ran in two papers. One was in a special pull-out section devoted to the World Cup games, right next to a picture of the Colombian team.

Frank Panessa had returned to Rome, to his usual burden of heroin investigations and an in-tray heaped with telexes and messages. When he spoke to Panessa later than morning, Mockler tried to soothe his agitated colleague. 'The story didn't say Cali, it said Medellin, and these guys know they're hunted, they know we're always on the look out for them, but in spite of this they travel around the world. This is no different from any other investigation. We have to expect that things will go wrong, we have to be flexible, we have to adapt and bend.'

On Sunday afternoon the Luxembourg trio left Bologna. Richie Crawford with a Guardia di Finanza team and Sam Meale (the case agent on the 1975 investigation in which Gilberto Rodriguez and Chepe first emerged) followed them to Rome.

Later that day Richie reported to Mockler, 'They are very edgy.' En Route to Rome the trio had stopped in Florence for a twenty-minute tour of the Piazza San Giovanni. The agents had started to follow on foot, then pulled back and waited in their cars after they saw their targets looking over their shoulders. 'Then coming out of Florence, they started playing games.' They pulled off the autostrada at the very first exit, made an abrupt U-turn just before the toll booth, then waited in the service area before returning to the autostrada.

The Guardia di Finanza, which temporarily lost them, searched the little town lying beyond the toll booth, then returned to the autostrada several exits south. They were cruising along in the direction of Rome when they spotted the blue Opel Turbo coming up behind them. They dropped back, let it pull ahead and managed to keep pace, although for most of the trip the Opel was averaging 130 miles an hour. 'If I ever rob a bank,' Richie told Mockler, 'I'm going to ask Luigi to be my driver.'

In Rome, Jurado Rodriguez deposited two cheques, totalling $210,000, in a Rome bank account. The name on the account was Heriberto Castro, the father of Chepe's wife Emparo. It had been opened in 1987 with a $57,000 deposit and had lain dormant until Jurado's deposit.

The Luxembourg trio spent two days in Rome, staying at the Vittoria Hotel. They left on Tuesday, 12 June. Their next destination, according to staff at the Vittoria, was Portofino, a luxurious resort on the Ligurian coast a few miles south of Genoa.

Because the Luxembourg trio appeared to be on the look-out for surveillance, the Guardia di Finanza and the DEA had decided not to follow them from Rome to Portofino. Instead, on the Tuesday, Richie Crawford, Sam Meale and a Guardia di Finanza team drove from Bologna across the Apennine mountains to the Ligurian coast. They were in two cars, a silver BMW and a white Fiat Turbo, one agent paired to one of the Guardia. Richie's companion, a young Sicilian, spoke no English and since Richie's knowledge of Italian was equally deficient, he was alone with his thoughts for most of the four-hour trip.

He was happy to be working again with Kenny, Mockler and Jerry McArdle. This operation was like a class reunion and he was grateful to Mockler for having included him. He often thought of himself as Operation Calico's prodigal son.

If his work were his home – and with no wife, no children, what else did he have? – then he had left home in 1982, his last year with Group Five, and returned in 1987, the year he testified in Colombia. The period in between was a rock bottom time during which he had got divorced, his father had died and his brother, an alcoholic, had committed suicide. In his last year in New York, he had been wild. (Jerry McArdle could remember him showing up late for a trial and the woman prosecutor, understandably furious, saying, 'He's your buddy, you find him,' and Jerry thinking, 'Where do I start? The guy sleeps with a different girl every night.')

The destruction of his roots in New York had been the impetus for Richie Crawford's transfer to Florida. But when he moved to Tampa he was drinking heavily and came close to losing his job before he went down to Colombia. His desire to make amends was the unspoken factor in his decision to testify against Gilberto Rodriguez, a decision he would never regret. It was one thing to read the *Miami Herald*'s editorials raging against Colombia's uncooperative government. It was another to experience the situation first-hand – the police armed with machine-guns who had met his flight, who insisted he wear a bullet-proof vest, who whisked him back to Bogota at the end of each day because they could not protect him in Cali if he stayed overnight. Then to see the inadequacy of the judicial system, the lax rules of evidence, the primitive resources, the tiny court which was barely large enough to hold the judge, the interpreter (niece of a convicted Cartel money launderer, Isaac Kattan), the defendant, his four lawyers, and the half dozen news photographers eagerly snapping the picture of the only DEA agent who ever testified in Colombia.

(For reasons he found hard to explain – was it a talisman, a souvenir, a badge of courage? – Richie had brought with him to

Italy a story in *El Tiempo* that referred to his briefcase from which he pulled forged documents as his '*caja de sorpresas*', his box of surprises.)

He had felt neither surprise nor defeat at the judge's verdict; instead, he had returned to the States with a renewed sense of purpose. Before testifying in Colombia, he had reviewed the papers seized from Gilberto in Spain, which the Spanish police had turned over to the DEA. Among them he had noticed a business card for the Amazon Trading Company, Mike Tsalickis, President. (This was one of the things Kenny Robinson had taught him – 'Keep everything, everything's important.') When he eventually learned that the Cartel was using Mike Tsalickis to smuggle cocaine into the US in hollowed-out mahogany logs, a method used since 1978, he had played a major role in the ensuing investigation. It resulted in the seizure of 7200 pounds of cocaine from a warehouse in Tarpon Springs, Florida, and the arrest of Tsalickis.

After Tsalickis's arrest, Richie returned to Colombia, to its Amazon frontier on the border of Brazil, to retrace the movements of the shipment of lumber. In a piece of ex-post facto deduction of which he was justifiably proud, he discovered that the lumber originated in Benjamin Constant, a small Brazilian town at the junction of two tributaries of the Amazon, only a few miles from the larger Colombian town, Leticia, where Tsalickis had lived in the early part of his career. (Tsalickis, who owned a hotel and had helped build the local hospital, once earned his living by shipping monkeys to the States for medical research.) It was moved by barge down the Amazon to another small town, Amataura, where a saw-mill was located. There it was banded together with the cocaine. (The cocaine had been processed in laboratories near Santa Clara, a Colombian town on the Putumayo River, thirty miles north of Amataura.) From the Amataura saw-mill, the shipment moved by barge to the city of Macapa, at the Amazon's mouth – a distance of nearly 1500 miles – before it was transferred to the *Amazon Sky*, one of Mike Tsalickis's boats, which moved it to St Petersburg, Florida.

This investigation had led to other cases, including, to Mockler's delight, the arrest of Chepe's half-brother Lucho, who had been convicted and sentenced to prison. But Richie had been more complimented when he heard what Miguel Rodriguez had said. 'I don't want to send anything through Tampa because of that pain in the butt DEA agent Crawford.'

The team of DEA agents and Guardia di Finanza arrived at Santa Margarita Ligure, a few miles south of Portofino, at five o'clock. They parked their cars by the beach, opposite a row of hotels interspersed with cafés and boutiques. Here they were joined by several more men from the Guardia's office in Genoa.

The senior Guardia was Giuseppe Versaci, a tall handsome man with gentle brown eyes, ten years younger than Richie and Sam Meale. He parked his motorcycle in front of the white Fiat, took off his helmet and shook Sam's hand warmly. The two men had worked together when the DEA agent was stationed in Milan. Giuseppe briefed Sam on what he had arranged.

'They're all set up at the Hotel Splendido,' Sam translated for Richie. 'Vincenzo's going to be in there and he'll be able to get pictures. Jurado Rodriguez made a call. They're expected in by nine o'clock. They've got two double rooms.'

'Do they have any indication as to how long they're supposed to stay?' Richie asked.

'Yes, one night.'

'Just one night?' Richie asked, puzzled.

'Yeah ... I don't know what they're going to do.'

'That tells me more and more that ... I mean, they're not getting here until nine o'clock, they're not here to enjoy the sunshine. I think they're meeting somebody.'

Sam nodded his head. 'You may be right. Two other people arrived together today, one a Brazilian, the other American. I've given Mockler their names. We're going to follow Giuseppe. He says the best place to wait is the parking lot behind Portofino.'

Portofino was the last village on a spit of land jutting into the Ligurian Sea. The narrow two-lane road that led to it, bounded on one side by the sea and the other by cliffs, snaked through a succession of towns before ending in Portofino's car-park. Once a fishing village, Portofino was now a luxury resort and in the stone buildings fronting the sea, where fifty years ago fishermen had repaired their nets, some of the fanciest retailers in the world had set up shop. Docked in its deep-water cove were millionaires' yachts and a few hundred yards from the village, perched on a bluff, was the Hotel Splendido, a magnificent white villa where for $200 a night guests could bathe in an Olympic-size pool that overlooked Portofino's castello and the azure blue sea. It was the perfect spot for the Luxembourg trio, concerned about surveillance, for it was impossible to observe the hotel from the road; a private guard kept watch at the foot of its drive.

The team parked their vehicles in the car-park behind Portofino (In addition to the BMW and Fiat, they now had a small surveillance van with a video camera and Giuseppe's motorcycle.) As darkness fell, more cars pulled into the car-park – there was a fancy restaurant in the village and several cafés – and the tempo of nightlife began to pick up. Sitting in the BMW's front seat, Richie listened to the slamming of doors, the chatter of Italian, and when a tall, slim blonde passed his car he couldn't resist trying to engage her attention with a low-voiced 'Hello'. (Although his brown hair had gone grey, he was still at forty-four a good-looking man, very fit, with striking blue eyes.)

Suddenly, he heard Sam's voice coming over the radio. 'They're here! They've just pulled in, they're in the blue Opel.'

'Are there any new players or is it just the three original guys?'

'We can only see three so I don't know if they're here to meet anybody or not. We'll just have to see where they go now and wait. They didn't check into the hotel.'

'They haven't checked in yet?'

'No, they bypassed the hotel, they came straight into the village.'

'I'm going to take a look at these guys.'

Richie got out of his car and walked into the village. He stopped at a café, bought an ice-cream and, licking it, strolled along the quay. He was always well dressed and tonight was no exception, so he fitted in easily with the well-heeled Italians. His wide, pale-blue eyes seemed to be fixed on the yachts in the harbour but as he ate his ice-cream, he studied three stocky figures. They had, he noted, typical Colombian faces, a mixture of Spanish and Indian, wide across the eyes and brow, with high cheekbones, thin lips, aquiline noses, small dark eyes and thick black hair. They stood on the quay for no more than five minutes, then walked back to their car when they had finished admiring the village.

Ten minutes later Giuseppe checked with the hotel staff. His newly arrived guests had booked a table for three for dinner at eleven o'clock.

The DEA agents and Guardia spent the night in Santa Margarita Ligure in a hotel with cracked tiles in the shower and lumpy mattresses, but one they could afford on their government allowances. On Wednesday morning they set up their surveillance. There was only one spot between Portofino and Santa Margarita Ligure that provided some cover, the car-park of a restaurant and discotheque on a slight promontory a few miles east of the village. Here they parked their vehicles facing the coast road. 'I'd rather not sit like this,' Sam told Richie, 'because we look a little weird. We ought to face the sea. What do you think?'

'Yes, but we might not have time to turn round. If they're going fast, we could lose them right away, we could get stuck behind a car and on this road it's hard to overtake.'

Giuseppe had already discovered that their targets had gone to their rooms after eating dinner together. They had not left the hotel or met anyone else, although Jurado Rodriguez had called two numbers in Nice and one in Portugal.

Was it possible, Giuseppe wanted to know, that their next destination was Nice? That might make sense, Richie said, because when he was in Bologna, Jurado had sent a fax to France.

They had taken up their positions at nine o'clock. By midday they were restless, hungry and bored with the view – three topless girls sunbathing on the rocks below.

'What can these guys be doing?' Richie said. 'I can't figure this out. They come here last night at nine o'clock, they don't meet anybody, they don't do anything other than make a couple of calls to France. It doesn't seem as if they're in a hurry. Maybe they're killing time before going back to Bologna.'

A few minutes before one o'clock word came from the hotel – a porter was carrying their bags to the car, the Luxembourg trio were about to depart. The agents and Guardia jumped into their cars and moments later Richie Crawford saw the blue Opel. It swerved into the restaurant's car-park at fifty miles an hour. He saw Edgar Garcia, his head and shoulders stuck out of the passenger window. It was an extraordinary sight, lasting only a couple of seconds, but the impression was unforgettable because of the jeering look on Edgar's face, which was not more than ten feet away from Richie. It was almost as though he knew they were there, as though he were issuing a challenge, 'Follow us if you dare!'

Then, just as abruptly, the Opel swerved back on to the road. Giuseppe kicked his motorcycle and took off with a roar, and a cavalcade of vehicles tore along the coast road, through Santa Margarita, making a sharp left turn, zigzagging, climbing, high up into the hills, through the toll booth, on to the autostrada, past the exit to Genoa. Richie had the BMW's accelerator depressed flat on the floor. 'I can't keep up. He's going like a bat out of hell.' Nor could any of the other cars match the Opel's power – it was speeding along at 150 miles an hour, making surveillance almost impossible – and a few miles south of Milan the last car left in the cavalcade, the white Fiat Turbo, lost the blue Opel.

While Richie Crawford and Sam Meale were in Portofino, Mockler passed a sleepless night in his brown room in Bologna. He listened to the bells of San Petronio ring two o'clock, three o'clock, four, five.... Finally, at six in the morning he fell asleep, only to be awakened three hours later by Richie Crawford calling from the car-park near Santa Margarita, asking Mockler to check the French and Portuguese numbers.

'Ok, ok,' Mockler mumbled and, as he knocked over a lamp fumbling for a pencil, he thought, 'Time is our enemy – we don't have enough time.'

It was now Wednesday morning and in twenty-four hours Colombia would play its last game in Bologna and then the traffickers would move on, probably to set up in new hotels in Milan. Since the day of the first game, the investigators had succeeded in identifying some twenty people who had past or present links with the Cartel, including an old-timer who had been involved in the laboratory end of the business and three people from Jaime Orjuela's California organization. They had even discovered a Houston, Texas, resident whose telephone number had appeared in various investigations. These were the threads they were trying to follow in the hope they would lead to more significant targets. But it was the type of investigation that normally took months and Mockler was trying to compress it into a handful of days.

On the premise that some of the traffickers would be travelling legitimately, he and Sandy Smith, the analyst from Washington, had put an extraordinary effort into reviewing Colombian passports. (On the day of the first game the police had brought them two hundred.) But he knew some of the traffickers would emulate Edgar Garcia, Chepe's accountant, travelling with Jurado Rodriguez, who had used one passport in Milan and a different one in Bologna. Although the DEA's office in Bogota had offered to help – if Mockler would fax them a list, a Colombian official would check names against numbers – this process would take too many days.

Later that morning he told Jerry McArdle, 'We have got to keep looking,' but even as he said it, Mockler was sceptical. Their best hope, he felt, now lay in Rome with the hard intelligence they had developed out of Argentina. This instinct proved right, for the second Bologna game yielded nothing save the reassuring presence of Kenny Robinson, who had come up from Rome to view the game as a 'spotter'.

On Saturday Mockler packed his bags, thanked the manager of Al Cappello Rosso, said goodbye to its black-haired waitresses and, with the rest of the team, departed for Rome. 'It is a beautiful city,' he thought as he left Bologna, 'but I would have seen more of it from an intercity train window.'

Mockler was cheered, however, by what was happening in Rome, where events seemed to be unfolding as their intelligence had predicted. As he moved into a box-sized room in the Hotel Jumbo Sicilia, conveniently located a few streets from Panessa's office and whose grim courtyard was pockmarked with bullet holes from Rome's liberation, he felt a renewal of optimism.

On the previous Sunday 'Q' had arrived with his travelling companions (not their targets but three former soccer players). He stayed the Sunday night at an apartment in one of Rome's suburbs and the following day moved into the Imperiale Hotel, booking three rooms and a suite at the nearby Ambasciatore, where he left a cash deposit of $30,000. Since the Ambasciatore was one of Rome's most luxurious hotels, built in the 1930s, with beautiful art deco interiors, Panessa was certain these rooms were intended for Miguel and his family. There were also the two double rooms at the Vittoria, which Jurado Rodriguez had booked when the Luxembourg trio stayed in the hotel at the beginning of the week; this booking began on 22 June. And significantly, these three hotels – the Imperiale, the Ambasciatore and the Vittoria – were within walking distance of each other, all in streets near the Via Veneto.

During the week that Mockler was in Bologna, Kenny Robinson had been watching Leonardo Da Vinci Airport. He drove out to the airport at least twice a day, watching incoming flights from several Latin American countries and using flight passenger lists to try to identify the parties. Meanwhile the Italians kept a close watch on 'Q'. On 18 June their patience was rewarded by a burst of activity on his phone.

He had intended that day to go to Naples where his home team, Argentina, was playing Cameroon, but he cancelled these plans. He sent a bouquet of flowers to the Ambasciatore, the five-star hotel where he had booked three rooms plus a suite and left the $30,000 deposit. He called Alitalia airlines, wanting to know the time the eight o'clock flight from London to Rome was arriving. When the Italian police checked the flight list, they found that one of the passengers bore the name Rodriguez. (Unfortunately, the list did not show the first name or initial.) Surveillances were set up at the hotels and airport. The flight, however, was delayed several hours.

At eleven o'clock Kenny Robinson telephoned Frank Panessa's office to report that 'Q' (who had earlier called the Ambasciatore to say that the Rodriguez party should telephone the Imperiale on arrival) was leaving the hotel with four men and a woman. 'They're walking up the hill,' Kenny reported.

'They're probably going out to get something to eat. The game's over – they've been watching it on the television – and maybe he's checking to see if the Rodriguez party has arrived.'

'Yes,' Kenny said, 'but Richie's in the Ambasciatore and I don't know if he knows 'Q'.'

'Don't worry. The Italians have the desk covered. They'll let Richie know if he makes an inquiry.'

At midnight a frustrated Jerry McArdle called from the airport. The Polizia and Guardia were involved in a territorial battle which had only just been resolved, with the agreement that if the arrivals included one of the principal targets, the Polizia would take him.

If not, the Guardia would be allowed to inspect their luggage. It was absurd to think they were going to find anything but the DEA had at least obtained the concession that they would search everyone on the flight so as not to arouse suspicions.

Ten minutes later the Alitalia flight landed but the Rodriguez who was on board was not the one they were looking for. He was Juan Miguel Rodriguez Arbalaise, Miguel's only son – 'Miguelito', the DEA agents called him – a thirteen-year-old boy with delicate features, the embodiment of childish innocence, accompanied by a chaperon and a boy of the same age, another trafficker's son.

Miguelito and his companions were met by a car that took them to the Ambasciatore. The following morning they got up early and were driven back to the airport, where they boarded a nine o'clock flight. 'Q' was taking them to Milan where that afternoon Colombia would probably be playing its last game in the series.

There was only slight disappointment that it was not Miguel Rodriguez because Miguelito's coming was an excellent sign – if the son were here, the father could not be far behind. Indeed, it was possible he was already in the country – the father of the boy who travelled with Miguelito had left a message at the Ambasciatore for his son to call him in Rimini – and, if that were the case, they were likely to meet up in Milan.

But with their target so close, almost within their sights, the team had to tread cautiously; they could not afford a mistake. At a late-night meeting in Frank Panessa's office, the Offsides team decided to reduce their surveillance. They would pick up their targets at the game. Following this plan, a group of twenty agents and Italian police walked into the stadium in Milan on the afternoon of 19 June.

With some modifications, they had decided to follow the same routine they had used in Bologna. They had an observation booth with video cameras and here they secreted the Colombian CI, the one who had identified Chepe's bodyguard, attended by the Italian police and an agent from Bogota. The former members of Group Five pushed into the crowd, which, with the West German team playing and a much larger stadium, was three times the size of the crowd in Bologna.

Mockler and Bill Snipes were at the back of the stadium. 'I

can't tell if that's where they are or if they're down from there,' Mockler was saying as he peered at the stands through a pair of binoculars. 'Ok, ok, you see the guy with the glasses leaning forward?'

'Yes,' said Bill Snipes.

'I think they're right up in there. I'm trying to see if it's the kid. That may be one of the kids with the sunglasses on – although he looks a little older. I can't see the kid, though, that's what I'm looking for....'

Kenny and two Carabinieri moved to the front of the stands. 'Where should we start?' one of the Italian policemen was saying when Kenny, who hadn't the faintest notion, turned and saw sitting directly behind him 'Q', Miguelito and his young travelling companion. Sitting near to them, Kenny noticed, were two men he had seen at the games in Bologna, one of whom closely resembled Chepe's second-in-command, Jaime Orjuela, a top-ranking figure on their list of second-tier targets. He asked the Italian policemen to take some photographs, then he made his way to the back of the stadium.

'The CI,' Mockler started to tell Kenny, 'the CI says Jaime Orjuela is here and they're going to arrest him.'

'Where?' Kenny asked roughly.

Mockler pointed to the bench where 'Q' and the kids were sitting. 'The CI thinks he's the guy in the red shirt near 'Q'.'

'I don't think so,' said Kenny. 'It's close, I know, he's got the Orjuela features.... I'll go down and take another look.'

He came back a few minutes later. 'It's not him, it's definitely not him. Tell them not to arrest him. He's too close to the 'Q' guy. It's going to cause us problems.'

'It's too late. They're going to take him....'

'But,' Kenny said angrily, 'they're putting everything on what the CI says, and he's full of shit. The guy was two feet from me and I'm telling you, it wasn't him!'

'I couldn't stop them,' Mockler protested. 'It was too late, they were already moving in and there wasn't a discussion, they were going to take him.'

Kenny was right, the man was not Jaime Orjuela, although when Kenny later looked at him through the one-way mirror at the police station, he realized he was someone he had seen before in Jackson Heights. Within a few hours he was released, along with the two men he had been sitting by, with the apologies of the Italian police.

Did the Colombians buy the Carabinieri's story that it was all a mistake; that they had been pointed out as having been involved in a fight – there had been several fisticuffs in the stadium – and, when the police discovered they had no identification papers, they had to take them in for questioning?

Mockler was looking at their world from the outside in, so how could he ever know for certain? But he was always worried that something might cause a problem, that the wrong interpretation would be placed on something mild. Now what he feared most had actually happened and he was sufficiently concerned about its impact on the operation that there were several telephone calls between Rome and DEA headquarters in Washington.

On the very next day, 20 June, more of the Rodriguez family arrived – Miguel's sister and brother-in-law, and their three children, who moved into the rooms in the Vittoria booked by Jurado Rodriguez. The following day it was Miguel's wife's turn. She, her mother and her two teenage daughters arrived on a flight from Madrid. Over the next few days other friends trickled in, including 'Q's family – his wife and Miguel's wife were supposedly best friends – and the president of their football club, the America de Cali, who was staying in the Hotel Boston. All the rooms were now filled except one, in the luxurious Ambasciatore, where Miguel's wife and children were staying.

'His whole family's here,' Frank Panessa told Mockler. 'And it doesn't make sense for him not to be coming but continually sending everybody else in. He's going to come. I know he is. We just have to wait, we have to be patient.'

But although Mockler excelled at the waiting game, on this occasion he had run out of time. He was no longer the supervisor of a small group with the freedom to pursue the case of his choice. He was a division chief commanding sixty men and there were other investigations that needed his guidance. One in particular, into Queens Central Printing, had been a source of intermittent anxiety throughout his stay in Italy.

The QCP investigation had been initiated the previous summer by Kenny Robinson, who had come up with a new technique for identifying Cali Cartel calls: the computerized analysis of known traffickers' telephone 'tolls'. (US telephone companies keep billing records which show every number dialled from a customer's phone. These records are an important law enforcement asset since they are not protected by the Fourth Amendment and police agencies can obtain them through the simple legal mechanism of a Grand Jury subpoena.) Through this analysis, combined with other intelligence, Kenny had identified Luis Delio Lopez.

Known to his own people as Leto, Luis Delio Lopez was the cousin of Omar Sanchez, the chief defendant in the 'seven customers' case and one of the second-tier targets of Operation Offsides; they came from the same part of Colombia, the city of Pereira, and Leto was married to Omar Sanchez's sister. Leto began working for the Cartel in 1982 as an errand boy for Omar Sanchez. But by 1989, when he was targeted by Kenny, Leto – like Chepe ten years earlier – was supervising the import of tons of cocaine into the New York area and distributing it in bulk amounts to the top tier of customers. He had a network of apartments in New York and Philadelphia but his nerve centre was Queens Central Printing, a small business located in a shop on Queens Boulevard in Jackson Heights. Here, he communicated by telephone and fax machine with the heads of the Cartel in Colombia.

When Kenny first proposed the investigation, it had seemed to Mockler a perfect project. It promised substantial results in a reasonable time period; and it was a manageable size given the available resources. Because QCP kept shop-business hours – it was open eight hours a day, six days a week – one group (twenty men and women) could monitor a wire. Had the project been larger, Mockler would have had to decline it for lack of manpower.

Mockler assigned the investigation to Group 98, whose supervisor, Marty MaGuire, had recently joined the Task Force after a stint in Germany. (Before QCP, Group 98 was working on the Jamaican gangs who ran crack houses. These gangs of street distributors, ranging in size from five to fifty people, took one- and two-kilo lots of cocaine and broke them down into crack vials, which were supplied to crack houses. The gangs often employed addicts, paid in crack, to dispense the vials to customers, and kept the addicts chained in the crack houses to prevent them from stealing the drugs and money.)

Mockler explained to the group what he wanted: a period of surveillance to develop the evidence to apply for a court order for a wire-tap on QCP's phone. This would hopefully lead to a major seizure, a shipment of cocaine or possibly money, giving sufficient evidence for a conspiracy charge, followed by the arrest of Luis Delio Lopez and the mopping up of his cell.

But there is as much friction in law enforcement as there is in war, a truth that Mockler knew all too well. (And one he hoped to expound some day, for he dreamed of writing a book on the Cartel, doing for investigations what Clausewitz had done for war.)

In the middle of October 1989, Group 98 began the surveillance of QCP. From their observation post in a building across the street, they saw the usual signs of a Cartel cell's activities, people they recognized from past investigations, men surrounded by bodyguards carrying bags into the store, cars whose licence plate numbers were traced to fictitious addresses. With high-powered binoculars, through the shop's plate-glass windows they watched Leto standing by the counter, holding a cellular phone to his ear. ('Ah,' they said to each other, 'he must be saying some pretty good stuff is he's not using the store phone!')

Everything seemed to be going smoothly until they hit a major bump on 3 November. Marty MaGuire was getting ready for work when he heard the news over the radio. Five tons of cocaine, a record-breaking seizure, wrapped in red, white and blue plastic and stamped with the words 'Baby I', had been found by Customs officials; it was packed in drums of sodium hydroxide which had been stored in a two-storey brick warehouse in Long Island City on the East River near the Queensboro Bridge. It was a billion dollars worth of cocaine and, concerned lest the robbery of the century compound the crime, for the next three days New York City police guarded the warehouse round the clock while a team of police officers wearing grey protective suits, masks and oxygen tanks, worked twenty-minute shifts to salvage the contraband. (Sodium hydroxide, commonly known as powdered lye, is a caustic material used in oil refining, rubber-making and drain cleaners. It burns the skin and, if breathed in, can destroy lung tissue and cause pneumonia.)[1] On the second day they briefly suspended their labours because the path of the New York City Marathon went by the warehouse.

Meanwhile, Marty conducted his own internal investigation – who did the coke belong to and how had the seizure happened? He learned that the seizure was based on an informant's tip that a large quantity of cocaine, concealed in powdered lye, was moving from Spain to Panama to Philadelphia by ship, in a commercial vessel called the *New York Senator*. When Customs checked the bill of lading to identify the importer, they saw it was the Arenal Company, whose name was so similar to a legitimate company, Arenol, a regular importer of powdered lye, that the Customs agent neglected to investigate this aspect further. In fact, Arenal was a dummy company – 'they were cute,' Marty said, 'they only changed one letter' – and had Customs examined its publicly registered papers, they would have seen Luis Delio Lopez listed as its secretary and would have asked for a NADDIS check. Learning of the DEA's investigation, Customs and the Task Force would then have joined forces and Mockler would have got what he wanted, a conclusion to QCP as quick and spectacular as the seizure of the $7.8 million.

But the Customs agent who was handling the case did not have the expertise of Mockler, Kenny Robinson or Jerry McArdle. (One of the problems the DEA faced was not enough investigators in enough cities and agencies with the institutional knowledge that Cali Cartel investigations required, a problem Mockler and Robinson tried to remedy with frequent lectures to other law enforcement agencies.) Since the Customs agent did not know the hallmarks of a Cali Cartel scheme, the shipment was treated as an isolated event.

Using a *modus operandi* perfected over the years, Leto's people first moved the powdered lye to a Philadelphia warehouse. There they separated the 252 two-foot-high, ten-gallon drums stamped 'POISON' that contained the cocaine, stacked them on wooden pallets (eighteen drums on each of fourteen pallets) and then moved them by truck to the Long Island City warehouse.

Customs followed the truck from Philadelphia to New York where they hoped to arrest the recipients of the cocaine. But their cars were seen and the people inside the warehouse who were unpacking the drugs abandoned their project and ran out of the building. (Wearing oxygen masks and dressed in protective clothing, they had been using a commercial vacuum pump, a Vacu-Max, which had been rented for cash in October, to extract the chemicals.)

Group 98 later discovered that within an hour of the seizure there were telephone calls from QCP to Colombia. Events thereafter followed a familiar pattern. Leto switched cars and apartments, his appearances at QCP became less frequent and when he did show up he drove so evasively that Group 98 decided it was counterproductive to follow him.

With Customs' seizure of the five tons of cocaine on 3 November and the links to Luis Delio Lopez and to QCP, coupled with intelligence accumulated during several weeks of surveillance and research of historical files, Group 98 and the federal prosecutor working with them decided they had sufficient probable cause to obtain a wire-tap order. But when the wire-tap application with its probable cause affidavit (approximately forty-five pages of circumstantial evidence) was submitted in the third week of November to the Justice Department in Washington, it was rejected. (The prosecutor reviewing it was accustomed to probable cause affidavits based on informants). Although the DEA's legal counsel disagreed, this decision bound Group 98.[2] The group spent another four weeks collecting evidence. Finally, on 15 January 1990, three months after they started the wire-tap application process, a judge signed the wire-tap order.

As they monitored the wire from the observation post across the street, the agents were listening for evidence to connect Leto to the five tons of cocaine. But four days after they began the wire-tapping, the investigation encountered another obstacle. Under rules promulgated by New York State's Public Services Commission, the telephone company is obliged to tell a customer if its 'tolls' have been subpoenaed unless there is a request from law enforcement that this requirement be waived. But when the case agent for QCP, Harry Brady (a young agent with tight black curls, bright, jaunty), hand-delivered the Task Force's request that notification be postponed, the New York telephone company was in the middle of a strike. The letter was lost, and QCP was told.

Group 98 first learned of this not from the telephone company but by monitoring the wire. They overheard the woman who ran the shop, Dollie Arias, a naturalized citizen of about fifty years, with no criminal record and who spoke English well – a perfect front-person for a little business which ostensibly published wedding and christening announcements – make a panicky call to Leto's number two. 'The cops have got my telephone records. I need a good lawyer. What should I do?'

When the lawyer, one of those who regularly represented the Cartel, came to the Task Force office to find out why they were interested in his client, he was put off with a story. 'It must have been somebody arrested outside New York who had the phone number so, as a matter of course, we obtained the telephone records and because we didn't see anything wrong, we let the phone company notify Mrs Arias.'

With this incident coming on top of the five-ton seizure, Leto stopped using QCP's phone. He still, however, came into the store and, although he did not use its phone, he was meeting people there. Mockler succeeded in obtaining a new wire-tap order to install a listening device inside the store and put a wire on one of Leto's cellular phones.

Eight months after Group 98 began surveillance of QCP, the investigation was still not concluded. It was active when Mockler left New York for Italy. At any moment the wire in QCP might be productive, yield a damning admission, reveal a new shipment, the whereabouts of Leto (who was probably now in Colombia). If opportunities were missed because of Mockler's absence, it would be the disastrous equivalent of a farmer losing his harvest.

So on 21 June Richie Crawford drove his ex-boss to Leonardo Da Vinci Airport. As Mockler got into the car he waved to his colleagues, 'Maybe now that I'm gone, your luck will change.' Although he was smiling, there was little cheer in his voice.

It wasn't Mockler who was the source of the curse. At the start of each football game, the investigators' hopes were high, and at the end of each game they left feeling depressed. This pattern held true for the World Cup final, on 8 July, when Argentina played Italy.

Among the spectators was Kenny Robinson, looking, he hoped, like an American tourist, with his baggy grey slacks belted around his wide midriff. As he stood in the stands, opposite the VIP section, staring at the spectators with a pair of high-powered binoculars and hoping no one would notice that his back was turned to the game, he saw, sitting not far from the President of Italy, a man who looked like Chepe. He was sitting next to a Hispanic woman and, although he had no beard, he was dressed sloppily, which was Chepe's style. But what really struck Kenny was his strange demeanour.

Kenny spoke to the agent he was working with. 'Nancy!' he said sharply. 'You see that guy? He's looking all around, he's not watching the game. Let's try to move in for a closer look.' He found one of the police photographers but with all the VIPs at the game, the threat of terrorism and the problem of soccer hooliganism, security at this last game was especially tight and he was told by the stadium police, 'You'll have to wait for half-time, then we'll take you through.' But when half-time came and Kenny crossed the stadium, the seat was empty and the man never returned.

Two days later Miguel's wife and children, his mother-in-law and 'Q' left Italy. For the Italian police, Operation Offsides had finished. But in the hope that somewhere along the line Miguel's children and spouse would meet the head of their family, Kenny and Sam Meale followed the Rodriguez party to Athens, where the family stayed for several days before embarking on a cruise of the Aegean. At Piraeus the surveillance was picked up by two Greek anti-narcotics detectives and was continued in Israel, Nice and Paris by DEA agents and their counterparts.

On 1 August 1990, as the Rodriguez family disembarked at John F. Kennedy Airport – they had flown on Concorde from Paris to New York – and walked towards Immigration, Kenny Robinson stood in the background awaiting them. The Immigration inspectors had already been briefed. It was hit or miss who would do the interrogation but, as luck would have it, the family joined the queue of a young Chinese-American inspector, a natural investigator.

Miguel's wife, a handsome woman in her late thirties, with high cheek bones and auburn hair, sophisticated looking and beautifully dressed, left her oldest daughter, whose English was perfect, to act as the family's spokeswoman. She explained that they were staying in New York for five days at the Helmsley Palace (New York's equivalent of the Ambasciatore) before flying to Miami.

'Where is your father and what is his business?' the inspector asked, not showing any eagerness.

Miguel's daughter explained that her father was an attorney and too busy to come on this trip. Then, as the inspector made a small joke, hoping she would say more if he dispelled her discomfort, she volunteered that her father would be coming to America in December. The inspector, knowing how important this was, instinctively glanced at Miguel's beautiful wife, who was staring at her daughter with cold, angry eyes.

Later that day, repeating a scenario enacted thousands of times, Kenny walked into Mockler's office to report what had happened. Mockler listened attentively, occasionally nodding, taking everything in, scheming, plotting and, finally, told Kenny, 'I want you to put it all together so we can move in December.'

It was typical of Mockler to ask Kenny, an analyst who had surrendered his gun and shield when he had retired from the New York police, to put together an operation as though he were still a detective; to give him an assignment which was probably hopeless, as difficult as spotting a familiar face in the stadium at Bologna, for Miguel's daughter had not given any date in December or what part of the States her father was coming to. For the thousandth time since he had met Mockler, Kenny repressed a sense of irritation at his impossible demands. 'Why do I put up with him?' he asked himself, which was a rhetorical question since he knew the response. He was sustained by the compliment of this extraordinary man's trust.

Later, as Kenny walked to the garage where he parked his car, he mentally prepared himself for the long trip home, a two-hour drive when traffic was light. He had been born in Manhattan, in St Vincent's Hospital in Greenwich Village, and he had grown up in Queens, but he could not live in the city. The New York that he worked in was a place for the rich and the poor, and with the exception of a few small enclaves, the old working-class ethnic neighbourhoods had been lost to drugs and crime.

But how he dreaded that journey into work, which he had tried to reduce by juggling his hours, starting at six am so that he could leave by two in the afternoon. But he had ended up working twelve-hour shifts because Mockler usually worked from midday to eight and just as it was time for Kenny to leave, his boss would be reaching a full head of steam – and, of course, if Mockler had something for him to do, he was constitutionally incapable of saying 'no.'

As he drove his car down the car-park's ramp, Kenny wondered, 'What's wrong with me?' Ever since coming back from Europe, he had felt ill. Was it simply fatigue? He had taken only two days off during the operation's six weeks and in his last fortnight in Italy he had been working twelve-hour shifts; as the days wore down to the final game, the team was reduced to a skeletal force. The prospects for Operation Offsides had once looked so good. Now Kenny asked himself 'What went wrong?' Had they made serious mistakes? Had they tried to throw too wide a net? Should they have exercised more control over the Colombian informant whose reliability Kenny had always found suspect? (He had watched the CI before the first game in Bologna, looking through albums Kenny had helped compile and skipping over people he claimed to know.) Was it the little newspaper article that appeared on day two? Or the botched arrests that took place in Milan?

Although neither incident had obviously helped, in retrospect, they were not critical events. Nor did the problem lie with their original intelligence. Everything that happened had proved it correct. Everything except Miguel's not coming, everything except that empty room in the Ambasciatore. But in the aftermath of the operation they had come up with an explanation, an informant's report from inside Colombia – that Operation Offsides had been betrayed by one of their counterparts, a high-ranking officer in Colombia's security police, which was why at the last minute Miguel had changed his plans. This interpretation of events was probably correct because of something one of the DEA agents had learned – a scrap of conversation, very telling, between Miguelito in Rome and his father in Cali. 'When are you coming?' the boy had asked and Miguel had replied, 'Hush. These are not things we discuss on the phone. . . .'

As for the man that Kenny had seen at the final, the one with the open-necked white shirt who wasn't watching the game, could he have been Chepe? Kenny would always wonder. It was certainly possible and perhaps three years from now they would find an informant, another Robert Lafferty, to solve this puzzle. 'It was Chepe and you were so close, within a hair's breadth, but he saw you guys. . . .'

9 The Enemy's Retreat

At the end of June 1990, two weeks before the World Cup final game in Rome, the investigation of the Luxembourg trio came to a head with the arrests of Edgar Garcia, Jurado Rodriguez and Ricardo Mahecha by the Sûreté Publique. This investigation, which in Italy had been a side-show, was to become one of law enforcement's greatest successes against the Cali Catel.

Of all the investigations that Jerry McArdle had worked on, the Luxembourg case brought him closest to Chepe. For the first time since he began working for the Task Force the enigmatic Jose SantaCruz Londono became a flesh and blood creature. This was partly because the case was 'pure Chepe'. Many of the people involved were his family – his daughter, his wife, his wife's parents, his paramour – and the money the agents seized, all $70 million, was part of Chepe's personal fortune.

For the DEA agents and analysts who were involved in the case – Jerry, Robbie Michaelis, Cheryl Holmes, Kenny Robinson and, in the background, Bill Mockler – it was the culmination of a decade's work. They were able to draw together so many threads, dribs and drabs of intelligence that had been obscure loose ends.

They also enjoyed the ironic twists of the case. The way, for instance, Cheryl Holmes had met Pierre Kohman at a money laundering conference organized by the Brussels office that the DEA had financed with traffickers' assets.[1] Or the way that Luxembourg's Sûreté Publique were led to Jurado Rodriguez. An irate citizen had called the police because one of his neighbours was disturbing his sleep operating an electric money-counter at all hours of the night. The police checked the name on the lease:

Jurado Rodriguez, a Colombian national with no obvious employment, no source of income, who was living in a luxury flat and had a fax machine; they found that his telephone records showed calls to Colombia and that he was receiving banking instructions from Miguel Rodriguez, a Cali businessman. That was, of course, just the beginning. Much more was learned through wire-taps and surveillance and the analysis of documents found in Jurado's Luxembourg residence and the apartment and office he maintained in Paris.

When Richie Crawford and Sam Meale last saw Jurado, in June 1990, he was in the blue Opel speeding north from Portofino on the autostrada. They had no idea where he was going, though they had speculated it might be Milan, Bologna or Nice. In fact, Jurado and his two compatriots returned to Luxembourg, where the Sûreté Publique resumed their surveillance. In the last two weeks of June, they and their counterparts in Scandinavia and Germany followed the three men to Copenhagen, where they opened four bank accounts and deposited $600,000, then to Stockholm, Amsterdam and Berlin where they opened more bank accounts and deposited more cheques. Then, at the end of June as the trio again left Luxembourg, the Sûreté Publique made the decision to arrest them. On 28 June they seized Ricardo Mahecha at Luxembourg airport, and on the following day they arrested Jurado Rodriguez and Edgar Garcia as they drove towards Germany.

Cheryl Holmes was immediately notified. She went first to the US Attorney's Office in the Eastern District of New York which was prosecuting Chepe and Gilberto Rodriguez. Here she helped prepare the 'letters rogatory', the request of a US court to the court of a foreign jurisdiction, so that they could identify and freeze the bank accounts. Then she flew to Luxembourg, where she sifted through boxes of documents, trying to identify every bank account they had opened. (Much of this evidence came from documents found on Jurado when he was arrested and in his two apartments and his Paris office. It consisted of notes, business cards, bank books and statements which Jurado retained to keep track of the money and to account to Chepe for its management.)

During this critical first week and the following months, Cheryl Holmes identified nearly three hundred bank accounts in five continents. With the help of other analysts, the New York Drug Enforcement Task Force, the Sûreté Publique, Scotland Yard and the Italian and Danish police, she was able to piece together Jurado's money laundering scheme.

The money was not, as Frank Panessa had originally surmised, to be used to set up distribution networks in Europe. Nor did it come from European drug sales. Most of it had originated in America and been smuggled out as bank drafts or cash, deposited in a Panamanian corporation, then funnelled into bank accounts in North America, Latin America, Europe, Asia and Australia. It was pure profit 'parked' outside Colombia.

Of the three hundred bank accounts that Cheryl discovered, not all were active when Jurado was arrested. In an effort to distance the money from its original source, Jurado had shifted it from country to country, sometimes transferring money within a bank to take advantage of more favourable interest rates. The bulk of the money was concentrated in the United States, Panama, England, France, Luxembourg and Germany but there were also accounts in such unlikely places as Denmark, Finland, Austria, Hungary and Israel and in countries as far flung as Japan, Australia and Uruguay. Many of the accounts – the ones opened in Rome and Norway, for instance – contained hundreds of thousands rather than millions of dollars. It was part of Jurado's scheme to spread the money through many small accounts, often choosing countries with few Hispanics and little experience of narcotics traffic. This was to avoid arousing the banks' suspicions, make the process of locating funds more difficult and give Chepe time to shift and hide the money in the event that the scheme was discovered. (The death of Rodriguez Gacha, one of the leaders of the Medellin consortium, who was killed by the Colombian police in late 1989, had made an impression on his colleagues in Colombia. In the search of one of his *estancias* after his death, the police found bank records concealed in barrels; the DEA blocked $62 million within five days.)

Having identified the accounts, Cheryl Holmes began the process of backtracking in an effort to identify the source of the money. Much of it came from Siracusa Trading Corporation, a Panamanian company whose president, Edgar Garcia, was intimately linked to the heads of the Cartel as the former director of the First InterAmericas Bank and the current vice-president of America de Cali.

There was no difficulty in proving that Jurado was laundering money given the sums involved and their zigzagging movement. But that fact alone, both in Luxembourg and the United States, was not sufficient to convict the Luxembourg trio. Prosecutors in both jurisdictions had to connect the money to a drug trafficking organization.

This was a task which Jerry McArdle tackled on his return from Italy, assisted by Kenny Robinson and Robbie Michaelis, a young agent with a cheerful and innocent face, known to the rest of the group as 'Little McArdle', who was 'doomed', Jerry said, 'to inherit my mantle'. Largely through their historical files, knowledge of names, notations in the Justo Guzman and Luis Ramos ledgers (the latter had been seized with the $7.8 million), they were able to establish a close family relationship between the names on the accounts and Jose SantaCruz Londono.

Some of the accounts 'belonged' to Marley Fuqueen, who had been Chepe's mistress since at least 1980 and was the mother of three of his children. She had had an account at the First InterAmericas Bank and there was a condominium in Miami in her name. (The DEA had identified it in 1988. They watched the place for several years, hoping that some day they might see Chepe there. Then in March 1990, three months before Operation Offsides, Jerry learned an attempt had been made to sell the property while, at the same time, Jurado switched various accounts out of Marley's name. This, coupled with other intelligence, suggested Marley had met with some disaster and in November 1990, to forestall Chepe selling the property, the DEA seized the Miami condominium.)

The majority of the accounts were, however, in two other names: Heriberto Castro and Esperanza Rodriguez Castro. Jerry believed them to be Chepe's parents-in-law but this was a connection that had to be proved in court with indisputable evidence that was also legally admissible. To obtain this proof, the investigators went back to Chepe's daughter, Ana Milena.

Kenny had discovered the existence of Ana Milena in 1983 when he arrested Justo Guzman and found in his apartment a scrawled note on a slip of paper – 'Brookline Trust, Brookline,

Massachusetts 02146', the name 'Ana Milena SantaCruz' and an account number. He contacted the bank, learned Ana Milena's address and that she was a student at Pine Manor College in Boston. He and other members of Group Five later attended one of the college's parents' weekends, hoping Chepe might visit his daughter. With Task Force vehicles scattered round the parking lot, Kenny spent the day inside the guard's booth at the entrance to the college watching each vehicle that entered its grounds. Neither of Ana Milena's parents appeared but a young drug trafficker, Jairo Escobar, did visit her, and when he left, Tommy Deignan followed him back to New York. (Escobar was one of the defendants in the 'seven customers' indictment; he was accused of keeping the Guzman cell's drug ledger. He was tried, convicted and sentenced to prison. Jerry McArdle was the case agent and a portion of the proof came from a handwriting expert's analysis.)

Eventually they learned that in 1988 Ana Milena and her mother were living in Boston. When they seized the $7.8 million and Luis Ramos's ledgers, they found notations showing that some of the drug cash Ramos collected had been sent to a doctor to pay the women's medical expenses. Following this lead, they obtained records which showed that Jose SantaCruz Londono was Ana Milena's father and Esperanza Castro her maternal grandmother. Through birth and marriage certificates obtained in Colombia, they linked Esperanza Castro to Heriberto Castro. With this, the genealogical picture was complete; the ostensible owners of many of the suspect accounts were in fact Chepe's father- and mother-in-law. After the arrest of the Luxembourg trio, they obtained additional proof connecting Ana Milena to Chepe. She was listed on the board of directors of 'legitimate' Colombian companies involved in construction and real estate – directed by her grandfather Heriberto Castro – which they knew SantaCruz had set up with drug trafficking profits.

The trial of Chepe's three accountants in Luxembourg was scheduled to take place in the summer of 1991. After that, the US Attorney for the Eastern District intended to pursue a prosecution in New York City. (The likely charges would be money laundering and conspiracy to distribute cocaine, carrying maximum penalties of life imprisonment.) In fact, it will take years to complete the Luxembourg case as analysts, agents and prosecutors follow its ramifications through.

As Jerry McArdle helped to prepare the indictment (a project which consumed most of the autumn of 1990), he was occasionally tempted to indulge in a feeling of triumph. Surely, in seizing this huge amount of money, $70 million, all of it profit and all of it Chepe's, they must have dealt the trafficker a heavy blow. But then he would think of the First InterAmericas Bank case, of travelling to Panama at the end of 1984 and being told that one of the groups using the bank was depositing $8 million a day. If Chepe were making that kind of money, he would recoup what they had seized in a few months time and from intelligence reports, informant debriefings, the number of leads generated by Mockler's Division, Jerry McArdle was forced to conclude that Chepe's organization was more powerful than ever. Its three chairmen of the board had recently been seen at a party in Cali attended by one prominent senator and numerous local politicians. The party was held at the Intercontinental, the city's best hotel, where in 1989 Amazon Trading Company's president, Mike Tsalickis, had stayed while working out the details of a shipment of cocaine.

The party took place in October 1990. Miguel Rodriguez, according to his daughter, intended to visit the States a few weeks later. But Mockler's grandiose scheme to locate and arrest the trafficker came to nothing, for when Miguel was expected in December, Kenny Robinson was ill in hospital.

He had been taken ill in Panama City where he and Robbie Michaelis had gone at the beginning of September on a mission that should have been simple: to obtain certified copies of bank and business records that the US Attorney needed for the Luxembourg prosecution. 'It was a routine request,' Kenny said, 'which I thought we could do one, two, three.'

But for reasons he did not understand – was it incompetence, obstructionism, corruption, anti-Americanism? – they were made to wait for nearly two weeks. Finally, Kenny told the Panamanian prosecutor who had been assigned to help the American investigators obtain the records, 'You're obviously a very busy man. Why don't you give us a couple of cops and they can help us get this thing done.' But even this was no solution – the Panamanian detectives would not budge without the prosecutor's authorization.

This was very frustrating but no more so than some of Kenny's experiences in Italy – and frustration was after all as much an element of his work as hydrogen is a component of water. This was one of the reasons he did not believe the diagnosis when, after weeks of tests, he was told by his doctors that the illness which caused him to be rushed to hospital in Panama was a biochemical imbalance caused by stress.

'But,' Kenny argued, 'how can that be? I'm an analyst now, not a detective, my job isn't as stressful as it used to be. I don't work the same crazy hours . . .' (How could he say this after his performance in Italy?)

'You're older now,' came the reply. 'It's stress accumulated over twenty-five years.'

Perhaps he found this diagnosis incredible because it seemed so unpalatable. That a man of his strength, his temperate habits, who had never been ill, who was his colleagues' emotional ballast, 'Mr Reliable', should succumb to an illness whose origins were psychological! And if the diagnosis was correct, what was the cure? To give up his job? That was inconceivable – he loved his work. To work less hard? 'You're forty-eight years old,' his doctor had said. 'Is there anything left that you have to prove?'

Although his body was telling him the doctors were right – he had gone back to work for two weeks in November and had suffered a relapse coming out of Mockler's office – he did not know whether he could change. It wasn't just a matter of altering his habits, getting more exercise, going on a diet. He hated, for instance, delegating work to others. If he asked an agent, 'Please check the hotel records,' and the agent came back saying the records were 'negative', he would not be satisfied until he had double-checked them – unless the agent was Jerry McArdle or perhaps Robbie Michaelis.

The relationship between those two, he had noticed, was reminiscent of his old partnership with Jerry. He could still remember when he realized Jerry had 'it', not the day or month or year but – and he laughed as he recalled this – what they were doing: picking over some trafficker's rubbish. (In a helpful decision for law enforcement agencies, the US Supreme Court has ruled that an individual has no 'expectation of privacy' in material they discard or abandon so no warrant is required to search someone's rubbish.) It might have belonged to Jairo Escobar who had been Ana Milena's visitor in that long ago parents' weekend at Pine Manor College; a party invitation found in his rubbish bin had helped to convict him. Kenny could remember lifting the plastic bag from the metal dustbin that had been left on the kerb for the early morning collection and explaining to Jerry, 'We've got to take this to some deserted spot where we can sort it out, the papers from the wet gunk, then let them dry out.' He recalled Jerry's reaction – not dismay or disgust but a quiet interest and eagerness to learn.

Before he became sick, before they went to Panama, Kenny had noticed the same qualities in Robbie Michaelis when the three of them had been in Jerry's office, searching through his and Jerry's files. They had been looking for links between Chepe and Jurado and Jerry had found some scrap – was it a telephone number? – and was leaping about in excitement while Robbie Michaelis had looked on delighted. The thought then had crossed Kenny's mind, 'He's got the enthusiasm, he's got the interest, he'll carry it on. He's the next generation.' For Kenny Robinson had no illusions. They would be working on this investigation long after he had retired.

A few blocks away from the New York hospital where Kenny Robinson lay, Bill Mockler was submitting to an annual ritual: briefly diverting his troops from the Cali Cartel investigation so that they could make a few 'buy and bust' cases to improve the Task Force's statistics. But what of his own criteria for success? What inroads had they made into the Cartel that year? Like Don Ferrarone, he was an optimist – in their line of work, you couldn't be a defeatist – so in the débâcle of Operation Offsides he saw accomplishments.

The operation had generated a whole new database of violators, Colombians in Italy, Italians working with the Cartel. It had taught the police forces of two different nations how to coordinate and manage the logistics of a cross-European operation, which would become particularly important with the relaxation of the Common Market's national border controls in 1992. And it had helped with the Luxembourg case, which was a great success, not just because of the amount of money involved but because they had arrested such important players, in particular Edgar Garcia. In fact, of all the people they had arrested since Nelson Gomez was seized with his brick of cocaine in 1978, only Chepe's half-brother Lucho had a higher rank.

The other major investigation of 1990 was Queens Central Printing which, despite the bumps and stumbles at its beginning, had reached a more or less successful conclusion. The wire in the store, which had been active while Mockler worked on Offsides in Italy, picked up several long conversations between Dollie Arias and other cell members in which they 'spilled their guts' over the five-ton Customs seizure.

'It was arranged all wrong,' she was overheard saying. 'The police know about everything, they know about Leto.' She described how Leto had spotted the surveillance as he was helping to unpack the cocaine from the drums of poison chemicals. He slipped a gun in his waist belt and escaped from the warehouse. When he returned to QCP, he 'looked a wreck'. When she asked, 'What's wrong?' he had said, 'Turn on the television and you'll see.'

Shortly after the five tons of cocaine were seized, Leto had returned to Colombia, having earned in the space of three short years millions of dollars from selling cocaine in America. He owned car-parks and garages in Colombia, three rental properties in Queens, a $900,000 house in Scarsdale, New York, and a $550,000 house in Delray Beach in Florida. 'Five acres of land, right on the water, four bathrooms, no mortgage, it was gorgeous,' said the case agent, Harry Brady, who was the same age as Leto, in his late twenties. (Delio also owned a Mercedes, a Porsche, a 1990 Acura Legend, a motorcycle, a Forerunner truck and an Oldsmobile Tornado.)

On 25 July 1990 most of the members of Leto's cell were arrested. These included the men who had moved the five tons of cocaine from Philadelphia to Long Island City as well as two people involved in providing Leto with stash-houses – a Peruvian, Luis Echegarry, and an Irish girl from Birmingham, Kathy Leahy, his assistant.

Luis Echegarry, who had worked for the Cartel since at least 1985, had been the best man at Leto's wedding. He owned Melizzo Realty, an estate agency located on the floor above Queens Central Printing, which supplied the Cartel with flats and houses, false identification and cellular phones. (In order to frustrate electronic surveillance, Echegarry rented mobile phones from a private phone company, then sublet them to cell members. If the DEA identified a suspect number and contacted Echegarry, the official subscriber, he could put them off – 'I rented the phone to a guy name Pablo, I don't know his last name, I don't have his address, he pays in cash' – then contact the cell member. 'Pick up a new phone, the old one's burnt.' But it was his role in providing stash-pads for the Cartel that led to Echegarry's arrest and prosecution.

In the late 1970s, as Chepe developed his New York distribution network, he realized that he could not keep drugs or money in traditional Hispanic neighbourhoods like Washington Heights or the Lower East Side of Manhattan because the local street people in these high crime areas would steal his money and drugs and kill his workers. So he started looking for stash-pads in middle-class neighbourhoods, first in Manhattan and Queens, and later in Long Island and Westchester. As the organization and its need for an infrastructure expanded and the requirements for stash-pads became more sophisticated (houses with attached garages, similar to that of Luis Ramos, or high-rise apartment buildings in Manhattan with underground garages), the Cartel invested in companies like Melizzo Realty, which had access to a wide range of properties. Like Echegarry, their owners had permanent resident status and spoke perfect English; no one suspected that they were involved in a criminal enterprise. They would prepare the rental application, sign the lease, pay the rent, obtain electricity and gas, arrange for the phone and prepare all the documents in false names.

Luis Echegarry – described by Harry Brady as 'a slick dresser and classy-looking guy' – was an accomplished con man; some of his tricks were wonderfully brazen. Posing as George Lozano, a wealthy Madrid businessman whose son was a student at Princeton University, he rented a townhouse on West 90th Street in Manhattan. He had several telephones in his office listed under the names of fictitious businesses. When the landlord called to check his reference, Echegarry's assistant, Kathy Leahy, answered the phone in her Irish accent, 'Molten Consultants. Can I help you? Yes, George Lozano does work here, he's been a manager for the last eight years and he's very conscientious, a very good worker. . . .' The building's unsuspecting owner never realized that his real tenant was a Cartel money launderer.

Sometimes Kathy Leahy rented the apartments. Posing as Vicky Perks, she sublet the ground floor of a three-storey brownstone building on East 75th Street, then passed the keys to a Cali Cartel woman who passed them on to another cell member. When the rightful tenant, a French woman, reclaimed her apartment at the end of September, two months after Leahy and Echegarry were arrested, the only evidence of its occupation was a black trunk left behind by her sub-tenant. Two weeks later, when no one had claimed it, Miss Françoise Masson called the New York City Police and the FBI. They opened the trunk and found seven pipe-bombs, twenty machine guns, eighteen silencers, ten thousand rounds of 9 mm ammunition, bullet-proof vests and anti-bugging devices.

This discovery coincided with a visit by Margaret Thatcher to the United Nations. Because the apartment had been sublet to an Irishwoman, the incident was reported in the British press as an IRA assassination plot.[2] In fact, the police quickly realized that it was a Cali Cartel arms cache. The Frenchwoman gave them Vicky Perks' contact number; they checked it in NADDIS and discovered the QCP investigation and the name of the case agent, Harry Brady, who added an additional dollop of evidence to his weighty case file. (Other stash-houses obtained by Echegarry were an apartment on East 66th Street, where $1.5 million was found, and two Long Island houses containing a total of $2 million.)

In the end QCP proved a classic example of the techniques developed and perfected by Robinson, Mockler and McArdle. Starting with a jumble of phone numbers and a computer, Group 98 concluded with eight arrests, five tons of cocaine, five houses, six vehicles, a cache of weapons – and more leads than Mockler had the manpower to follow, enough spin-off investigations to occupy the entire Division. The case would have been perfect except for one thing: they never laid their hands on Luis Delio Lopez.

The Colombian anti-narcotics police arrested him in his hometown of Pereira, a city of two hundred thousand people and the capital of Risaralda province, a coffee-growing region in the north-west of Colombia, halfway between the cities of Medellin and Cali. The Justice Department requested his extradition but as of March 1991, he was still in Colombia.

Was he at least in jail in Colombia? When asked this question,

Harry Brady sounded deflated. 'I call the office in Bogota, they tell me he's there but I don't know, it's so hard to tell...'

This was the most difficult thing about working on the Cartel. 'It is like fighting the war in Vietnam,' Mockler said, 'where the enemy could retreat to Cambodia or Laos or North Vietnam and the soldier, the GI, could only go to the border.'

Everything in the end went back to Colombia, to the largest of that trio of Andean countries which were trapped with the United States in a web of social, political and economic forces that were beyond the manipulation of any agency or individual.

On 18 August 1989, when Kenny Robinson was developing his computer analysis of Cali Cartel telephone records, a Colombian Liberal Party politician, Luis Carlos Galan, was assassinated in Soacha, Colombia. This was hardly a surprising event. For a country not at war, Colombia has the highest murder rate in the world; homicide is the main cause of death for men aged fifteen to forty-five. In the seven weeks preceding Galan's murder, there had been six other assassinations. Two judges had been murdered, two union activists, a governor and, on the morning of Galan's death, Colonel Franklin Quintero, the police commander of the Antioquia Department whose capital, Medellin, Colombia's second largest city, is home to Colombia's other drug consortium.[3]

The murder of Luis Carlos Galan was, however, especially shocking. Since its formation in 1981 by cocaine traffickers Pablo Escobar, Jorge Luis Ochoa, Carlos Lehder and Gonzalo Rodriguez Gacha, the Medellin Cartel had killed many public officials, including mayors, councillors, governors, policemen, judges, a Justice Minister and an Attorney General. But it had never struck so high into the ruling elite. Luis Carlos Galan was the heir designate of President Virglio Barco, a popular reformer who would probably have been the country's next president. He had pledged to fight the drug barons and he was committed to opening up Colombia's moribund and corrupt oligarchical power structures. He was 'the maximum expression of honour and honesty on the national political scene', Colombia's best hope of escaping from an abyss of violence.[4]

Galan was murdered at an open-air political rally in the suburbs

COLOMBIA

Gulf of Mexico
Gulf of Uraba
Panama City
PANAMA
URABA
VENEZUELA
R. Magdalena
Medellin
Puerto Boyaca
Pereira
PACIFIC OCEAN
Bogata
Soacha
Cali
ANDES
COLOMBIA
R. Yari
R. Putumayo
ECUADOR
Santa Clara
R. Amazon
Amataura
Leticia
Benjamin Constant
R. Amazon
PERU
BRAZIL
N
0 150 300 kilometres
0 100 200 miles

of Bogota. There had been an attempt on his life two weeks earlier and he was wearing a bullet-proof vest and surrounded by twenty-two bodyguards. His assassins, however, were professionals. While six men fired into the air to distract Galan's bodyguards, a seventh pushed close and, at point-blank range, cut down the presidential candidate with an Uzi machine-gun. Judging from their skill, their weapons, their *modus operandi*, they had probably been trained at one of the Medellin Cartel's schools for assassins in Puerto Boyaca. This town on the Rio Magdalena, which prided itself on being 'the anti-subversive capital of Colombia', was one of the many safe havens of the Medellin Cartel whose leaders owned vast chunks of land in the fertile river valley between Bogota and Medellin.[5]

The assassination of Luis Carlos Galan triggered a new campaign in Colombia's on-again, off-again war against its cocaine mafia. In the fortnight following his death, Colombian anti-narcotics police arrested 11,000 workers in the cocaine industry (most low-level, most later released), confiscated property, destroyed laboratories and seized over 1200 weapons and 900 vehicles and aircraft. But the most threatening development to the Medellin Cartel was President Barco's decision to resume extraditions to the United States; these had been suspended when the Colombian Supreme Court ruled the US–Colombian extradition treaty unconstitutional in 1987.

When the extradition treaty had been signed in 1979 by the administration of President Julio Cesar Turbay Ayala, it was considered sufficiently important for the State Department to reward Colombia by tripling its anti-narcotics assistance to $16 million, which gave Colombia more than a third of the $42 million fund allocated to worldwide drug policing.[6] By 1982, when the treaty was meant to come into effect, it had become a central plank of the US government's anti-narcotics policy in the cocaine source countries.

The Colombian cocaine industry had been established in the mid-1970s and grew by leaps and bounds over the next decade. Between 1976 and 1982 annual exports to the US increased from between 14 and 19 metric tons to 45 metric tons, generating foreign exchange earnings of $2.5 to $3 billion, making cocaine the country's principal export earner. (Colombia's next most significant export earner, coffee, brings between $2 and $2.5 million into the country.) It created fabulous fortunes for a handful of men. In October 1987 *Fortune* magazine put Jorge Luis Ochoa and Pablo Escobar among the twenty richest men in the world. Most of these *nouveau riche* traffickers came from the lowest ranks of Colombia's society. A study of twenty middle- and top-ranking drug traffickers from Antioquia in 1988 found that seventy-seven per cent were of peasant origin and thirty per cent from the urban lower class.[7] Pablo Escobar was a one-time car thief, a child of the Medellin slums.

These men used their wealth to buy and bully their way into power, to protect their interests, to extend their influence. When Colombia's notoriously inefficient and archaic judicial system collapsed under the twin pressures of bribery and intimidation, the US government saw extradition as the antidote. American law enforcement agents would build cases against Colombian traffickers, obtain their return to the States and prosecute them in a court system free of taint.

As much as the US government wanted extradition, it was feared by the Colombian drug barons. In 1982 the Medellin Cartel was financially involved in many legislators' campaigns; Pablo Escobar himself ran for office on the Liberal Party slate in his home department of Antioquia. The Medellin group also financed a nationwide publicity campaign to arouse nationalist sentiment against the extradition treaty, which was denounced as an abandonment of Colombian sovereignty.

When President Turbay's successor, Belisario Betancur Cuartas, took office in 1982, he refused to honour the treaty on nationalist grounds, stating his intention to try Colombian traffickers in Colombian courts. But he balanced this with the appointment of an aggressive Justice Minister, Rodrigo Lara Bonilla, who set out to destroy the cocaine industry's manufacturing facilities. On 10 March 1984 Colombian police and DEA agents jointly raided Tranquillandia, the Medellin Cartel's huge cocaine-refining complex on the Yari River, seizing 27,500 pounds of cocaine, the largest foreign seizure on record.

Seven weeks later the Cartel retaliated by murdering Rodrigo Lara Bonilla in Bogota and also assassinating the head of the narcotics unit of the national police who had led the raid against Tranquillandia, Colonel Jaime Ramirez Gomez, and the Bogota judge who had implicated the Cartel in Lara's murder.

In the wake of Lara's assassination, Betancur dropped his previous opposition to the treaty. He signed an extradition order for Carlos Lehder and ordered his narcotics police to crack down on the Medellin Cartel. The unprecedented wave of arrests, confiscations of property and destruction of laboratories forced the Medellin Cartel leaders to flee across the border to Panama, where, for a $5 million fee, they took refuge under General Manuel Noriega's wings.

There, they secretly met with the Colombian Attorney General, Carlos Jimenez Gomez, and attempted to negotiate a peace treaty whose key elements were their withdrawal from the drug business and the repatriation of billions of dollars in drug profits (enough to offset Colombia's $15 billion foreign debt), in exchange for freedom from extradition and reinstatement in society. They promised to turn over their clandestine laboratories and airstrips, calculating that it would take at least ten years for others to redevelop the industry. They also pledged to stay out of cocaine trafficking, to stay out of politics and to help substitute other crops for coca and marijuana. A treaty with these terms might have spared Colombia the orgy of corruption, terror and murder which followed but there was outrage both in Colombia and the US when a Colombian newspaper publicized the negotiations. Betancur was forced to renounce them; in the next two years he extradited thirteen people to the States.

The Medellin Cartel's next target was a more vulnerable institution, the Colombian Supreme Court. They hired fifty lawyers to demand the treaty's annulment, then sent the following death threat to each of the judges who were to rule on this issue:

> We are writing to you to demand favourable positions for our cause. We do not accept resignations, we do not accept sabbaticals, we do not accept fictitious illnesses.... Any position taken against us we shall take as an acceptance of our declaration of war. From prison, we will order your execution and with blood and lead we will eliminate the dearest members of your family.

In November 1985 four magistrates connected with the case were killed in an attack that took place in the Palace of Justice.

When, by December 1986, another eleven judges had been murdered (bringing the total death toll to fifty judges for the period 1981–86) the Supreme Court declared the extradition treaty unconstitutional. The decision was based on a technicality: a government minister rather than President Turbay had signed the treaty.

But within two weeks the treaty was restored, signed by Colombia's new President, Virgilio Barco, on 14 December 1986. (The Colombian constitution limits a president's term to four years.) Four weeks later Cartel hitmen in Budapest shot and seriously wounded Colombia's Ambassador to Hungary, former Justice Minister Enrique Parjeo Gonzalez – he had been sent to Budapest after the Cartel threatened to kill him – in retaliation for his 'traitorous' support of extradition. The Cartel also renewed its threats to the judiciary and in June 1987 the Supreme Court, despite President Barco's signature, again ruled the treaty unconstitutional, resulting in the suspension of extraditions.

Then, on 25 January 1988, after the Cartel murdered the Colombian Attorney General, Carlos Mauro Hoyos Jimenez, President Barco responded with, among other measures, a pledge to renew extradition. A few months later his government was wavering. Barco was considering unilateral repudiation of the 1979 treaty when the Cartel assassinated his protégé, Luis Carlos Galan.

Following President Barco's renewal of extradition in September 1989, the Medellin Cartel launched a new wave of terrorism. It threatened to kill ten judges for every one of their members extradited. Pablo Escobar offered a $4000 reward for every policeman killed in Medellin. It began a bombing campaign, targeting banks, newspapers, the headquarters of political parties, commercial centres and schools. At the end of November 1989 a bomb destroyed an Avianca jet, killing all 107 passengers. The following month another bomb blew up the headquarters of the DAS, whose head, General Maza Marquez, was in charge of the government's anti-narcotics offensive. Over sixty people, mostly civilian passers-by, were killed.

A year after the murder of Galan the Cartel stepped up its pressure by kidnapping Diana Turbay, a magazine editor and television correspondent, the daughter of ex-President Julio Cesar Turbay whose government had negotiated the 1979 extradition treaty; they also kidnapped eight other journalists with close family ties to Colombia's governing Liberal Party.

Eighteen months into the campaign, the government could claim only modest successes. With the exception of Gonzalo Rodriguez Gacha, killed in an arrest attempt in November 1989, the other leaders of the Medellin Cartel, Pablo Escobar and Jorge Luis Ochoa, were still at large. Considerable assets (over 400 ranches, 470 planes, 600 vehicles, millions of dollars) and tons of cocaine had been seized but the human cost was terrible – five hundred murders attributed to the Medellin Cartel's extradition counter-offensive.

On 7 August 1990, a few weeks after the conclusion of Operation Offsides, a new Colombian president, a forty-three-year-old economist, Cesar Gaviria, was sworn into office. Within six months he concluded a peace treaty with 'the Extraditables' – the name adopted by the Medellin Cartel – promising immunity from extradition for traffickers charged with drug crimes who surrendered. This treaty was unlikely to result in the punishment of traffickers but it promised relief from the maelstrom of violence, a breathing space in which President Gaviria could attempt the Herculean task of transforming his country's political institutions, the source of almost continuous turmoil since the great Latin American liberator, Simon Bolivar, triumphantly marched into Bogota in 1819.

Colombia has been described as 'a society that has long demonstrated an extraordinary capacity for unrevolutionary self-destruction'.[8] During the nineteenth century, after the bloody War of Independence which resulted in its liberation from Spain and the formation of Gran Colombia (consisting of Colombia and Ecuador and Venezuela from which it seceded in 1830), it experienced eight general civil wars, fourteen local civil wars, countless small uprisings, two international wars with Ecuador and three *coups d'état*.[9] Its worst civil war, the Thousand Day War, 1899–1903, resulted in the deaths of 100,000 people and the loss of Panama. (The US instigated Panama's secession in order to build the Panama Canal.)

At the heart of these conflicts have been its two political parties, the Liberals and the Conservatives, founded in 1848 and 1849, which still control its government. In terms of their class, ideologies and ethnic characteristics, there were and are few distinctions between them. But most of the wars which caused the deaths of hundreds of thousands of Colombians resulted from power struggles between these two political parties as they fought for control of a government that was perceived as the property, the booty, of the party who won office.

Colombia inherited from the Spanish Empire a large administrative apparatus which dispensed salaries, licences, exemptions, profits, privileges, contracts and public offices. Under the Constitution of 1886, the President and Congress were democratically elected but the President appointed governors, governors appointed mayors, mayors appointed police chiefs. Almost every administrative position at all levels of government down to the humblest employees, the village clerk and policeman, was filled through patronage. This patronage, which gave unparalleled opportunities for wealth and advancement in what was then Latin America's poorest country, belonged to the party that captured the country's presidency. The party that did not control the state could expect only discrimination from it.

Although formally a democracy, Colombia's government has always been controlled by a small number of families. (Today, these families own many of the major newspapers, radio and television stations. The cocaine mafia has developed an alternative power base in part by buying up radio stations and newspapers.) During the nineteenth century, this ruling elite mobilized the people into their political conflicts with the promise of bounties, salaries, jobs and rewards. But as the participants saw their families and friends killed, wounded, driven off their lands, atrocities committed, the conflicts evolved into blood feuds and vendettas. Like the children of Catholics and Protestants in Ulster or Jews and Arabs in the Middle East, the children of Liberals and Conservatives were socialized into their parents' antagonisms.

In the worst twentieth-century civil war, La Violencia, 1948–58, triggered by inter-party conflicts, thousands lost their lives and the centre of Bogota was destroyed. Violence spread to the countryside; village exterminated village, paramilitary groups roamed the country and, on both sides, there were horrifying atrocities, torture, decapitation, mutilation, sexual crimes. La Violencia was finally damped down when the parties agreed to form the National Front. This arrangement provided that, regardless of election results, both parties were to receive half the membership of all legislative bodies, have parity in the Cabinet, the Council of State, the Supreme Court, governorships and mayoralties and in the executive's administrative bureaucracy.

But although the National Front resolved the immediate problem of La Violencia, it left intact Colombia's oligarchical power structure and governmental institutions characterized by patronage, corruption, inefficiency, and insensitivity to the needs of the majority. Nor did it abate the Colombian tradition of resolving conflicts through violence.

Since La Violencia, Colombia has gone through a period of enormous social upheaval. Its government's *laissez-faire* economic policies have produced rapid development, with an average annual growth rate of five per cent during the last two decades, and diversification of the economy, which has enabled it to escape from its traditional dependence on coffee. (It is now a major producer of sugar, cut flowers, coal, gold and oil.) It has the distinction of being the only Latin American country that was not forced to reschedule its $16 billion debt during the 1980s.

But despite this the majority of its people live in 'absolute poverty' or 'absolute misery'; there has been little investment in roads, sewerage, electricity, drinking water, in public health and housing.[10]

There has been an exodus from the countryside to the city, spurred by the development of agro-industry. The urban population doubled between 1964 and 1985 without any concomitant increase in housing or employment opportunities and huge shanty towns have grown up around the major cities. Over half the employment in urban areas is in the informal sector, adults and children earning a living by washing cars, shining shoes, collecting rubbish for resale, as pedlars, thieves, prostitutes, as assassins employed in the cocaine industry.

Social upheaval, economic growth, inequitable distribution of wealth, rising expectations, the closed political system, have spawned a myriad of anti-government groups and movements, some committed to armed struggle against the government, others non-violent. In the mid-1980s President Betancur, a Conservative

Party reformist who had criticized the traditional parties for failing to introduce urgent reforms, made two important moves to defuse political violence and democratize government. He offered an armed truce to the left-wing guerrilla movements who wished to participate in the electoral process, and he took the historic step of making city and town mayors an elected rather than an appointed office. (The first local government elections took place in 1988 and were marred by corruption and violence. In the town of Barrancas, for example, 17,000 people were registered to vote, although the total population was only 18,756. Altogether, 327 candidates, mayors and councillors were murdered in the run-up to the elections and their aftermath.)[11]

The reforms profoundly threatened conservative elements of the country's elite and helped forge an alliance between extremists within the security forces, large landowners and the Medellin Cartel. During the mid-1980s the Cartel's leaders invested heavily in agro-industry and bought huge chunks of land in north-central Colombia, in the fertile Magdalena river valley. Situated between the two mountain ridges of the Cordillera Central and Cordillera Oriental on which the cities of Medellin and Bogota are sited, this area has a long history of conflict between large landholders, peasants, farmworkers, unions and guerrilla organizations. The cocaine barons brought to their new enterprise the same thuggish tactics used in their anti-extradition campaign and with the connivance of local landowners and elements of the military and police, they financed, organized and trained paramilitary death squads.

There are now an estimated 140 death squads in Colombia, whose victims include police, judges, politicians and journalists who directly threaten the cocaine industry, as well as union and civic activists, peasant organizers, intellectuals and left-wing guerrillas. A particular target has been the Patriotic Union (UP), formed in 1985 following President Betancur's truce with the guerrilla movements. Since then, over a thousand UP activists, including the head of the party, Jaime Pardo Leal, and its presidential candidate in the 1990 elections, Bernardo Jaramillo, have been murdered. The death squads are responsible for most of the political killings that have occurred in the last five years.[12] They are the greatest destabilizing force in Colombia today, a state within a state, murdering with impunity.

In 1988 DAS, the civilian detective force that has played a major role in the government's anti-narcotics campaign, investigated the massacre of twenty workers on a banana plantation in the Uraba department on the border of Panama and the Caribbean coast.[13] Six months after the massacre, in September 1988, Pablo Escobar, Gonzalo Rodriguez Gacha, three military officials, a police lieutenant, a local mayor and eleven other civilians were charged with either planning or executing the massacres.

According to the DAS report of 20 July 1988, 'Organization of Hired Assassins and Drug Traffickers in the Middle Magdalena', the Medellin Cartel has established four training schools for *'sicarios'* in Puerto Boyaca, where some two thousand assassins were trained by British and Israeli mercenaries.[14] The commander of the local army garrison, who allowed it to be used as the death squads' communication centre, attended their graduation ceremonies and issued weapons permits.

During its investigation, DAS discovered several mass graves that contained the remains of an estimated two hundred bodies. This hardly reflected the number of people killed by the death squads. 'To eliminate witnesses, evidence and traces of crimes, the killers prefer to make their victims disappear,' a death squad deserter reported to DAS. 'They chop them into pieces and scatter the body parts in common graves or along riverbeds near the site of sacrifice.'[15]

Neither Escobar nor Gacha were arrested for their role in the Uraba banana plantation massacre. Instead, the judge who issued the arrest warrants, Martha Lucia Gonzalez, was forced to flee Colombia after repeated death threats. Unable to exact revenge on her, Medellin Cartel assassins murdered her father, Alvaro Gonzalez Santana, a university professor and former governor of Boyaca department. The judge who took over the case, Maria Elena Diaz, was one of the victims of the six political killings that occurred in the seven weeks preceding the murder of Luis Carlos Galan.

When Barco's predecessor, Cesar Gaviria, campaigned for the presidency in the spring of 1990, he promised to fight trafficker violence without concessions, a pledge that endeared him to the governments of the cocaine-consuming countries. But when Gaviria took office in the summer, his country was experiencing levels of violence – murders, disappearances, kidnappings, massacres – as widespread and grisly as in the worst years of La Violencia. To the dismay of the right, he offered one seat in his cabinet to M-19, an important guerrilla faction which had renounced force and paticipated in the presidential election, where it won thirteen per cent of the vote. He pushed through plans for a seventy-member constitutional assembly to be elected in November 1990 and he began negotiating a peace treaty with the Medellin Cartel.

On 8 October 1990, ten days after one of the men charged with the murder of Luis Carlos Galan walked out of Bogota's toughest jail simply by putting on a false beard, President Gaviria's Justice Minister, Jaime Giraldo, announced 'measures to strengthen the justice system'. This was a euphemism for Gaviria's peace terms with the Medellin Cartel. In exchange for their surrender, the government agreed that traffickers would have to confess to only one crime; there would be no pressure to cooperate against former colleagues; the maximum terms they faced would be reduced by one half; and they could select the judge who would try their case. But, most importantly, under no circumstances would they be extradited to the States. Indeed, the National Assembly to reform Colombia's undemocratic constitution, whose seventy members would be elected in November, was likely to ban extradition altogether.

Over the next few months a 'Committee of Leading Citizens' negotiated additional concessions on behalf of the traffickers. Its members included former President Alfonso Lopez and his ex-Justice Minister Alberto Santofimio who had brought Pablo Escobar into the Liberal Party; both of them were members of the Liberal Party's central committee. The government agreed to appoint a delegate to protect traffickers' human rights, create special jails and return all property previously confiscated.

Shortly after these concessions were made, on 15 January 1991, the number two leader of the Medellin Cartel, Jorge Ochoa, surrendered in a church in Caldas just outside Medellin. He had helped organize and finance the right-wing death squads, he had been arrested in Madrid with Gilberto Rodriguez Orejuela and he was facing four indictments in the United States. As an outlaw, he had bribed and killed scores of judges. Under the terms of the extradition treaty, he could now choose the judge who would preside over his case.

Three months after Jorge Ochoa surrendered, the Medellin Cartel's hitmen continued to ply their bloody trade. On the seventh anniversary of the assassination of Rodrigo Lara, who had ordered the 1984 raid on Tranquillandia, they murdered Enrique Low. As President Barco's Justice Minister from 1987 to 1989, Low had been an outspoken proponent of extradition. Forced to resign because of death threats, he was appointed Ambassador to Switzerland. When the election of Cesar Gaviria brought his diplomatic career to an end, he became dean of economics at Colombia's La Salle University. On 30 April 1991 the fifty-two-year-old professor, whose distinguished public service career included terms as a Supreme Court Justice and director of the Inter-American Development Bank, was gunned down as he waited for a taxi after teaching a class. 'Life is short for every man,' Low had said in an interview in 1988, 'and what we must do is to work for something that is useful and significant for other people.'[16]

How did the trio of law enforcement agents who had made the pursuit of the Cali Cartel their vocation react to President Gaviria's peace treaty with the cocaine cartels? After the surrender of Jorge Ochoa, was there any hope of prosecuting Jose Santacruz Londono and Gilberto and Miguel Rodriguez in America? Were all those years of work a wasted effort? Would those weighty legal instruments, the US indictments, be tossed like yesterday's newspapers into some prosecutor's wastebin?

Jerry McArdle, who had been taken off the Luxembourg case to work on a new investigation of Mockler's – this time their target was Chepe's likely successor Jaime Orjuela – found this thought too painful to contemplate. 'They still travel,' he said, clinging to a sliver of hope, 'to Europe if not to the States, to countries like Italy that will extradite to us. And Chepe, we think, is still coming in and out....'

Kenny Robinson, who was gradually healing, planned to return to work full-time after Easter. ('You have to come back to the meat grinder,' his superviser in the Unified Intelligence Division told him. 'Does he mean my job or Manhattan?' Kenny had wondered.) He was devastated when he heard the terms of the treaty. 'It's so frustrating,' he said, 'when we know where they are, what they're doing, that they're still operating in the United States. It means we'll only be able to work on the organization here. I can't understand how a government can do such a thing and after so many brave people have lost their lives. When you think of the cops and judges, the politicians, the journalists, the ordinary people who've spoken out against them.... It just doesn't seem right.'

But Bill Mockler expressed no sense of indignation. 'That's what we have to live with,' he said. 'What can I tell you?' Still, he was struck by the paradox of his government's power – 'We can win the war in Iraq in a matter of weeks and we can't resolve the problem of drugs in America.' He also understood that the first priority of the Colombians was to quell the violence. In any event, although the shift in policy might make his job harder, was the extradition of Chepe ever a realistic option? The Colombian government had never pursued the leaders of the Cali Cartel and why should it when they managed their drug ring like a legitimate business, not threatening the state, not engaging in terrorism, making cocaine capitalism almost respectable.

Perhaps, also, Bill Mockler's serenity flowed from a certain self-awareness, that it did not matter what he was investigating so long as the challenge was sufficient. 'Sometimes, people say to me, "Suppose they legalize drugs – what are you going to do then?" But I belong to the world's second oldest profession. There will always be crime, there will always be work for me. If I had lived two thousand years ago I would have done the same thing. I am an investigator. That's what I will always be.'

10 Breaking Out of the Circle

Recently I came across an article entitled 'Snowed In' which had appeared in an American magazine, the *New Republic*, in March 1990. Its author, Mark A.R. Kleiman, a drug policy analyst for the US Justice Department in the early 1980s, had previously written a thorough and well-reasoned study of the impact of tougher law enforcement on marijuana consumption.[1] I looked forward to reading his thoughts on the cocaine problem.

For reasons evident in the DEA operations described in this book, Mr Kleiman concluded that neither crop eradication nor crop substitution nor the efforts to destroy the cocaine industry of the Andean countries were likely to reduce drug abuse in the United States. 'Nothing that happens in South America has any real chance of significantly reducing the cocaine problem in North America,' he wrote.[2] Border policing was equally futile. What then should the federal government be doing? According to Mr Kleiman, it should be putting more resources into local law enforcement to enable police and prosecutors to arrest, convict and imprison more of the thousands of inner city youths who make a living by dealing in drugs.

From the cities of America, to the US borders, to the Andean countries and back to the streets of New York – law enforcement policy revolves in a circle. Every strategy tried has a common goal: to reduce the supply of cocaine and increase its price so that fewer people are willing and able to purchase the drug. But none of these strategies has been particularly effective. Today, five years after the crack epidemic began, cocaine is more plentiful and cheaper than ever before.

Is this because law enforcement has never had the chance to

prove its mettle? Would we do better if our drug laws were tougher, if we had more resources?

Since the crack epidemic of 1985, the federal government and many states have enacted laws that make prison terms mandatory for convicted drug dealers. At the same time, police and prosecutors have stepped up arrests and convictions of street traffickers. This combination has resulted in a huge increase in the nation's prison population, which more than doubled between 1980 and 1990, growing from 329,821 to 771, 243 inmates.[3] When defendants serving sentences of less than a year in county jails are included (396,000), the total inmate population in 1990 rises to over one million. Most of the new inmates are street drug traffickers sentenced to prison in the five years since 1985.[4] The United States now has the unhappy distinction of having the world's highest imprisonment rate, incarcerating a higher percentage of its population than South Africa or the Soviet Union, the two runners-up.[5]

Between 1981 and 1990 the federal government increased its drug budget by nearly eight hundred per cent. In 1990 it spent $9,483.2 billion on the DEA, border policing, international programmes, research, treatment, drug education, on everything that relates to drug control except prisons.[6] Of this $9 billion, seventy per cent went to law enforcement. This is a paltry sum compared to what the Pentagon receives or the estimated $150 billion that Congress plans to spend to bail out America's bankrupt Savings and Loan institutions. But what would be the impact if the DEA's budget was doubled? If Bill Mockler commanded two divisions instead of one, would he be able to break up the Cali Cartel? The answer 'no' leaps out of these cases. Lack of resources is an irritant but Mockler's greatest obstacles are not financial. They are the legal restrictions imposed by the US Constitution; the political situation within Colombia; and the extraordinary profitability of the cocaine trade which ensures that even if he captured the heads of the Cartel, a younger generation would take over, as eager to make their fortunes as twenty-eight-year-old Luis Delio Lopez, 'Leto'.

In 1984 the Rand Corporation, a Californian think tank which has used market analysis of the drug trade to evaluate different strategies for curbing drug use, published a study which reached a similar conclusion. According to the study's authors, if the total budget of all federal law enforcement agencies was doubled, it would enable them to triple the number of high-level drug dealers imprisoned. But the impact on the drug market would be very modest. The price of cocaine would rise by fifteen per cent, which would increase the cost of a vial of crack by less than one dollar.[7]

Recently, a group of academics, journalists and public figures – the University of Chicago's Dr Milton Friedman, *Economist* magazine, President Reagan's Secretary of State George Schultz, among others – have pronounced themselves in favour of drug legalization, largely because they think this will reduce the cost and disorder of drug-related crime and violence. Drug users, they argue, would not have to commit crimes to support their habits. The black market would wither and, with it, the assaults and murders which drug dealers now use to discipline workers and protect their business.

But the only way to undercut the black market is to make drugs cheap and readily available, which would inevitably increase the number of drug abusers. This is what occurred in America after cheap crack was introduced in 1985, in mid-nineteenth-century China after opium was legalized and in England during the seventeenth century when soldiers campaigning in the Netherlands brought home the Dutch habit of drinking gin. After the Glorious Revolution of 1688 and the accession of Prince William of Orange to the throne, English consumption of gin increased twenty-fold, from 527,000 gallons in 1685 to 11 million gallons in 1725. In 1750 an estimated 200,000 Londoners, a quarter of the capital's population, drank a pint a day in addition to prodigious quantities of beer. Gin with brand names like 'Royal Poverty', 'Strip Me Naked', 'Cuckold's Comfort' and 'Last Shaft' was sold on market stalls and hawked about the streets in barrels. There were six or seven thousand dram shops in London and Westminster. The result, according to one commentator, was a 'perfect pandemonium of drunkenness'.[8]

We have now had several centuries of experience with alcohol. Many social rules regulating how much, what, when and where to drink have developed to control its abuse. In spite of this, our legal drug takes a high toll. In America it is involved in approximately half of all violent crimes and in one quarter of admissions to general hospitals. Drunk driving results in approximately fifteen thousand road deaths each year.[9]

If cocaine, heroin, LSD, amphetamines, or any other dangerous drugs people may devise, were freely available, the public health bill would be enormous. To give some idea of its scope, it has been estimated that Florida – one state out of fifty and not the most populous – will spend $700 million on health care, social services and special education to prepare for kindergarten the 17,500 children born in 1987 who were exposed to cocaine in their mothers' wombs. In New York City in 1988 the cost of intensive hospital care for each cocaine-affected baby was estimated at $90,000.[10] The *New York Times* recently reported that the charge for a week-long cocaine detoxification programme is $5000; a ten-day heroin detoxification programme costs $6500.[11]

Moreover, the black market is unlikely to disappear. Governments would be forced to regulate and tax legal drug consumption, just as they do with alcohol and tobacco, if only to protect minors and fund prevention programmes and the public health bill. The result would be the worst of scenarios, more drug abuse and a thriving black market. (In America the traditional Italian-American organized crime families continue to make millions of dollars a year from illegal gambling despite the introduction of government-controlled betting and lotteries. There is also a black market in 'bootleg' cigarettes and alcohol.)

Between increased law enforcement and drug legalization, there are other options that offer a greater chance of success in the long term. When President Bush's National Drug Control Strategy was announced in the late summer of 1989, Sheriff Clarence W. Dupnik of Pima County, Arizona, was reported as saying, 'I know it would be heresy for a cop to say this, but we need to quadruple our effort on the demand side.'[12] In fact, Sheriff Dupnik's heresy is the secret belief of many law enforcement agents.

In the United States a two-tier pattern of drug use has developed. While among the middle class there has been a marked decline in casual use, in the inner cities drug abuse is entrenched. Although the crack epidemic seems to have peaked – street researchers for the New York State Division of Substance Abuse Services report few new converts to the drug in New York – it has left behind a population of addicts which the government estimates at 1.7 million people.[13] Now heroin use may be on the rise. The DEA reports large amounts of the drug entering New York from South-east Asia; the price has been halved, from $2 to $1 for a pure milligram of heroin; more people are smoking or snorting instead of injecting the drug; and there has been an increase in heroin addicts seeking treatment.

Given the conditions in the inner city, it is hardly surprising that a higher percentage of minorities – in New York State, twice as many blacks as white – should seek a release from their misery in the euphoria of drugs. My first trip to Harlem, in the company of a police officer to visit a robbery crime scene, was an unforgettable descent into Hades. Thirty blocks north of the Metropolitan Museum of Art, which faces the luxurious Fifth Avenue apartment house where Jackie Onassis lives, are burnt-out shells of buildings with urine-stained halls, back yards knee deep in rubbish, rusting hulks of cars and, hanging out on street corners at midday, the unemployed – young men and old.

In the last twenty years, in New York and many other northern American cities to which southern blacks immigrated en masse in the years 1940–60, hundreds of thousands of manual jobs have been eliminated as these cities' economies have shifted from manufacturing to services. Harlem, for instance, has lost most of its industrial facilities. Jobs in central Manhattan's garment industry, once a major employer of unskilled blacks who hustled racks of clothing from one loft factory to another, shrank from 300,000 in 1960 to 90,000 in 1980.[14] With a new wave of immigration, bringing a flood of Asians and Latin Americans into the city, there is intense competition for the jobs that are left.[15]

In Harlem over sixty per cent of households have incomes below the federal poverty line. The majority of children are raised by their mothers. Forty per cent of Harlem high school students drop out before achieving the minimum qualification of a high school diploma. Barely literate and numerate, they are unqualified for New York's white-collar job market. For some of the same reasons as the Altiplano *campesinos* of Bolivia, a substantial proportion of poor youths gravitate to the drug industry.[16] Street dealing is the ultimate dead-end job. It culminates for many in prison, violent injury or death. But no shortage exists in the supply of recruits. Few young people make their fortunes – the teenage drug dealer draped in gold chains and driving a Mercedes is rare – but wages in the drug trade are greater than what they can make legitimately.[17]

For historical and cultural reasons, we treat drug use as a

criminal matter. In fact, inner city drug abuse is one of the spectrum of social problems from which black Americans suffer disproportionately – others include teenage pregnancy, single parent families, high rates of infant mortality and, for black men, low life expectancy – while drug trafficking proliferates for mainly economic reasons. Law enforcement plays a vital role in containing violence and the street market's excesses. But it is, at best, a holding action against superior economic and social forces.

Since 1985 federal and state governments have spent billions of dollars constructing new cells to house convicted drug dealers.[18] With prisons throughout the country operating at over-capacity, billions more will be spent over the next few years. But is this money wisely spent? Every young man imprisoned returns to the streets, less capable of finding legal employment.

While history does not repeat itself and conditions vary from culture to culture, historical analogies are sometimes helpful, if only because they provide a sense of perspective. In nineteenth-century England, drunkenness was endemic among poor people. One social commentator wrote in 1844 of his Saturday evenings in Manchester, 'I have seldom gone home without seeing many drunkards staggering in the road or lying helpless in the gutter.'[19] Although the causes of drunkenness were largely environmental, it was treated as a criminal offence, a defect of the individual. In one year alone, 1876, 23,665 mostly working-class people in England and Wales were imprisoned for 'drunk and disorderly' behaviour.[20] Within sixty years, by the beginning of the 1930s, widespread drunkenness had disappeared. This was not through the efforts of police, magistrates or prison warders. It was due to social and religious reformers, to education, improved living conditions, the development of 'counter-attractions' – alternative forms of recreation – and non-alcoholic beverages, including drinkable water, that were substituted for beer, to the shift from an agricultural to an industrialized economy. Factory work required sobriety.

To treat the causes of the disease rather than the symptoms is not, for now, a politically popular solution. Americans are stuck in the circle of law enforcement. The majority do not want more money spent on drug education, rehabilitation and treatment. Nor do they favour budget increases for social services that benefit the inner cities – improved schools, housing, job training, summer employment, after-school recreation programmes, support for single mothers.

The reasons for this are complex; to elaborate them would be a book in itself. America's success-oriented ethos, which has created such extraordinary wealth, breeds contempt rather than compassion for society's weakest members. The majority are angry about crime and the decay of the cities. Fear and resentment of the underclass have been exacerbated by confrontational racist politics.

There is also, among American elites, a mistrust of social programmes aimed at blacks. This is based in part on the failures, real and perceived, of President Lyndon Johnson's War against Poverty, the most ambitious scheme since the Great Depression to improve the lot of America's poor. It was waged at the same time as the Vietnam conflict by an administration committed to both 'guns and butter'. Both conflicts were characterized by waste, misconceptions and failures of strategy.[21] American failures in the Vietnam War have been widely publicized abroad; the deficiencies of the War on Poverty are less well known. Its ideological commitment to 'maximum feasible community participation' occasionally led to excesses. For example, a prominent member of the liberal establishment, John Kennedy's brother-in-law, Sargent Shriver, consulted a notorious Chicago youth gang, the Blackstone Rangers, on how the federal government should spend money in the ghettos. As a result of weaknesses in government management, some of the money intended for the poor ended up lining the pockets of dubious 'community leaders'.

But as Don Ferrarone saw in Bolivia, as the world witnessed in the war with Iraq, the American military learned from its mistakes. The younger officers who served in Vietnam, including Generals Maxwell Thurman and Norman Schwarzkopf, spent many years analysing what went wrong. In the realm of social policy, there has been a similar round of self-critique.[22] Its generals – those who plan and execute social programmes – should be given the same opportunity to put it right.

Notes

1. The Tidal Wave

1. 'Drug Misuse in Britain, 1990', Institute for the Study of Drug Dependence (ISDD), London, p. 9. ISDD, an independent national information and research centre on the misuse of drugs and drug dependence in Britain, is an excellent source of descriptive and statistical information.

2. See John Kaplan, *The Hardest Drug: Heroin and Public Policy* (Chicago: The University of Chicago Press), 1983, and David F. Musto, *The American Disease: Origins of Narcotic Control* (New York and Oxford: Oxford University Press), 1987.

3. Quoted in Musto, p. 27.

4. D. E. Owen, *British Opium Policy in China and India* (New Haven: Yale University Press), 1934, p. vii.

5. Quoted in Arthur Waley, *The Opium War Through Chinese Eyes* (London: George Allen & Unwin), 1958, pp. 33–4.

6. Kaplan, p. 60.

7. Owen, p. 266.

8. Andrew Tyler, *Street Drugs* (London: New English Library), 1986, p. 183.

9. See V. Berridge and G. Edwards, *Opium and the People: Opiate Use in Nineteenth-Century England* (London: Allen Lane), 1981.

10. Virginia Berridge, 'Drugs and Social Policy: The Establishment

of Drug control in Britain, 1900–1930', *British Journal of Addiction* 79 (1984), pp. 17–29.

11. Musto, p. 254.

12. Kaplan, p. 113.

13. Of addicts notified to the Home Office in 1989, 10,479 were male, 4306 female. 'Drug Misuse in Britain, 1990', p. 17.

14. See Martin Plant, *Drugs in Perspective* (London: Hodder & Stoughton), 1987.

15. See Eric D. Wish and Bruce D. Johnson, 'The Impact of Substance Abuse on Criminal Careers', in A. Blumstein, J. Cohen, J. Roth and C. Visher, eds, *Criminal Careers and 'Career Criminals'* (Washington, DC: National Academy Press), 1986.

16. For a thorough and well-reasoned discussion of the pros and cons of marijuana legalization, see Mark A. R. Kleiman, *Marijuana: Costs of Abuse, Cost of Control* (New York and London: Greenwood Press), 1989.

17. Quoted in Musto, p. 265.

18. For a description of the health consequences of cocaine and heroin use, see 'Cocaine and Crack', ISDD Drug Notes 5, and 'Heroin', ISDD Drug Notes 1, Institute for the Study of Drug Dependence, London, 1989.

19. Kaplan, p. 122.

20. There are exceptions to this simplified description of the division of responsibilities between local and federal law enforcement agencies in New York City. For instance, the US Attorney for the Southern District of New York in the 1980s, Rudolph Giuliani, prosecuted street dealers. He had aspirations to elected office and in 1989 he was the Republican mayoral candidate, running against Democrat David Dinkins on a law and order platform. As US Attorney, he claimed that he could obtain tougher sentences for street dealers in the federal court system. In fact, there was little difference between the penalties meted out to street dealers in the state and federal court system, and the federal judiciary was critical of Giuliani's intervention in local law enforcement.

21. Figures given by the Drug Enforcement Administration.

22. A. M. Washton and M. S. Gold, 'Crack', *Journal of the American Medical Association*, 1986, p. 711, cited in 'Crack', a briefing from the ISDD, London, August 1989, p. 5.

23. Figures from the New York City Office of Biostatistics.

24. Testimony of Robert M. Morgenthau before the House Select Committee on Narcotics Abuse and Control, 31 May 1989.

25. 'Drug Study Faults Role of State Department', *The New York Times*, 6 February 1990, D24.

26. *New York Times*, 28 May 1989, p. 14.

2. *Lawrence of Latin America*

1. The phrase 'abject underdevelopment' comes from James Dunkerley's moving and complex study of modern Bolivia, *Rebellion in the Veins* (London: Verso Editions), 1984.

2. For a description of the politics involved in the creation of the South Florida Task Force and its successor agency, National Narcotics Border Interdiction System, see Elaine Shannon, *Desperados, Latin Drug Lords, U.S. Lawmen, and the War America Can't Win* (New York: Viking Penguin, 1988), pp. 84–91.

3. US General Accounting Office, 'Drug Smuggling: Capabilities for Interdicting Private Aircraft Are Limited and Costly' (Washington, DC: Government Printing Office), 1989, p. 10.

4. Fixed land radar do not work well in mountainous regions (much of the Mexican–American border is mountainous) and have trouble detecting small, low-flying aircraft; airborne radar (such as the E-3 AWAC system, a radar platform mounted on a Boeing 707) also miss many of the relevant targets; aerostats (balloon-floated radars costing

from $12 to $22 million) do not work in the stormy conditions which frequently prevail on the south-west border; and no radar system has the capacity to distinguish the smuggler's aeroplane from the myriad legitimate small aeroplanes entering the United States. For further explanation of the radar shield's defects, see Peter Reuter, Gordon Crawford, Jonathan Cave, *Sealing the Borders: The Effects of Increased Military Participation in Drug Interdiction* (Santa Monica, Calif.: Rand Corporation), 1988.

5. 'Airborne Drug War is at a Stalemate', *New York Times*, 30 July 1989, p. 1, col. 5.

6. In 1989 Congress designated the Department of Defense as the lead agency for monitoring and detecting drug traffickers because it possessed and was familiar with the military assets increasingly involved in border interdiction. But the traditional law enforcement functions of apprehension and seizure still rest with Customs and the Coast Guard and to a lesser extent with INS. The Coast Guard, which is part of the Department of Transportation, provides marine interdiction; Customs provides inshore marine coastal, air and land interdiction; and INS covers land border interdiction, particularly along the Mexican–American border.

7. See Peter Reuter, 'Eternal Hope: America's Quest for Narcotics Control', *The Public Interest*, pp. 90–91.

8. Hectares under cultivation are 1989 figures. See US Department of State, Bureau of International Narcotics Matters, Report to the Congress, *International Cocaine Strategy*, 1 March 1990, pp. 9–10.

9. See Peter Andreas and Coletta Youngers, 'US Drug Policy and the Andean Cocaine Industry', *World Policy Journal*, Summer 1989, p. 540.

10. Reuter, 'Eternal Hope', p. 90.

11. See Col. Howard Lee Dixon, 'Low Intensity Conflict: Overview, Definitions, and Policy Concerns', CLIC Papers, Army-Air Force Center for Low Intensity Conflict, Langley Air Force Base, Virginia, 1989.

3. Ready, Aim, Fire!

1. James Dunkerley, *Rebellion in the Veins* (London: Verso Editions), 1984, p. 316.

2. Dunkerley, pp. 318–19. Dunkerley reports that in 1980, 300 kilos of cocaine sulphate (whose ownership Banzer eschewed) were discovered in a raid on Banzer's *estancia*, 'El Potrero'.

3. Madeline Leons and William Leons, 'Land Reform and Economic Change in the Yungas', in *Beyond the Revolution*, eds James M. Malloy and Richard S. Thorn (Pittsburgh: University of Pittsburgh Press), 1971, pp. 270–1.

4. James Dunkerley, 'Political Transition and Economic Stabilization: Bolivia, 1982–1989', University of London, Institute of Latin American Studies research papers, no. 22, 1990, p. 34.

5. Dunkerley, 'Political Transition and Economic Stabilisation', pp. 40–3.

6. The enabling statute was the Anti-Drug Abuse Act of 1986 which requires the US government to withhold foreign aid to all major illicit drug-producing and transhipment countries, unless the President certifies that such countries have cooperated fully with US drug control efforts or that national security considerations justify certification.

7. 'International Cocaine Strategy, 1 March 1990', Bureau of International Narcotics Matters, Department of State, pp. 10–11.

8. US Senate Caucus on International Narcotics Control, 'Narcotics-Related Foreign Aid Sanctions: An Effective Foreign Policy?' (Washington, DC: US Government Printing Office, 1987) pp. 8–12.

9. Ethan A. Nadelmann, 'The DEA in Latin America: Dealing with Institutionalized Corruption', *Journal of Interamerican Studies and World Affairs*, vol. 29, No. 4, Winter 1987–88, p. 12.

4. The Six-Thousand-Pound Gorilla

1. For a history of the struggle between the government of Bolivia and the coca lobby, see James Dunkerley, 'Political Transition and Economic Stabilization: Bolivia, 1982–1989', University of London, Institute of Latin American Studies research papers, 1990, pp. 39–47.

2. General Carl Von Clausewitz, *On War* (London: Kegan Paul, Trench, Trubner & Co.), 1918, vol. 1, pp. 77–81. 'Every war ... is an unexplored sea, full of rocks which the General may have a suspicion of, but which he has never seen with his eye, and round which, moreover, he must steer in the night. If a contrary wind also springs up, that is, if any great accidental event declares itself adverse to him, then the most consummate skill, presence of mind, and energy are required, whilst to those who only look on from a distance all seems to proceed with the utmost ease.'

6. The Investigation without an End

1. The New York Drug Enforcement Task Force draws its manpower from the DEA, the New York City Police Department and the State Police. It was founded in 1970 to consolidate resources and reduce bureaucratic wrangling among the agencies that share jurisdiction over narcotics crimes in New York City.

7. 'You Have to Wish and Dream and Hope'

1. Medellin trafficker Pablo Escobar financed the Atletico Nacional which, in 1988, won South America's coveted Libertadores Cup; its former president, Hernan Botero Moreno, is serving a thirty-year prison term in the United States for money laundering. See 'Colombian Soccer: RIP?', *Newsweek*, 26 February 1990, p. 35.

2. Ochoa was returned to Colombia two weeks later, where he was indicted in Cartagena for smuggling 128 fighting bulls from Spain to his father's Colombian ranch. Despite instructions from the Colombian Justice Minister, Enrique Parejo Gonzalez (later seriously wounded in a Medellin Cartel assassination attempt), that he should be jailed pending trial, the judge released Ochoa on $11,500 bail, then convicted and sentenced him to twenty months in jail. Ochoa never returned to court to serve this sentence. For detailed accounts of the arrests of Gilberto Rodriguez and Jorge Ochoa and the extradition proceedings, see Guy Gugliotta and Jeff Leen, *Kings of Cocaine* (New York: Simon and Schuster), 1989.

8. The Waiting Game

1. *The New York Times*, 5 November 1989, Section B, p. 1.

2. All federal wire-tap applications, in every jurisdiction – New York, Los Angeles, Miami, Houston – must be approved by the US Attorney General.

9. The Enemy's Retreat

1. In 1989 the DEA seized $973.9 million in assets – real estate, boats, vehicles, jewellery, cash – which was nearly twice its $535 million budget. A large portion of this money was ploughed back into law enforcement. Most of the vehicles used by Bill Mockler's division were seized from the Cali Cartel.

2. 'Arms Swoop Foils IRA Plot to Kill Maggie', *The Sun*, 24 September 1990; 'Arms Find Fails to Deter PM', *The Guardian*, September 1990.

3. The other victims were: Antonio Roldan Betancur, the Governor of Antioquia; Judge Maria Diaz Perez, who ordered the arrest of Pablo Escobar and Gonzalo Rodriguez Gacha for their involvement in the March 1988 massacre of twenty-two union activists on banana plantations in Uraba province; Carlos Ernesto Valencia, the magistrate who called for the prosecution of the drug barons responsible for the 1986 murder of Guillermo Cano, the crusading anti-drug editor of Colombia's second largest newspaper, *El Espectador*; Henry Cuenca Vega, President of the National Federation of Cement Workers, the twelfth cement union activist killed since December 1988; and Daniel Espitia, national treasurer of the peasants union, ANUC, whose brother and father had been assassinated in separate incidents before him. Jenny Pearce, *Colombia: Inside the Labyrinth* (London: Latin America Bureau), 1990, p. 265.

4. Jorge Child, *El Espectador*, 26 August 1989, quoted in Pearce, p. 266.

5. Pearce, p. 248.

6. Bruce Bagley, 'Colombia and the War on Drugs', *Foreign Affairs,* vol. 67, pt 1, 1988, p. 80.

7. Pearce, p. 114.

8. Alexander W. Wilde, 'Conversations among Gentlemen: Oligarchical Democracy in Colombia', in *The Breakdown of Democratic Regimes, Latin America,* eds Juan J. Linz and Alfred Stepan (Baltimore: The Johns Hopkins University Press), 1978, p. 69.

9. Pearce, p. 17.

10. 'Absolute poverty' (40 per cent) means the majority of basic living and subsistence needs are not satisfied; 'absolute misery' (18 per cent), means an inability to meet even basic nutritional needs. In rural areas, where 30 per cent of the population live, 88 per cent of the inhabitants lack sewerage, 72 per cent are without access to potable water, 59 per cent lack electricity. These figures were compiled by Colombia's National Administrative Bureau of Statistics. See *Colombia Besieged*, Washington Office on Latin America (Washington, DC: 1989), p. 9.

11. See Pearce, pp. 225 ff.

12. There were 2342 political killings in the first quarter of 1989. Between 70 and 80 per cent were attributed to right-wing death squads. *Financial Times Survey, Colombia*, 28 July 1989, p. 15.

13. Between 1 January and 4 March 1988 one hundred workers were murdered on the banana plantations of Uraba. After the 4 March assassinations, there was a demonstration by 22,000 workers. This was followed by the massacre of twenty-five more workers; some of their bodies were found floating in the sea with their hands tied and bullet wounds in their heads.

14. In testimony before the US Senate Permanent Subcommittee on Investigations, a British citizen, David Tomkins, an explosives expert and the leader of one of the mercenary groups, said he was paid $2000 a week. He justified his association with the notorious drug gangs by saying that Colombian military officials forged a financial and political alliance with the drug traffickers in order to combat leftist insurgents. 'Report Says Mercenaries Aided Colombian Cartels', *New York Times*, 28 February 1991, p. A20.

15. *Colombia Besieged*, pp. 75–6. See this book for a detailed discussion of the Colombian Army's involvement in narcotics-funded right-wing paramilitary organizations.

16. Quoted in 'Victim of the Cocaine Cartels', *The Guardian*, 8 May 1990.

10. Breaking Out of the Circle

1. Mark A.R. Kleiman, *Marijuana: Costs of Abuse, Costs of Control* (Westport, Conn.: Greenwood Press), 1989.

2. Kleiman, 'Snowed In', *New Republic,* 23 April 1990.

3. Robyn L. Cohen, 'Prisoners in 1990', *Bureau of Justice Statistics Bulletin*, US Department of Justice, May 1991.

4. According to Henry Donnelly, head of research for the New York State Division of Correctional Services, during the years 1970–84 drug offenders made up on average only ten per cent of New York's prison population but in 1990 nearly half the defendants sentenced to prison were convicted of offences related to drug trafficking.

5. The US incarceration rate is 426 per 100,000; South Africa, 333 per 100,000; Soviet Union, 268 per 100,000. American black males are imprisoned at four times the rate of black men in South Africa. See 'Americans Behind Bars: A Comparison of International Rates of Incarceration' (Washington, DC: The Sentencing Project), 1991.

6. The figure for 1981 was $1,230.7 billion. Source: Drug Enforcement Administration.

7. J. Michael Polich, Phyllis L. Ellickson, Peter Reuter, James P. Kahan, *Strategies for Controlling Adolescent Drug Use* (Santa Monica, Cal.: Rand Corporation), 1984, pp. 75–6.

8. John Kaplan, *The Hardest Drug: Heroin and Public Policy* (Chicago: University of Chicago Press), 1983, pp. 141–2.

9. See James B. Jacobs, *Drunk Driving: An American Dilemma* (Chicago: University of Chicago Press), 1989.

10. Mathea Falco, 'The Substance Abuse Crisis in New York City', unpublished paper prepared for the New York Community Trust, Fall 1989, pp. 15–16.

11. James B. Jacobs, 'Imagining Drug Legalization', *The Public Interest,* No. 101, Fall 1990, p. 36. In working out the practical implications of drug legalization, which its proponents have not done, the author presents an overwhelming case for not legalizing drugs.

12. 'After Studying for War on Drugs, Bennett Wants More Troops', *New York Times,* 6 August 1989.

13. 'US Almost Triples Estimate of Hard-Core Cocaine Users', *New York Times*, p. D24, 7 February 1991.

14. Terry M. Williams and William Kornblum, *Growing Up Poor* (Lexington, Mass.: D.C. Heath & Co.), 1985. The young Harlemites

I met as a prosecutor are very similar to the youths described in this ethnographic study of poor young people in four American cities.

15. In 1969 the national unemployment rate for inner city black males aged 16 to 24 was 13 per cent. It was 37.1 per cent at the beginning of New York's crack epidemic in 1985. Peter Reuter, Robert MacCoun, Patrick Murphy, *Money from Crime: A Study of the Economics of Drug Dealing in Washington, DC* (Santa Monica, Cal.: Rand Corporation), 1990, pp. 2–3.

16. In a 1988 Urban Institute survey of poor teenagers in Washington, DC, despite their view of drug dealing as a degrading occupation, one in three youths older than sixteen and a half claimed to have sold drugs. See Reuter, MacCoun and Murphy, pp. 46, 79.

17. Ibid., pp. 75–6.

18. In New York, where it costs $25,000 to maintain a prisoner for one year and an estimated $70,000 to build a new cell, the state added 20,785 new cells between 1985 and 1990. Source: New York State Division of Correctional Services.

19. Quoted in Brian Harrison, *Drink and the Victorians* (London: Faber and Faber), 1971, p. 364. This is an excellent study of alcohol abuse in nineteenth-century England and the temperance movement.

20. Ibid., p. 398.

21. See Nicholas Lemann, *The Promised Land: The Great Black Migration and How It Changed America* (New York: Knopf), 1991, and Harry G. Summers Jr, *On Strategy: A Critical Analysis of the Vietnam War* (Novato, Cal.: Presidio Press), 1982.

22. See Sheldon H. Danziger and Daniel H. Weinberg, eds, *Fighting Poverty: What Works and What Doesn't* (Cambridge, Mass.: Harvard University Press), 1986.

Index